The German Choral Church Compositions of Johann David Heinichen (1683-1729)

American University Studies

Series XX
Fine Arts
Vol. 14

PETER LANG
New York • Bern • Frankfurt am Main • Paris

Melvin P. Unger

The German Choral Church Compositions of Johann David Heinichen (1683-1729)

PETER LANG
New York • Bern • Frankfurt am Main • Paris

Library of Congress Cataloging-in-Publication Data

Unger, Melvin P.
   The German choral church compositions of Johann
David Heinichen, 1683-1729 / Melvin P. Unger.
      p. cm. — (American university studies. Series XX,
Fine arts ; vol. 14)
      Includes bibliographical references.
      1. Heinichen, Johann David, 1683-1729. Choral
music. 2. Choral music—Germany. 3. Cantata—
Germany. I. Title. II. Series.
ML410.H44U5   1990   782.2'4'092—dc20   89-29831
ISBN 0-8204-1236-8   CIP
ISSN 0890-412X

Excerpts from *J.S. Bach and Liturgical Life in Leipzig,* copyright © 1984 Concordia Publishing
House. Reprinted by permission from CPH.

© Peter Lang Publishing, Inc., New York 1990

Printed in the United States of America.

Table of Contents

Preface

My interest in the German cantata was initially stimulated in 1974 by classes in choral literature and conducting under Helmuth Rilling at the music conservatory in Frankfurt. What particularly interested me was the manner by which German composers used texts to generate their musical ideas. In pursuing the matter I was led to a survey of the literature dealing with rhetoric in music and eventually to Heinichen's systematic discussion of the *loci topici* in the preface to the second edition of his treatise. Because Heinichen so explicitly demonstrates ways that texts can generate musical invention, his cantatas seemed the logical starting point for an investigation of this subject.

Another reason for choosing the church works of an eighteenth century *Kleinmeister* was the potential significance such works have for establishing the context of Bach's cantatas. The aesthetic ideals of German music had begun to shift by the early part of the eighteenth century as they came under the influence of the Enlightenment. In his treatise, Heinichen clearly identifies this transition; the more progressive composers, he tells us, are guided by good taste, naturalness, and reason rather than by artifice. As history's reverence for Bach has grown, however, it is Bach's works that have come to be regarded as the highest musical expression of his age. Although this assessment is undoubtedly accurate, it tends to obscure the prevailing cultural trends of the time, for these trends are more clearly exemplified in the works of his contemporaries. It is only when we comprehend these trends that we can fully understand the resistance Bach's music encountered, or, on the other hand, properly evaluate the efforts of his contemporaries. Because the music of J.S. Bach so overshadows the works of these composers, we may easily tend to view their works only in relation to Bach's comparable ones, instead of evaluating them in their rightful historical context. This is especially true in the case of the cantata, whose development is very diffuse and embodies many diverse elements and trends. It is hoped that the present study will contribute to a further understanding of Heinichen's compositions on their own terms and according to their own merit. Thus, with the opportunity to test and demonstrate Heinichen's explanation of musical rhetoric by analyzing his own works, and with the works of this typically progressive composer under examination, the present study aims at contributing to a more nearly complete picture of the cantata's significance and development in Germany during the early eighteenth century by clarifying its aesthetic basis, illuminating its range of musical styles, and placing these in the context of contemporaneous culture and society.

This book was written originally as partial fulfillment for the D.M.A. degree from the University of Illinois. In that form it included a lengthy appendix of the actual compositions under study as transcribed by the author. Since the following work does not include this appendix, the musical examples used in the text have been somewhat lengthened. We hope the reader will find them adequate to illustrate the points being made. Two of the compositions under discussion are being published by Carus-Verlag of Stuttgart and should be available shortly: *Heilig is Gott der Herr*, and *Herr, nun lässest du deinen Diener in Friede fahren*.

I am especially indebted to the Sächsische Landesbibliothek in Dresden and the Deutsche Staatsbibliothek in Berlin for providing the microfilms of Heinichen's manuscripts. The librettos proved almost illegible at times, and I am particularly grateful to my mother, Susie Unger, for her assistance in deciphering them. Craig Westendorf was instrumental in providing me with data on the historical Lutheran pericopes. Linda Unger's help in procuring interlibrary loan materials and producing an accurate typescript was invaluable. John Walter Hill of the University of Illinois was helpful with succinct and insightful comments, and his own fine scholarship spurred me on. Wolfgang Horn contributed valuable information regarding Heinichen's handwriting. Finally, my wife freed me from many tasks so that I could devote the countless hours required to transcribe Heinichen's works and complete this project. To them all I acknowledge my indebtedness and express my thanks.

S.D.G.
Melvin P. Unger

The German Choral Church Compositions of Johann David Heinichen (1683-1729)

1.
Heinichen and the Protestant Cantata

Introduction

When Heinichen published the greatly expanded second edition of his musical treatise on the thorough-bass in 1728, he firmly established himself as one of the foremost music theoreticians of his time. This book was the first "really complete treatise on the thorough-bass, one of the most instructive works for musical composition written in Germany in the first half of the eighteenth century."[1] His work received high praise from his contemporaries, including Charles Burney, who called him the "Rameau of Germany,"[2] and Johann Mattheson, who wrote, Heinichen "does not just compose, he contemplates and thinks...and shows the world what knowledge is."[3]

Heinichen was also highly regarded as a composer. As Kapellmeister at the court of August the Strong in Dresden, Heinichen held one of the most prestigious posts in Germany, the same position for which Bach later applied when he presented the *Kyrie* and *Gloria* of his *B Minor Mass* to August II (successor to August the Strong). Such fame led Mattheson to rank Heinichen along with Handel and Hasse in a triumvirate of German "Hs."[4] Johann Scheibe (1708-1776) wrote, "Nature guides his every note,"[5] and later writers, too, emphasized Heinichen's mastery of compositional techniques.[6] Thus, Hiller writes,

> Mr. Heinichen fully understood harmony and its laws and did not merely appropriate the old rules but pondered them and, through personal, constant, practical application, became master of them. He understood counterpoint no less thoroughly, but he also realized the proper use and limits of such artifices.[7]

Heinichen's greatest fame arose from his operatic successes, and it was for this skill in the Italian operatic style that he was engaged in Dresden. He composed, however, in almost every popular form of his day, and his output includes concerti, suites, sonatas, sinfonias, operas, Masses, Magnificats, Italian secular cantatas, German church cantatas, and smaller church works.

Scholarly research on Heinichen's work presently includes five studies:[8]
1. A biographical study with thematic catalogue by Gustav Adolph Seibel (1913).[9]
2. A study of the dramatic music by Richard Tanner (1916).[10]
3. An examination of the instrumental music by Günter Hausswald (1937).[11]
4. A study of Heinichen's treatise by George Buelow (1966).[12]
5. A study of the Masses by Eberhard Schmitz (1967).[13]

Until now, the German church compositions have been left, and it is to that group, more specifically, to the choral works, that the present work is devoted. Most of these compositions are cantatas; a few might more appropriately be called motets.

Terminology

Within the German Protestant context the term *cantata* "may be defined in terms of function as the principal music of the Lutheran service, and in terms of structure as a vocal work comprising a number of relatively independent movements."[14] Not always has the term been defined so broadly. Indeed, the term did not even appear in German church compositions before 1700. Instead, such pre-1700 compositions were designated *Concerto, Motetto concertato, Corale concertato, Psalm, Ode, Aria, Dialogo, Actus musicus, Actus funebris, Actus tragicus*, or in the case of a collection of such works, *Musikalischer Andacht, Kirchenandacht*, etc.[15] Today, however, many such seventeenth century compositions are included as part of the cantata genre.[16]

Even after 1700, when the operatic forms of recitative and aria, with their requisite kind of poetry, were incorporated into Lutheran church music, the term *Kantate* was originally reserved for *solo* works with continuo accompaniment comprising a sequence of recitatives and arias on a madrigalian text.[17] The ordinary "church pieces" (*Kirchenstücke*) with their mixture of chorale stanzas, scripture, and madrigalian verse, and their inclusion of choral movements and instrumental accompaniment, often carried no designation at all other than the Sunday or feast day for which the work was intended.[18] In the contemporary literature, such works are called *Kirchenmusik* or *Kirchenstücke*. If an entire liturgical cycle is meant, they are called a *Jahrgang* or *Kirchenjahrgang*.[19]

By 1739 some writers were evidently broadening the meaning of the term *cantata* to include these normal church pieces, for Mattheson registers his objections to such a wider usage of the term, pointing out that the normal *Kirchenstücke* employ several styles, only one of which can rightly be called the "cantata style."[20]

By 1800, however, the broader definition had been generally adopted. Thus, for instance, a musical lexicon of the time equates cantata with "the usual church compositions."[21] Nevertheless, the term *Kirchenmusik* was still by far the preferred term well into the ninteenth century.[22] Bach's cantatas, too, were not called "cantatas" until the term was applied to them in the ninteenth century by the editors of the Bach Gesellschaft.[23] Thereafter, however, the accepted meaning of the term broadened rapidly, extended by Philipp Spitta and others to include "older analogues of the genre from the time of Schütz onward."[24] Even in recent times, the genre has been defined by means of reference to Bach's cantatas.

> That which all the works now called cantatas have in common, is an...approximate similarity of their textual and musical forms: more precisely, their similarity with Bach's cantatas.[25]

The fact that, for a long period, neutral terms like *Kirchenmusik* and *Kirchenstück* were preferred even for the madrigalian cantata indicates that, in the view of contemporary writers, such works were defined more by their liturgical function than by their formal and stylistic characteristics. Especially significant was the relationship of their texts to the pericopes. How this evolved is described by Alfred Dürr:

> Previously (in the Lutheran church as well) the liturgist had chanted [the] lessons in the lesson tone; now, however, parts of them (especially words of Jesus or other sententious sections) are taken over by the choir in newly composed sections, and finally the development reaches the point that the choir does not perform it as part of the lesson but performs it after the reading. Here we stand at the birthplace of what, in the terminology of the day, still carried various designations such as *motet, Kirchenstück, Kirchenmusik*, often simply *Musik, Musikalische Andacht, Concerto*, etc, but is finally also called *cantata*, and this name is the only one that has sifted through to later generations.[26]

That the cantata had not always been related to the pericopes is made clear by Krummacher:

> Whereas before [the eighteenth century] there was no typological difference between the *Hauptmusik* of the divine service and other figural music, cantata production after 1700 concentrated on music linked to the sermon, and cantatas in other positions were rare.[27]

For this reason, numerous writers distinguish between the *Evangelienkantate* or "seasonal cantata" (i.e., a cantata related to the pericopes) and other types.[28] Although the present usage of the term *cantata* is quite confused,[29] a return to the narrower sense of the word (i.e., restricting the term to madrigalian works) would be "to ignore the similarities that exist between [the two types]; similarities that were already obvious to contemporaries such as Walther and Mattheson."[30] Furthermore, we would then be left with the original designations for the pre-1700 works, and these designations were used inconsistently by the composers themselves. Often the same term was used for works that are typologically different.[31]

This leaves us, then, with our original definition, which, admittedly, is somewhat imprecise. As "principal music of the Lutheran service, defined structurally by a number of relatively independent movements,"[32] the term *cantata* subsumes some works that could otherwise be called motets, especially those types often called *sacred concertos*. Indeed, "the baroque vocal concerto is the transitional form between the motet and madrigal of the sixteenth century and the church cantata of the eighteenth century."[33] The actual transition point, however, cannot be precisely determined.[34] These sentiments are echoed by Christoph Wolff:

> Implicit in the sacred concerto is a complex range of possible combinations of vocal and instrumental parts in conjunction with the sectional structure of the motet. In the second half of the seventeenth century this resulted in its being split up into separate units, which in turn led to its developing into independent sections of movements using elements foreign to the motet such as aria, chorale and finally recitative. The cantata derives from this development of the concerted motet.[35]

According to Spitta,

> The form of church music accompanied by instruments (or, as I shall henceforth call it, the older Church Cantata) which was the predominant form from 1670 to 1700, resulted from a combination of the different forms of church music which had previously been in use separately.[36]

Because there are definite distinctions between the seventeenth-century cantata, with its mainly heterogenous textual origins, and the madrigalian cantata of the eighteenth century,[37] Spitta's terminology of "older cantata" and "newer cantata" is useful. Within these two broad categories, still further distinctions can then be made on the basis of text type (biblical text, ode, madrigal, chorale, or any combination thereof) and also on the basis of their musical form (concerto, aria, recitative, chorale).[38] To a certain degree, these two bases for distinction run parallel to each other. Thus, for example, settings of biblical texts often employed vocal and instrumental forces in a concerto mold. A final distinction, that between solo and choral cantata, although not useful from a typological perspective, nevertheless also has merit because of its implications for performance.

Chapter 1. Notes

1. George J. Buelow, *Thorough-Bass Accompaniment according to Johann David Heinichen* (Berkely & Los Angeles: University of California Press, 1966), p. 1.

2. Charles Burney, *A General History of Music* (London, 1776-1789), New Edition, Frank Mercer (London, 1935, reprinted New York, 1957), 2:459.

3. Johann Mattheson, "Ode auf des S.[alvo] T.[itulo] Hrn. Capellmeister Heinichen(s) schönes Werck von General-Bass," printed as an Introduction to Heinichen's *Der General-Bass in der Composition* (Dresden, 1728) cited in Buelow, *Thorough-Bass*, p. 1.

4. Johann Mattheson, *Der Vollkommene Capellmeister*, trans. by Ernest C. Harriss (Ann Arbor: U.M.I. Press, 1981), p. 136.

5. Johann Scheibe, *Der critische Musikus*, 2d ed. (Leipzig, 1745), p. 764.

6. A complete summary of biographical sources is provided by Richard Tanner, *J.D. Heinichen als dramatischer Komponist* (Leipzig, 1916), pp. 13-15.

7. Johann Adam Hiller, "Lebenslauf des Herrn Johann David Heinichen, *Wöchentliche Nachrichten und Anmerkungen die Musik betreffend* (Leipzig, 1766 and following years; reprint ed., Hildesheim: Georg Olms, 1970), 1:224.

8. See also Wolfgang Horn, *Die Dresdner Hofkirchenmusik 1720-1745* (Stuttgart: Carus-Verlag, 1987).

9. Gustav Adolph Seibel, *Das Leben des Königl. Polnischen und Kurfürstl. Sächs. Hofkapellmeisters Johann David Heinichen...und thematischen Katalog seiner Werke* (Leipzig, 1913).

10. See previous note.

11. Günter Hausswald, *J.D. Heinichens Instrumentalwerke* (Leipzig, 1937).

12. George J. Buelow, "Johann David Heinichen's Der General-Bass in der Composition" (Ph.D. dissertation, New York University, 1961) published in 1966 without appendix as *Thorough-Bass Accompaniment according to Johann David Heinichen*. See above.

13. Eberhard Schmitz, *Die Messen J.D. Heinichens* (dissertation, Hamburg, 1967).

14. Friedhelm Krummacher, "The German Cantata to 1800," *The New Grove Dictionary of Music and Musicians*, ed. Stanley Sadie (London: MacMillan, 1980), 3:703.

15. Georg Feder, "Die protestantische Kirchenkantate," *Die Musik in Geschichte und Gegenwart*, 16 vols., ed. Friedrich Blume (Kassel: Bärenreiter, 1949-1979), vol. 7 (1958), col. 582.

16. Feder, col. 582.

17. Feder, col. 581.

18. Feder, col. 581.

19. Feder, col. 581.

20. Mattheson, *Capellmeister*, pp. 436-437.

21. H.Ch. Koch, *Musikalisches Lexicon*, 1802. cited in Feder, col. 581.

22. Feder, col. 582.

23. Krummacher, "The German Cantata," p. 703. In an examination of Bach's cantatas, Zander found only six that were expressly called cantatas, and five of these are solo cantatas. See Ferdinand Zander, *Die Dichter der Kantatentexte Johann Sebastian Bachs* (Ph.D. dissertation, University of Cologne, 1967), p. 3.

24. Krummacher, "The German Cantata," p. 703. See also Feder, col. 582, Philipp Spitta, *Johann Sebastian Bach*, 3 vols., trans. Clara Bell and J.A. Fuller-Maitland (New York: Dover, 1951), 1:292.

25. Feder, col. 582, trans. M. Unger.

26. Alfred Dürr, *Die Kantaten von Johann Sebastian Bach*, 2 vols. (Kassel: Bärenreiter, 1971), 1:14, trans. M. Unger.

27. Krummacher, "The German Cantata," p. 707.

28. Feder, col. 582, Christoph Wolff, "Motet" III, 3, *The New Grove*, 12:640. See also Günther Stiller, *Johann Sebastian Bach and Liturgical Life in Leipzig* trans. Herbert J.A. Bouman, Daniel F. Poellot, Hilton C. Oswald, edited Robin A. Leaver (St. Louis: Concordia, 1984), p. 152.

29. Feder, col. 582.

30. Krummacher, "The German Cantata," p. 703.

31. Feder, col. 582.

8

32. See Krummacher's definition cited earlier.

33. Adam Adrio, Arno Forchert, "Das Vokalkonzert," *Die Musik in Geschichte und Gegenwart*, 16 vols., ed. Friedrich Blume (Kassel: Bärenreiter, 1949-1979), vol. 7, col. 1566, trans. M. Unger.

34. Adrio, Forchert, col. 1568.

35. Wolff, p. 641.

36. Spitta, *Bach*, 1:292.

37. Krummacher, "The German Cantata," p. 703; Spitta, *Bach*, 1:73.

38. Krummacher, "The German Cantata," p. 703.

2.
The Development of the German Church Cantata

The development of the church cantata can only be properly understood within the context of Lutheran theology and liturgy. What particularly
influenced the development of the Protestant cantata (and did so in
increasing measure) was the Lutheran conviction that only preaching enlivens
the divine Word, that "the Word of God remains dead and ineffectual unless
it is proclaimed; that everything therefore, depends upon putting the Word
of God 'into motion.'"[1] In practice, "putting the Word of God into motion"
meant rhetorically amplifying, paraphrasing, and applying the Scriptures; it
meant preaching and singing in equal measure. Thus, the purpose of music
in the church service was to enliven the Scriptures themselves or to further
enhance a text that was in itself an amplification of the Scriptures. In either
case, the role of music was rhetorically and emotionally to serve the text and
its religious significance.

The idea that music could be used to "enliven the Word" had
influenced Lutheran service music from the start. At the beginning of the
Reformation, this objective had manifested itself in a concern for proper
declamation of the texts (which were now increasingly in the German
language) so that the music would fit the natural rhythm and inflection of
the language. Then, when the Italian monodic style, with its idealized goal
of "heightened speech," reached Germany in the 1600s, composers no longer
contented themselves with merely declaiming the text properly. They now
sought to heighten the emotional impact of the text by clothing the words in
a persuasive and passionate setting; an art of which Schütz was the
unexcelled master.[2]

In the late seventeenth century, the cantata, like the motet from which
it evolved, was dedicated to serving the divine Word[3] and defined primarily
in terms of this function. As a regular component of Sunday and feast-day
services, its purpose became increasingly specific; namely, to elaborate on the
lesson of the day,[4] and it was, therefore, normally placed between the Gospel
reading and the Credo, hence shortly before the sermon.[5] Since the motet
and the cantata were both "service music," defined more in terms of function
than musical form, and since the basic function had not significantly changed,
there was little need for distinguishing between the two genres. Such pieces
were all called service music (*Kirchenmusik*), or, if specifically linked to the

sermon, *Prädigtmusik* or *Hauptmusik*. This emphasis on function rather than musical form also explains, at least in part, the absence of any standardized label for the cantata before the Neumeister innovations of the 1700s. In fact, the motet (especially that type known as the sacred concerto) and the seventeenth-century cantata (or "older church cantata," as Spitta calls it) are at times virtually indistinguishable.[6]

Although the basic theological function of service music remained the same, the overall musical forms did change, evolving from motetlike structures in the mid-1600s to more sectionalized structures in the later part of the century, and finally to a form comprised of alternating arias, recitatives, and choruses in the first half of the eighteenth century. This change was due in large part to an evolution of the texts. As the librettos and their configurations changed, so did the musical structure. It was the text that provided the composer with his point of departure and largely determined the overall architecture of the work. In general, the trend was for the texts to become increasingly didactic (self-consciously so) and it is this sermonizing element that is the common thread uniting the diverse forms of Lutheran service music that we now call the church cantata.[7]

> The history of church music from Schütz to Bach is, therefore,
> the history of the penetration of service music by sermonizing
> elements (i.e., elements which enlighten or expound).[8]

The Lutheran cantata reached the peak of its popularity during the first half of the eighteenth century.[9] Few of these, however, appeared in published form; an exception can be found in the case of Telemann, who did, in fact, publish a few yearly cycles. Nevertheless, exchange of cantatas was common; it was made possible by an arrangement in which one cantor would pay another for the right to copy a cycle of cantatas.[10] Although some of the resulting manuscripts have not survived, those that do form a vast repertory, much of which is still not available in modern editions.

The Chorale Cantata

The older church cantata drew on three types of texts: biblical passages, chorale texts, and strophic poems called "odes." Of these, the latter two types lend themselves most readily to a sectionalized (cantata) structure because of their strophic nature. Actually, settings of chorale texts did not differ from ode cantatas, unless the composer chose to retain the actual chorale melody in his setting. In that case, the structure became a set of chorale variations, with each stanza presenting a different treatment of the chorale melody. Chorale variation was not a new choral technique. It had already been used in motets of the early seventeenth century.[11] What made the chorale cantata different from its motet predecessor (insofar as this characteristic was present) was an increased sense of sectionalization. One of the means composers used for making sections more independent of each other was to change the orchestration for each stanza. By giving each stanza of text its own distinct orchestration and making the orchestral material melodically independent from the vocal material, the structure as a whole became much less homogenous and each section more clearly delineated as a self-contained unit.[12]

Although the distinction between chorale motet and chorale cantata works well in theory, in practice the distinction is often not very clear-cut, and some works fall somewhere between the two categories.

As for the treatment of the chorale melody itself, while some chorale settings treated the tune quite strictly,[13] most chorale cantatas kept the chorale melody intact only in the tutti stanzas, where it appeared as a cantus firmus set against a contrapuntal background. By contrast, the solo stanzas presented free treatments of the tune. At times the chorale tune would be reworked and embellished; more often only motives remained to remind the listener of the original melody. Even in the tutti stanzas, the literal presentation of the cantus firmus was sometimes interrupted with free material.

Usually the cantata would present a series of free solo stanzas and end with the more literal tutti setting of the chorale. If the composer were interested in creating a somewhat symmetrical structure, he would also set the first stanza as tutti, thus framing the solo stanzas between two choral pillars. This effect could be strengthened by making these outer movements musically identical. Occasionally a composer would alternate the tutti (strict) settings with the solo (free) movements in a rondolike pattern. Some of Schelle's cantatas take symmetrical form even one step further by pairing the movements in an arch form (A B C D C B A).[14]

The Ode Cantata

The textual basis for the ode cantata is the ode: a strophic poem that is really no different from a chorale text in its structure but whose sentiments are generally more fervent in tone. With the rising influence of pietism during the last half of the seventeenth century, the desire for a deeper devotional life led to the composition of such strophic poems.[15] The musical beginnings of the ode cantata can be found in the service music of such composers as J.R. Ahle, who points out, in a foreword to one of his collections of strophic songs, that variety can be achieved in the performance of these works by assigning each stanza to a different performing medium (alternating soloists, choir, etc.)[16] Such differentiation between stanzas in performance produced a quasi-through-composed work and prepared the way for full-fledged strophic variation.

Real cantatalike differentiation between the strophes was achieved with the adoption of older Italian cantata models, which consisted of strophic variations over an unchanging bass. (In some cases the bass changed too.) Of such cantatas, the type using a vocal ensemble became most important.[17] During the course of time, it became standard to have outer tutti movements frame movements for alternating soli; a structure that was quite similar to that of the chorale cantata. The form might then be further delineated with instrumental ritornelli.[18]

Composers who used odes for their cantatas included Buxtehude, Schelle, Erlebach, Böhm, and Bruhns.[19] As in the case of the chorale cantatas, individual works of this textual type display varying degrees of sectionalization and contrast. This fact leads to a certain degree of semantic confusion. Should they be called sacred concerto, strophic aria, or cantata?[20]

The Biblical Cantata

In cantatas using only biblical texts, the words were most commonly taken from the Psalms, the Song of Solomon, the Gospels, Epistles, or the prophetic books; or they were assembled from several biblical books.[21] Although musical sectionalization was not necessarily suggested by the biblical texts (except in the case of verse compilations), composers, at times, still chose to contrast various sections or even to set them apart with instrumental or choral ritornelli in order to give the compositions a clearer architecture.

This was especially true of Psalm settings, occasionally also of Epistle settings, less often of Gospel settings. Where composers did sectionalize their works, they would sometimes frame them with choral sections, at times literally repeating the opening chorus at the end of the work. Inner movements were sometimes identified as recitatives despite the fact that their texts were still biblical (not yet verse). These were usually followed by movements with arialike characters.

Mixed-Text Cantatas

More common than the pure text-forms of chorale, scripture, and ode were the mixed forms in which two or even all three types were combined. Of these, the most common (in fact the most common of all early cantata types) was the kind combining scripture with ode. The desire to amplify the liturgical lesson of the day encouraged this tropelike technique in which the ode stanzas served as poetic commentary to the scriptural movements.

Whether the scripture-ode cantata[22] developed by inserting an ode into a biblical text, or whether the composer began with an ode and prefaced it with a mottolike scripture is debatable. The fact is that many of these cantatas frame an ode with identical tutti settings of a biblical text (*dictum*). Another tutti (also scripture) may appear in the center. Usually, the repeated closing choral section is not written out but is simply indicated with a rubric such as "ab initio," "da Capo," "ut supra," etc.[23]

Composers of the mixed cantata included Knüpfer, Buxtehude, Schelle, J.Ph. Krieger, Pachelbel, Zachow, Bruhns, Telemann, plus a host of less-well-known composers; in short, almost all church composers of the late seventeenth century. Differences between the cantatas of these composers were not so much architectural in nature as stylistic. The younger composers tended much more toward arialike melismas and a greater independence of the instrumental parts.[24]

In addition to the standardized scripture/ode combination just discussed, all sorts of text juxtapositions combining scripture, strophic poetry, and chorale stanzas in a variety of ways are to be found in the late seventeenth century. The common thread uniting these diverse types appears to be a desire to move beyond mere commentary to a kind of literary dialogue that was usually not possible in cantatas with unmixed texts.[25]

Actually, polytextuality and dialogue elements had already appeared in the sacred concertos (motets) of earlier composers like Hammerschmidt and do not in themselves require cantatalike structure.[26] Nevertheless, the greater sectionalization of the cantata lent itself readily to the contrast implied by multiple texts, especially if the composer sought to establish distinct emotional affects for each movement.

The dialogue in such cantatas was often allegorical rather than realistically dramatic in nature. Thus, for example, a dialogue might take place between the believing soul and the heavenly bridegroom. This fondness for allegory caused librettists to juxtapose all sorts of texts (Bible verses, stanzas of different chorales, individual chorale lines, poetic strophes, etc.). Whereas Scriptural passages whose structures lent themselves to responsive treatment had long been set as dramatic dialogues, this allegorical treatment often juxtaposed scriptural texts with other texts in ways that took them out of their original contexts and gave them new meanings.[27]

The Stylistic Sources For the "Old" Cantata

Thus far we have discussed mainly the textual bases of the "old" cantata, showing that the type and configuration of texts chosen primarily determined its large-scale structure. On the smaller scale, too, the type of text in any particular movement played an integral role in determining that movement's musical form, although, to be sure, the composers worked within the context of contemporary styles and forms. Each type of text, however, suggested its own musical form. Almost all contemporary musical forms and styles were incorporated: the motet, the concerto, the chorale, and the strophic aria. A variety of arioso and recitative movements can also be found in cantatas of the late 1600s, and these already foreshadow the adoption of full-fledged Italian operatic style; the style that characterizes the "new" cantata of the 1700s.[28]

Motet style was often used in setting biblical texts, especially those that functioned as *dicta*. In the traditional manner, each phrase of text was given a distinctive musical gesture, which was then treated imitatively throughout the texture. The techniques of word painting (which were themselves musical imitations of rhetorical methods)[29] played an integral role in determining the shapes of the individual phrases. The entire movement thus became a series of such "points of imitation." Although the motet as a form was outmoded by the end of the seventeenth century, the motet principle can still be found in many of the individual choral movements of cantatas.[30]

The concerted style was also useful for scriptural texts, especially those of opening movements that suggested an elaborate setting for voices and instruments. In this style, the instrumental lines were given equal status with the vocal lines, participating as equal and independent partners in a musical exchange. For responsorial texts such as Psalms, the composer might choose a full polychoral style for the maximum festal effect. On the other hand, the concerto principle might reveal itself in a number of other ways, including the elevation of a single voice or instrument to a prominent role, or the concertizing exchange of a few single voices over basso continuo. Often the concerted style was combined with the contrapuntal techniques of the motet style, and such movements were sometimes referred to as "motetto concertato."[31]

Of the musical forms originating in German tradition, the most important as a musical source for the cantata was the chorale, with its related cantus firmus techniques.[32] We have already seen how the chorale might become the basis for an entire cantata. Individual chorale-based movements were, however, also possible in cantatas with mixed texts. Even in movements with texts other than chorales and in forms other than chorale variation, a chorale might appear as a cantus firmus, with or without its text. This superimposition of the chorale on some other text and form served to heighten the interplay of musical and textual ideas and further unified the movement. Full-fledged chorale variation was essentially an old-fashioned technique, however; and so, with the notable exception of Bach's chorale-based movements, it slowly disappeared from the cantata genre, although simple homophonic settings still appeared.[33]

For the setting of odes, composers used the strophic aria, a simple, songlike form similar to the chorale. Unlike the chorale, these tunes were generally not superimposed on movements with other texts and forms but rather stood as independent settings for solo voice.[34] Each strophe of text was set as a musical unit, and these sections were often separated by instrumental ritornelli. In some cases the tune remained the same for each strophe, although it often shifted from one solo voice part to another. In other cases the tune was varied for each new strophe, while the bass line repeated unchanged.

Italian operatic styles began to enter the German church cantata toward the end of the seventeenth century. This trend can be seen in the replacement of strophic arias with arioso movements whose texts are metrically dissimilar, in the looser ritornello frameworks, and in the more significant instrumental accompaniments.[35] Some of these arias incorporated a da capo of their first lines.[36] Occasional movements labelled "recitative" can also be found in works by Krieger, Kuhnau, and others.[37] The full impact of the Italian theatrical forms, however, was really felt only after 1700, when a new style of poetry suitable for these forms was introduced in Germany by Erdmann Neumeister (1671-1756). The stylistic change that the cantata subsequently underwent was sufficiently radical that this cantata type has usually been differentiated from the older model by the use of terms such as "new-style cantata," "reformed cantata," or "Neumeister cantata."

The Neumeister Cantata

The poetry that Neumeister introduced in 1700 was specifically designed for recitatives and da capo arias. Those texts intended to be set as recitative are generally referred to as "madrigalian" because the rules for their composition are the same as those for the Italian madrigal. These rules had already been outlined by Caspar Ziegler in 1653:[38]
1. no fixed number of lines, usually between five and sixteen
2. freedom of line length, usually between six and eleven syllables
3. freedom of rhyme scheme (some unrhymed lines)
4. iambic meter for the most part
5. renunciation of strophic structure
Whether or not such "madrigals" by post-Ziegler poets directly influenced the operatic recitative is not clear, although Spitta thought so.[39] In any case, after Ziegler pointed out the relationship between the two genres, the terms "madrigal verse" and "recitative" were usually equated.[40] Neumeister's description of the recitative is very similar to Ziegler's of the madrigal, and Neumeister also acknowledges the similarity between the two poetic genres.[41]
Neumeister also lists the poetic characteristics of the aria:
1. one to two (occasionally three) strophes
2. focus on a central affect or moral
3. preferable repetition (at the end) of the poem's beginning[42]
He then stresses the complete freedom the poet is given in choosing the number of arias and recitatives as well as their arrangement.

In the composition of recitatives, additional musical characteristics distinguished the new form:[43]

1. syllabic text underlay, with no word repetition
2. melodic leaps, unless the voice was accompanied by orchestral ensemble
3. basso continuo accompaniment only (in most cases)

It is the madrigalian recitative that is the main distinquishing characteristic of the "new" or "reformed" cantata. To be sure, some of the characteristics of the new cantata had already appeared in earlier cantatas; the use of the da capo principle, the pairing of metrically different single-strophe arias, and a cautious use of recitative had all been found in what Feder calls "transition cantatas" by composers such as Zachow, Erlebach, Kuhnau, J.Ph. Krieger, and others.[44] Because of its operatic origins, the new cantata met with fierce opposition from opponents who considered its theatrical forms too worldly for sacred purposes. Some of their more vocal spokesmen included Johann Heinrich Buttstedt, Christian Gerber, and Joachim Meyer. Their objections were powerfully refuted by men like Mattheson, Telemann, Keiser, Stölzel, Tilgner (the publisher of Neumeister's *Fünffache Andachten*), and Neumeister himself. A summary of the arguments presented by both sides has been provided by Spitta.[45]

Erdman Neumeister wrotc tcn[46] liturgical cycles of poems in this new style.[47] The first of these cycles (1701/1704)[48] contains only verse settings, which are, hence, essentially intended to be set as solos. In the second cycle (1708), however, short movements marked "tutti" are also included.[49] Then in the third and fourth cycles (1711, 1714), the older scriptural (*dicta*) and choral movements for tutti ensemble return, although these movements do not occur in any standardized positions.

It was this latter form, which mixed recitatives, arias, *dicta*, and chorales, that became the most favored type and reached its peak in the cantatas of Bach's Leipzig period. Especially popular was the scheme: Scriptural tutti (*dictum*), alternations of recitatives and arias (also duets), closing chorale.

The combination of chorale/scripture movements, on the one hand, and recitative/aria movements on the other seemed to produce a happy balance between conservative tradition and modern innovation. Even the conservative chorale and *dicta* movements were modernized with time, however. Whereas the scriptural tutti movements were originally contrapuntal (usually fugal) with homophonic introductions, they gradually became ever more homophonic, with the upper voice gaining more and more melodic prominence, while the fugues, if not disappearing altogether, served only as brief codas. Chorale movements, too, became increasingly simple, usually appearing only at the end, with the instruments simply doubling the choral parts. In this regard, Bach's elaborate chorale settings are old-fashioned and do not typify the general practice of the period.[50]

The list of men who composed cantatas of this new type is almost endless. Johann Philipp Krieger, Kuhnau, and Zachow belonged to that older group of musicians who switched to the new style. Telemann, Graupner, Fasch, and Bach are just a few of the more well-known composers of the next generation (born after 1680), which brought the genre to its peak.

The new type of cantata, using mixed texts, was by far the most prominent type during the first half of the eighteenth century. Cantatas using only Biblical texts were almost nonexistent, although a few Psalm settings can be found. Chorale cantatas (with the exception of Bach's) generally abandoned variation technique and took on the character of the earlier ode cantata, so that some stanzas were kept as simple tutti movements, the others set as solo arias (no da capo) without cantus firmus. Bach's practice of using paraphrased texts for the solo movements, which were then set as recitatives and arias (with little, if any, reference to the chorale tune), was actually a unique departure from the norm, even though Spitta regards these cantatas as the "perfect flower"[51] of the cantata's development.

The cantata's development did not end with the Bach generation. As the intellectual and aesthetic climate changed under the influence of the Enlightenment, the dogmatic and moralistic aspects of the texts became offensive.

> Dogmatic instruction was now replaced by touching contempla-
> tions of God's goodness, moralistically zealous sermons by gentle
> calls to sympathy and an appreciation for profitableness, (and)
> baroque praise of God in the style of byzantine homage by the
> hymn-like "Praise of the God of Nature."[52]

Musically, the classicists objected to what they considered the contrived ornamentation of the baroque cantata, the use of rhetoric and tone painting, which was the basis of the baroque musical vocabulary, the da capo aria, and secco recitative style.

It becomes clear that Heinichen and his contemporaries stood on the edge of a major cultural transition that began in the philosophical principles of the Enlightenment and worked its way through religious thought and cultural endeavor. To the extent that a composer felt comfortable with these new directions, he tended to embrace the Classical style with its melody-dominated texture, symmetrical phrase structures, and appeal to nature and good taste.[53] To the extent that a composer rejected these trends, however, he tended to compose music that was considered contrived and artificial by the new guard. For this reason, it is well for us to remember that although Bach's cantatas are unsurpassed specimens of the genre, they are often not typical of prevailing trends and are, therefore, not necessarily the right yardstick with which to measure the efforts of his contemporaries.

Chapter 2. Notes

1. Dürr, *Die Kantaten*, 1:13.

2. Ibid.

3. Feder, col. 584; Dürr, *Die Kantaten*, 1:14-15.

4. Dürr points out that the reason for choosing the lesson as the textual basis for musical composition was that the lesson (especially the Gospel) contains the greatest potential for sermonizing. Dürr, *Die Kantaten*, 1:14. Before 1700 cantatas were not inevitably linked to the lesson. See Krummacher, "The German Cantata," p. 707.

5. Feder, col. 582.

6. Adrio, Forchert, "Das Vokal Konzert," cols. 1568-9.

7. One could perhaps argue that the trend toward increasingly didactic texts specifically related to the Gospel lesson (and hence to the sermon) indicates that the theological role of service music was itself changing.

8. Dürr, *Die Kantaten*, 1:14. See also Stiller, pp. 150, 155-56, 212-225, 230, 250-251, 253-55. At the start of the eighteenth century, the most productive German districts for the Protestant cantata were Thuringia and Saxony. Prominent cantata composers of this area included J.Ph. Krieger (1649-1725), Erlebach (1657-1714), Zachow (1663-1712), Kuhnau (1660-1722), Telemann (1681-1767), Graupner (1683-1760), Römhild (1684-1757), and, of course, J.S. Bach (1685-1750).

9. Krummacher, "The German Cantata," p. 708.

10. Feder, col. 583.

11. Feder cites the motets of Scheidt. See Feder, col. 586.

12. Feder, col. 586.

13. Examples of such cantatas can be found in the works of Kindermann, Tunder, Buxtehude, Topf, Schelle, and J.Ph. Krieger. Feder, col. 587.

14. Feder, col. 587.

15. Dürr, *Die Kantaten*, 1:15.

16. Feder, col. 588.

17. Feder, col. 588.

18. Dürr, *Die Kantaten*, 1:21.

19. More composers are listed by Feder, col. 589.

20. See Feder's discussion of Buxtehude's cantatas. Feder, col. 589.

21. Feder, col. 585.

22. Feder calls this the *Spruchodenkantate*. Feder, col. 590.

23. Feder, col. 591.

24. Feder, col. 592.

25. Feder distinguishes between monologue and dialogue types of cantata whether the texts are unmixed or not, but points out the affinity of polytextual librettos for allegorial dialogues. Feder, col. 593.

26. See Feder, col. 595 for examples.

27. Even the poetic texts themselves contained many references to a variety of Biblical texts. Helmuth Rilling points out that a particular recitative from Bach's cantata 113 refers to four totally unrelated Biblical stories. See Helmuth Rilling, "Bach's Significance," trans. Gordon Paine, *The Choral Journal* (June, 1985): 8-9.

28. Feder, col. 596. Krummacher, "The German Cantata," p. 707.

29. Dürr, *Die Kantaten*, 1:19.

30. Dürr, *Die Kantaten*, 1:19.

31. Krummacher, "The German Cantata," p. 703.

32. Dürr, *Die Kantaten*, 1:20.

33. Dürr, *Die Kantaten*, 1:21; Feder, col. 602.

34. An exception occurs in Heinichen's cantata *Einsamkeit, o stilles Wesen*. The tune of the soprano aria is a simple choralelike tune that is first heard in the sonata as a cantus firmus.

35. Krummacher, "The German Cantata," p. 707.

36. Feder, col. 596.

37. Other composers are listed by Friedhelm Krummacher, "The German Cantata," p. 706.

38. Karl Vossler, *Das deutsche Madrigal: Geschichte seiner Entwickelung bis in die Mitte des XVIII Jahrhunderts* (Weimar, 1898), p. 45, 46; and Feder, col. 599.

39. Philipp Spitta, *Musikgeschichtliche Aufsätze* (Berlin, 1894), p. 72, referred to in Vossler, p. 93.

40. Vossler, p. 93.

41. Erdmann Neumeister, Foreword to *Geistliche Cantaten statt einer Kirchen-Music. Die zweite Auflage Nebst einer neuen Vorrede auf Unkosten Eines guten Freundes* (Weissenfels, 1704), partially reproduced by Max Seiffert in a Forword to "Johann Philipp Krieger," vol. 53/54 (1916) of *Denkmäler Deutscher Tonkunst*, p. LXXVI, LXXVII. See also Christian Hunold [Menantes], *Die aller neuste Art zur reinen und galanten Poesie zu gelangen* (Hamburg, 1707), pp. 72-75. Hunold's book (published under the pseudonym "Menantes") was a plagerized version of lectures given by Neumeister in 1695 in Leipzig. See Kerala Johnson Snyder, "Erdmann Neumeister," *The New Grove* 13:155. See also chapter 8.

42. Seiffert, p. LXXVII; Hunold, pp. 216-229.

43. Feder, col. 599.

44. Feder, col. 597.

45. Spitta, *Bach*, 1:478-485.

46. Although Snyder gives the count as nine, Tagliavini lists ten. See Snyder, 13:155, and Luigi Ferinando Tagliavini, "Erdmann Neumeister," *Die Musik in Geschichte und Gegenwart*, vol. 9, col. 1402, 1403. Dürr also speaks of ten cycles. See Dürr, *Die Kantaten*, 1:17.

47. For a discussion of these cycles see Spitta, *Bach*, 1:475-478.

48. These texts were published individually in 1701; as a complete cycle in 1704.

49. J.A. Westrup suggests that Neumeister may have realized he had "gone too far" by excluding the chorus in works intended for the church. See J.A. Westrup, *Bach's Cantatas* (Seattle: University of Washington Press, 1969), p. 6.

50. Dürr, *Die Kantaten*, 1:21; Feder, col. 602.

51. Spitta, *Bach*, 3:105.

52. Feder, col. 603, trans. M. Unger.

53. For a further discussion see George J. Buelow, "In defense of J.A. Scheibe against J.S. Bach," Royal Music Association, London: *Proceedings* 1974/75, pp. 85-100.

3.
Biography

Early Life

Johann David Heinichen was born on April 17, 1683, in the small town of Krössuln, which was near the town of Teuchern and about ten kilometers from the city of Weissenfels, to which the court of Johann Adolph I had recently moved.[1] Heinichen's father, David, was the pastor of the small Lutheran parish in Krössuln; he had come there in 1673, directly upon completing his studies at the St. Thomas School and the University of Leipzig,[2] married the daughter of his predecessor, and then remained as pastor for forty-five years. At the time of his death in 1719, Johann was the only surviving male heir.[3] Heinichen's ties with the Lutheran parish of Krössuln continued even after he left: his sister married his father's sucessor in 1711.

The source of Heinichen's earliest musical instruction is unknown, but likely his father, who had studied for eight years under Sebastian Knüpfer as a student at St. Thomas,[4] first instructed him in composition. According to Heinichen's own testimony, he was already composing church works as a thirteen-year-old boy and would direct these himself at nearby locations.[5]

Like his father, Johann Heinichen enrolled at the St. Thomas School when he was thirteen years old. There he studied under Johann Schelle and, afterward, with Johann Kuhnau. His relationship with Kuhnau seems to have been especially close at this time; he went to Kuhnau for organ lessons even before Kuhnau became cantor of the St. Thomas school.[6] Then, when Kuhnau succeeded Schelle as cantor, Heinichen studied privately with him, a privilege that was reserved for exceptional students. Kuhnau's esteem for his student is further substantiated by the fact that Heinichen, along with another private student of Kuhnau's, Christoph Graupner, worked as Kuhnau's copyist.[7] Other classmates at St. Thomas included Christian Umblaufft, Johann Schieferdecker, Johannes Römhild, and Johann Fasch. That Heinichen apparently excelled at composition and its instruction can be surmised from the fact that his fellow student Graupner came to him for lessons.[8] Years later Heinichen was able to write a recommendation for his former classmate when Graupner applied for the position of cantor at St. Thomas.[9] Heinichen writes of these student days that his enthusiasm for counterpoint hardly left him enough time to eat, drink, or sleep.[10] He appears to have had an inclination for organizing his newly acquired knowledge into well-ordered and logical systems. Thus, for example, his claim of having independently discovered the circle of fifths during this time[11] shows him as a budding theoretician. This analytical ability may well have been the reason for his apparent popularity as a teacher and certainly contributed later to the success of his treatise on the thorough-bass. During his stay in Leipzig, Heinichen also came under the influence of Melchior Hofmann's operas, which were being performed at the Leipzig opera house.[12]

In 1702 Heinichen enrolled at the University of Leipzig as a law student. There he met Telemann, who had also originally enrolled as a law student but switched to music in 1702, founding a collegium musicum (of which Heinichen, Graupner, and, later, Pisendel, were members) and becoming musical director of the Leipzig Opera in place of Strungk, who had died a few years earlier.[13] By offering the services of this student choir to the New Church,[14] Telemann also got the job as organist there. This arrangement between Telemann's student choir and the New Church encroached on the jurisdiction of Heinichen's former teacher Kuhnau, who had previously provided choristers to Leipzig churches on an alternating basis and consequently now "complained bitterly about the students' 'rush to opera' for they ...flocked to join Telemann and no longer supported Kuhnau in providing music for the church services."[15]

Since lesser roles at the Leipzig opera were usually sung by university students, Heinichen, Telemann, Petzold, Grünewald, Graupner, Schieferdecker, and Fasch got some first-hand experience with the "theatrical style" of which he later wrote in his treatise.[16] Kuhnau's struggle against the intrusion of operatic style into church music must have given Heinichen much cause for reflection. No doubt some of the opinions expressed in his treatise about these matters were already being formulated at this time.

Weissenfels and Leipzig

Heinichen apparently graduated in 1705/6, although no archival record of the event survives.[17] He then moved to Weissenfels, where he presumably began a law practice. At the Weissenfels court, Johann Georg was now the duke (1697-1712), and musical life was elaborate and glamorous. Being interested primarily in theater and opera and less concerned with finances than his father, the duke began to import performers from larger centers.[18] Resident musicians included Johann Phillip Krieger (1649-1725), who served as Kapellmeister, and Christian Schieferdecker (the father of his former classmate), the city organist.[19] Krieger's exhaustive list of the works that he performed while cantor at Weissenfels indicates that on St. Michaels Day, 1711, a cantata for soprano and three instruments by Heinichen was presented.[20]

Other musicians with whom Heinichen had contact during these years included Christoph Förster, who came to him for lessons, and the opera composer Reinhard Keiser, who returned to his birthplace on visits to his former teacher, the organist Christian Schieferdecker.

In 1709 Heinichen was invited to Leipzig to compose some operas. The request was occasioned by a managerial conflict resulting in Melchior Hofmann's departure for England. In accepting the commission, Heinichen apparently abandoned his law profession forever. He moved to Leipzig and wrote two operas: *Mario*, and *Carneval von Venedig*, which were performed at the Easter Festival that year.[21] He also assumed the directorship of a collegium musicum, which met at Lehmann's coffee house in the market.[22] Another commission for the Naumburg opera followed for which Heinichen composed *Olimpia vendicata*. During this time he also completed the first edition of his treatise, which appeared in 1711 under the title *Neue erfundene und gründliche Anweisung...zu vollkommener Erlernung des General-Basses*.

Trip to Italy

Heinichen's growing popularity next led to an appointment to the court in Zeitz, but already in that same year Heinichen requested a release so that he might visit the musical establishments at various German courts.[23] Heinichen's desire to leave Zeitz so soon after his arrival was most likely occasioned by the death of the ten-year-old crown prince on February 17, 1710. The prince had been living in Halle under the tutelage of Enoch Buchta, an official hired by the king for that purpose.[24] With the death of the king's only child, a period of state mourning was no doubt declared, and Heinichen was relieved of all musical responsibilities.[25] Buchta, for that matter, likewise had no further duties. He invited Heinichen to accompany him on a trip to Italy, and Heinichen accepted the invitation, apparently dropping his earlier plans. Heinichen and Buchta arrived in Venice sometime in 1710.[26] In Venice, Heinichen was commissioned to write two operas for the Teatro Sant'Angelo. These operas, following legal proceedings that delayed their production, eventually appeared in 1713 and received an enthusiatic reception. Despite competition from such Venetian contemporaries as Pollarolo, Lotti, and Gasparini, the German composer's operas were in such demand that they were repeated more often than almost any others of the time.[27]

While in Venice, Heinichen also had opportunity to visit the four Venetian conservatories and meet their music directors: Michelangelo Gasparini, Antonio Biffi, Francesco Pollarolo, and Antonio Vivaldi.[28] Heinichen was accompanied by Gottfried Heinrich Stölzel, who was visiting Italy during this time. Schmitz suggests Heinichen may have studied composition under Vivaldi, as did his later colleague Jan Dismas Zelenka.

During the interval in which Heinichen's commission had been in litigation, he had travelled on to Rome. There he met Prince Leopold of Anhalt-Köthen (later Bach's patron), who wished to take Heinichen with him on his travels. Although the exact results of this contact are unclear, it is, nevertheless, certain that the prince eventually returned to Germany alone. Heinichen, meanwhile, had returned to Venice, where the legal proceedings had been resolved in his favor.

Once back in Venice, Heinichen gained an enthusiastic supporter in the person of Angioletta Bianchi, who, as a graduate of one of the Venetian conservatories, was a fine singer and a keyboard player. Her husband was a wealthy merchant whose business brought him into contact with the crown prince of Saxony, Friedrich August, who was in Venice from February 13, 1716 to July 20, 1717.[29] On the prince's occasional visits to her home, Angioletta had opportunity to play some of Heinichen's cantatas and to point out to the prince that the composer was a native Saxon.[30] Then, for a special birthday celebration on October 17, 1716, held in the prince's honor, she secretly commissioned Heinichen to write a serenata for the event. The serenata was performed on the canal outside their home and greatly impressed the assembled spectators. According to Hiller, it was this performance that moved the crown prince to hire Heinichen as Kapellmeister on a life-long appointment to the Dresden court.[31] Since the actual document[32] is dated August 28, 1716, however, it appears that the transaction had already been finalized a few months earlier. From the document itself we learn that the appointment was to take effect immediately and that the contract was made with the king's permission:

Ayant le consentement de Sa Majesté le Roÿ mon Père, j'a engagé à son service Jean David Heünichen pour maître de chapelle...et les appointements commenceront du mois d'Août 1716...[33]

During this time Heinichen probably met a group of Dresden musicians who had been sent to Venice in 1716 by August the Strong to provide chamber music for the crown prince: Johann Christian Richter, Christian Petzold, Jan Dismas Zelenka,[34] and their director Johann Georg Pisendel.[35] Of these, Petzold and Pisendal were likely known to him from encounters in Leipzig. Pisendel had come to Leipzig in 1709; the exact date of Petzold's stay in Leipzig is not known.

The crown prince had, in fact, become enamoured with Italian music and proposed to his father that an Italian opera company be hired by the Dresden court. Although the king was more inclined toward French culture,[36] he agreed to his son's request, and the Crown Prince went about making the necessary arrangements. In his enthusiasm for the project, he began spending so much on contracts that his father began to make objections.[37] Eventually the contracts were finalized, however, and an entire opera company with Lotti as director was hired. Some of the salaries reached 6000-7000 Taler, amounts five times that paid to Heinichen, Veracini, and other leading instrumentalists.[38]

Dresden

The opera troupe left Venice for Dresden on September 5, 1717.[39] It is possible that Heinichen had already arrived in Dresden toward the beginning of the year, for by February of that year, Mattheson had apparently already requested his biography for his dictionary of musicians, *Grundlage einer Ehren-pforte*, and was using Heinichen's new title: "Chur. Printzl. Sächsis. Capellmeister."[40] According to Fürstenau, Heinichen's appointment began January 1.[41] It is doubtful that Heinichen arrived in Dresden this early however, because on January 30, 1717, August the Strong still questioned the necessity of hiring Heinichen in addition to Lotti:

To what good [purpose] the composer Heinichen the German, since there is already a composer for the opera [Lotti] and since Schmidt is sufficient for the rest.[42]

The crown prince responded, defending his action, on March 28, 1717.[43] Heinichen, therefore, probably did not arrive in Dresden until sometime after this date. That Mattheson was already using Heinichen's new title in February of that year may simply indicate that the news of Heinichen's appointment reached Germany before Heinichen did.

Once in Dresden, Heinichen's duties as Kapellmeister placed him alongside Johann Christoph Schmidt,[44] who apparently had just received the title of "Oberkapellmeister,"[45] although Heinichen stresses in his treatise that Schmidt in no way ranked above him and never on any occasion had claimed to be his superior.[46]

There were, in fact, two chapels at the court, the old Protestant one, and the Roman Catholic one, which had been instituted in 1697, at the time of August the Strong's conversion to Catholicism. Apparently Heinichen worked mostly in the Catholic chapel, while Schmidt took care of the Protestant one. Indicators that suggest this conclusion include Fürstenau's statement that upon Schmidt's death in 1728 Heinichen took over the Protestant chapel,[47] the fact that Heinichen's choral output during his Dresden years is comprised mostly of Masses, and contemporary accounts that indicate that on occasion Schmidt was given the court orchestra for performances in the Lutheran chapel.[48] At all events, this is the conclusion drawn by numerous authors.[49]

In addition to fulfilling churchly duties, Heinichen also acted as Lotti's substitute in the opera, since Schmidt was unacquainted with the Italian operatic style.[50] In fact, the intrusion of the Italian musicians apparently met with considerable resistance (especially from Schmidt and the French concertmaster Volumier) so that the king had to make a special point of his support for the Italians.[51]

Shortly after he came to Dresden, Heinichen's health began to fail. He was apparently suffering from tuberculosis, a disease that had claimed numerous of his relatives.[52] To help Heinichen with the church services, Zelenka was appointed as his assistant.[53] Zelenka also succeeded Heinichen after the latter's death, although he never did gain the official title of Kapellmeister.[54]

Many of the musicians at Heinichen's disposal were outstanding. These included the violinists Volumier (at Dresden from 1709-1728), Pisendel, who studied some composition with Heinichen (at Dresden from 1712-1728), and Francesco Maria Veracini (1717-1722); the organist and composer Petzold (1697-1733), the oboist Richter (sometime before 1714 to 1744), the bass player and composer Zelenka (1710-1745), the flautists Buffardin (1715 to retirement in 1749) and his student Quantz (1727-1741), the lutenist Weiss (1718-1759); and Hebenstreit, the inventor of the pantaleon (1724-1750).[55]

Heinichen must also have met many of the leading European musicians who would visit the Dresden court from time to time. His very first year there, Bach came to play the organ in competition with the French organist Marchand. Then in 1719, the crown prince married Maria Josepha, daughter of Emperor Joseph I. The month-long celebration included the opening of the new opera theater and attracted many musicians, including his former classmate Telemann,[56] the famous Italian singing instructor Tosi, and Handel, who was apparently looking for singers for the London Opera.[57] A look at the calendar reveals a very hectic performance schedule:[58]

Mar. 23, 1719	Prince returns to Dresden after eight-year absence.
Aug. 20, 1719	Engagement in Vienna.
Sept. 2 (Sat.)[59]	Royal couple arrives in Dresden.
Sept. 3 (Sun.) a.m.	Te Deum in Catholic chapel and a banquet at which the orchestra played.
Sept. 3 (Sun.) p.m.	Opening of Opera House with Lotti: *Giove in Argo*.
Sept. 5 (Tues.)	French theater performance.
Sept. 6 (Wed.)	Italian theater performance.
Sept. 7 (Thurs.)	Opera: Lotti: *Ascanio*.
Sept. 10 (Sun.) p.m.	Celebration of the Sun (the first of seven "planet celebrations"). Heinichen cantata: *La Gara degli Dei*.
Sept. 11 (Mon.)	Theatre performance.
Sept. 12 (Tues.)	Probably the Mars Celebration.[60]
Sept. 13 (Wed.)	Opera: *Teofane* by Pallavicini (librettist) and Lotti (composer). Included ballets by Duparc to music by Volumier.[61]
Sept. 14 (Thurs.)	Theatre performance.
Sept. 15 (Fri.)	Jupiter Celebration: cantata by Lotti.

Sept. 17 (Sun.)	Turkish festival and hunt. Included Venetian acrobats and janissary music by 24 musicians.
Sept. 18 (Mon.)	Diana Festival (goddess of the moon): Heinichen cantata *Diana sul' Elba* performed on the Elbe river, followed by a hunt.
Sept. 20 (Wed.)	Mercury Festival: a multi-art event.
Sept. 21 (Thurs.)	Opera: *Teofane* repeated.
Sept. 22 (Fri.)	Theatre performance.
Sept. 23 (Sat.)	Venus Festival. Schmidt Divertissement: *Les quatre saison* with ballets by Duparc. The nobles took various roles.[62]
Sept. 24 (Sun.)	Opera: *Ascanio* (Lotti) repeated.
Sept. 25 (Mon.)	Theatre performance.
Sept. 26 (Tues.)	Festival of Saturn: Italian comedy.
Sept. 27 (Wed.)	Opera: *Teofane* repeated.
Sept. 28 (Thurs.)	Theater performance.
Sept. 29 (Fri.)	Opera: *Ascanio* repeated.
Sept. 30 (Sat.)	French play.

As can be seen from the above calendar of events, Heinichen contributed two cantatas to the celebrations; the first, *La gara degli dei,* had the prestigious function of introducing the seven festivals of the planets on September 10 and was, therefore, accompanied by elaborate staging. All seven planets appeared in a cloud above the castle wall by the gun turrets, while the orchestra played from their position below. Each planet, represented by one of the opera singers, invited the guests to its respective festival.[63] The entire spectacle concluded with fireworks in a representational presentation of the sun.

Heinichen's second performance (Sept. 18) was likewise accompanied by visually stunning effects. A specially built boat in the shape of a seashell carried by nymphs and drawn by four hinds presented Diana, goddess of the moon, in her legendary setting. Inside were the Italian opera singers and the orchestra members who performed the cantata *Diana sul Elba* under Heinichen's direction as this floating stage approached the assembled guests from the far side of the Elbe river.[64] The performance was followed by a hunt.

Both of these cantatas were so successful that the king immediately increased Heinichen's yearly salary by 300 Taler to a total of 1500; a raise that was made retroactive to September 1.[65]

The public festivities concluded at the end of September, and the court moved to the hunting castle of Moritzburg for a week-long hunting party from October 4 to 12. Here on October 7 a serenade of Heinichen's was featured during the formal banquet.[66] Seibel points out that the score is dated the 6th, so perhaps the performance already took place on that date.[67]

With the celebrations now over, Lotti and a few of the other Italian musicians returned to Italy that same month, while the rest of the opera singers, their contracts extended by a year, remained in Dresden. This arrangement left Heinichen in charge of the theater. He began composing an opera for the carnival of the following year but ran into a serious conflict with two of the singers, Senesino and Berselli, who complained that he had not set the text of a particular aria with proper declamation. The ensuing battle of personalities provided August the Strong with an excuse to dismiss the entire company, although the real reason for such drastic action was likely a depleted treasury.[68] Heinichen was retained in his position as Kapellmeister, however.

The dismissal of the Italian opera company proved to be a watershed in Heinichen's compositional output. With the opera now inactive, he turned his attention to providing music for the religious services of the Catholic chapel. Since the elderly Schmidt was no longer composing new works, most of the responsibility for providing new music now fell to Heinichen.[69] All twelve of his Masses date from this time, as do numerous smaller Latin works. To help him with his responsibilities, Louis André was appointed *Compositeur de la Musique* in September, 1720.[70] It is noteworthy that works by nonresident composers were not performed; apparently this exclusivity served to maintain the prestige of the Dresden court.[71]

In 1721 Heinichen married Erdmuthe Eubischens, the daughter of a Leipzig businessman. The wedding took place in Weissenfels and was a private affair.[72] On January 25, 1723, their only child was born: a daughter, Erdmuthe Friederica, who was baptized in the Lutheran Kreuzkirche in Dresden on January 27.

During this last decade of his life, Heinichen apparently concerned himself a great deal with theoretical and pedagogical matters. That one of his private students was the child prodigy Johann Siebenkäs from Nürnburg is evidence of his considerable reputation as a teacher. This twelve-year-old boy had so impressed a leading official of the Dresden court on a visit to Nürnburg that he had brought him to Dresden for further training.[73] Heinichen's preoccupation with theoretical matters during these years consisted of a complete revision of his book, which had occupied his time since 1722.[74] Eventually reaching 960 pages (more than three times its orginal length), the second edition of the book was eventually published in 1728 at his own expense and was available in most major German cities from agents that included Graupner in Hessen-Darmstadt, Bach in Leipzig, and Mattheson in Hamburg.[75]

Perhaps because they were both theoreticians, Mattheson and Heinichen seem to have been especially drawn to each other. As early as 1717, Mattheson had requested an autobiographical sketch from Heinichen, intending to use it in his book *Grundlage einer Ehren-pforte*.[76] Although Heinichen never did fulfill this request, the two men remained in contact. In December of that year, Heinichen wrote a lengthy letter in response to a questionaire Mattheson had sent him. To settle an argument with Heinrich Bokemeyer, Mattheson had formulated seven questions about matters relating to the study of counterpoint and directed them to three composers: Heinichen, Keiser, and Telemann.[77] Heinichen's response is reproduced in Mattheson's *Critica Musica*, Vol. II.

Then, on July 2, 1729, Heinichen wrote Mattheson a poignant letter in which he informed his friend that he was suffering from a severe illness and asked him to collect a certain outstanding debt in Hamburg so that his young daughter might not be impoverished in the event that the illness should prove fatal. In fact, Heinichen's fears proved to be true, and he died on the 16th of that same month. A Lutheran funeral was held three days later at the Dresden Kreuzkirche.

Chapter 3. Notes

1. Max Seiffert, Forword to "Johann Philipp Krieger," vol. 53/54 of *Denkmäler Deutscher Tonkunst*, p. XVI.

2. Seibel, p. 3.

3. Ibid., p. 4.

4. Ibid., p. 6.

5. J.D. Heinichen, *Der General-Bass in der Composition* (Dresden, 1728), p. 840, footnote.

6. Kuhnau was first appointed organist of St. Thomas then, later, cantor.

7. Seibel, p. 7.

8. Johann Mattheson, *Grundlage einer Ehren-Pforte* (Hamburg, 1740; reprint ed., Berlin: Leo Liepmannssohn, 1910), p. 411.

9. Seibel, p. 25.

10. Heinichen, p. 935.

11. Heinichen, p. 840.

12. Hermann Mendel, "Heinichen," *Musikalisches Conversations-Lexicon* (Berlin, 1875), 5:176.

13. Martin Ruhnke, "Georg Philipp Telemann," *The New Grove Dictionary of Music and Musicians*, 20 vols., ed. Stanley Sadie (London: MacMillan, 1980), 18:648.

14. The New Church was dedicated on September 24, 1699. It was a restored building that had not been used since the Reformation, but was now required because of the overcrowding at St. Nicholas and St. Thomas. See Günter Stiller, *Johann Sebastian Bach and Liturgical Life in Leipzig*, trans. Herbert J.A. Bouman, Daniel F. Poellot, Hilton C. Oswald, edited Robin A. Leaver (St. Louis: Concordia, 1984), pp. 40-41.

15. Ibid.

16. Arnold Schering, *Musikgeschichte Leipzigs von 1650 bis 1723* (Leipzig, 1926), pp. 437-471. Cited by Buelow, *Thorough-Bass Accompaniment According to Johann Heinichen* (Berkeley & Los Angeles: U. of California Press, 1966), p. 6.

17. Seibel, p. 9.

18. Seiffert, p. LXXIII.

19. Seibel, p. 10.

20. Seiffer, p. LVI.

21. Seibel, p. 11.

22. Hiller, p. 216.

23. The letters are reproduced in Seibel, pp. 12-13.

24. Arno Werner, *Städtische und fürstliche Musikpflege in Zeitz* (Leipzig, 1922), p. 2.

25. Werner, *Zeitz*, p. 82.

26. Some writers date their arrival 1711. Since there is no record of Heinichen visiting any German establishments, 1710 is a more likely date. This the conclusion reached by both Seibel and Werner. See Seibel, p. 15; Werner, *Zeitz*, p. 82.

27. Ibid.

28. Seibel, p. 18.

29. These dates are recorded in the ceremonial book of the *Eccellentissimo Collegio* of Venice, and reproduced in John Walter Hill, "The Life and Works of Francesco Maria Veracini" (Ph.D. dissertation, Harvard University, 1972), pp. 876-880, 900-901. This dissertation was published in 1979 by University Microfilms International Research Press, but without the appendix containing these relevant documents.

30. Hiller, 1:221.

31. Hiller, 1:222.

32. The document is reproduced in Seibel, p. 19.

33. The entire document is reproduced in Seibel, p. 19. See also Irmgard Becker-Glauch, *Die Bedeutung der Musik für die Dresdener Hoffeste bis in die Zeit Augusts des Starken* (Kassel: Bärenreiter, 1951), p. 23.

34. While in Venice, Zelenka studied composition under Vivaldi. See Schmitz, p. 119.

35. Fürstenau, *Zur Geschichte der Musik und des Theaters am Hofe zu Dresden*, 2 vols. (Dresden, 1862; reprint ed., Hildesheim: Georg Olms, ?), 2:73, 85. Pisendel led this group of chamber musicians from April to December of that year. See Seibel, p. 19.

36. Fürstenau, *Geschichte*, 2:98.

37. Fürstenau, *Geschichte*, 2:99. Hill reproduces some of the correspondence between king and crown prince in his appendix, pp. 884-896.

38. See Becker-Glauch, *Bedeutung*, pp. 24-25; Hill, pp. 22, 904-917; Seibel, p. 20.

39. Fürstenau, *Geschichte*, 2:101.

40. Mattheson, *Das beschützte Orchestre* (Hamburg, 1717), introduction, dated in Hamburg, February 21, 1717.

41. See Moritz Fürstenau, *Beiträge zur Geschichte der Königlich Sächsischen Musikalischen Kapelle* (Dresden, 1849), p. 120. The actual document (partially quoted by Fürstenau) states "...et les appointements commenceront du mois d'Août 1716." See earlier.

42. Quoted in Hill, p. 893 and translated in Hill, p. 76.

43. Excerpts from the correspondence between the crown prince and the king is reproduced in Hill, pp. 884-896.

44. At one point Fürstenau incorrectly identifies him as "Johann Christian Schmidt." Fürstenau, *Geschichte*, 2:13. Johann Christian was the father of Johann Christoph. See Dieter Härtwig, "Schmidt, Johann Christoph," *Die Musik in Geschichte und Gegenwart*, vol. 11 (1963), col. 1858.

45. Fürstenau, *Geschichte*, 2:15.

46. Heinichen, p. 960.

47. Fürstenau, *Geschichte*, 2:17.

48. Ibid.

49. Härtwig, "Schmidt, Johann Christoph," col. 1858; Schmitz, p. 6. In any case Heinichen's ties to the Lutheran church remained intact, for his daughter was baptised at the Kreuzkirche on January 27, 1723, and Heinichen's funeral took place there on July 19, 1729. The records are reproduced in Seibel, pp. 25 and 28 respectively.

50. Hiller, p. 222.

51. Fürstenau, *Geschichte*, 2:99, 100.

52. Seibel, p. 21.

53. Presumably because of Heinichen's ill health.

54. Fürstenau, *Geschichte*, p. 75.

55. For a detailed roster of musicians, see chapter 6.

56. Mattheson, *Ehren-pforte*, p. 354.

57. Fürstenau, *Geschichte*, p. 151.

58. See Fürstenau, *Geschichte*, 2:138-148; Becker-Glauch, *Bedeutung*, pp. 98-111.

59. Fürstenau incorrectly identifies Sept. 2 as a Wednesday. Since Protestant Germany had adopted the revised Gregorian calendar in 1700, the dates of the Protestant and Catholic areas now agreed and correspond with our present calendar.

60. This celebration involved a tournament. See Becker-Glauch, *Bedeutung*, p. 103.

61. Lasted from 7 p.m. to 2 a.m. See Fürstenau, *Beiträge*, p. 126.

62. It involved more than 100 performers, among them 48 chorus members. See Fürstenau, *Beiträge*, p. 126.

63. Fürstenau, p. 143.

64. Fürstenau, p. 145. A picture of the ship has been preserved in a copper etching. See: *Music in Geschichte und Gegenwart*, vol. 3, plate 18.

65. The original document is reproduced in Seibel, p. 22.

66. Fürstenau, p. 148.

67. Seibel, p. 23.

68. Henry Raynor, *A Social History of Music* (New York: Taplinger Publishing Co., 1978), p. 294.

69. Ernst Ludwig Gerber, "Heinichen," *Neues Historisch-Biographisches Lexicon der Tonkünstler*, 2 vols. (Leipzig, 1812-14; reprint ed., Graz: Akademische Druck und Verlaganstalt, 1969), col. 618.

70. Fürstenau, *Beiträge*, p. 127.

71. Fürstenau, *Beiträge*, p. 109.

72. Seibel, p. 25.

73. Ibid., p. 26.

74. Ibid., p. 25.

75. Werner Neumann and Hans-Joachim Schulze, eds., *Bachdokumente*, 3 vols. (Leipzig: Bach-Archiv, 1963-1972) 2:260.

76. Johann Mattheson, Introduction to *Das beschützte Orchestre* (Hamburg, 1717).

77. Seibel, p. 25.

4.
The Sources

List of Extant Cantatas

The manuscripts of Heinichen's fifteen German choral church compositions are presently preserved in two libraries, the Sächsische Landesbibliothek
in Dresden and the Deutsche Staatsbibliothek in East Berlin. In only one
case is there any duplication between the two collections. Those titles held
by the Staatsbibliothek are the ones listed in Seibel's thematic catalogue
under the heading "Kirchenlieder."[1] There are seven compositions in this
collection, and all are in score format.

> *Es lebet Jesus unser Hort* (à 6)
> *Meine Seele erhebet den Herrn* (à 8 in 2 choirs)
> *Ach, was soll ich Sünder machen* (à 4)
> *Einsamkeit, o stilles Wesen* (à 4) 1709
> *Heilig ist Gott der Herr* (à 4)
> *Gegrüsset seist du holdselige Maria* (à 5)
> *Gott ist unsere Zuversicht* (à 4)

In addition to these "choral" compositions, the Deutsche Staatsbibliothek also owns a bass solo cantata, *Warum toben die Heiden.*
The Landesbibliothek in Dresden contains ten manuscripts preserving
nine different works (one cantata exists in two versions). These works
formerly resided in Grimma[2] but have since been acquired by the library in
Dresden. Most of these manuscripts are sets of performing parts. They
comprise the following works:

> *Mag auch ein Blinder* (score)
> *Es naheten aber zu Jesu* (score)
> *Lass dich's nicht irren* (score)
> *Herr, nun lässest Du deinen Diener* (parts)
> *Gelobet sei der Herr* (2 copies, parts)
> *Der Herr ist Nahe* (parts)
> *Lobe den Herrn* (parts)

Der Segen des Herrn (parts)
Einsamkeit, o stilles Wesen (parts)

Taken together, the titles of both Berlin and Dresden collections equal Günter Hausswald's list of what he calls Heinichen's "German cantatas and motets." Hausswald's dual designation apparently reflects the difficulty in differentiating between the two genres. Seibel's catalogue also reflects this confusion over terminology by using the term *Kirchenlieder*. His thematic catalogue does not list any of the works in the Grimma/Dresden collection, however, with the exception of *Einsamkeit, o stilles Wesen*, a cantata that is common to both collections.

It is virtually impossible to determine whether this list is complete. The transmission of Heinichen's manuscripts, as described by Fürstenau, indicates that they were locked away by Queen Josepha until her death in 1758. At that time a chamberlain,[3] oblivious to their value, began selling them. They were rescued by another musician, however, and returned to the church archives.[4]

Authenticity of Sources

With regard to the questions of authenticity and accuracy of these manuscripts, matters that require specialized skills, only a preliminary study has been attempted here. Only the solo cantata *Warum toben die Heiden* is actually designated as an autograph. The designation can be found in the title itself, which is found in the top margin of the first page of music and states:

à Violino Fagotto (Concordat con Cont)
et Basso solo è Continuo
mus. ms autogr. 1 Di Giov Heinichen

The writing is neat and mostly vertical, although occasionally the stems slant to the right. In cases where half notes have stems pointing down, they are usually centered on the note head, without, however, entering the note head itself (♉). Treble clefs look like the letter G, with the tops beginning considerably higher than the top staff line. Bass clefs combine a reverse C formation with a double vertical bar (ɔ‖:). The flags of single eighth notes are straight and made without lifting the pen (♪). The flags of sixteenths are also usually made with one motion ($\mathcal{L}$), although exceptions can be found on the first page. Quarter note rests are written thus: ($\curlyvee$).[5]

According to studies made by Wolfgang Horn, however, this script bears no resemblance to that of Heinichen's other autographs. Horn concludes, therefore, that the designation "Mus. ms. autogr. J.D. Heinichen" was a librarian's error.[6]

There is one other cantata manuscript that resembles *Warum toben die Heiden*, the score of *Einsamkeit, o stilles Wesen*, in the Berlin library. Several differences can be noted, however. The writing never slopes to the right, being consistently vertical, the G clefs look more like a conventional G clef (with a reverse hook at the top: $\mathcal{G}$), the F clef lacks the double bar, and the few single sixteenth notes that can be found have separate flags. Quarter rests do not have the little hook at the bottom but otherwise look similar.

The other manuscripts were apparently written by several different copyists. In the Berlin group, four appear to be in the same hand.

Meine Seele erhebet den Herrn (score)
Gegrüsset seist du holdselige Maria (score)
Gott is unsere Zuversicht (score)
Es lebet Jesus unser Hort (score)

In these works, the handwriting is moderately cramped and angular. The clefs are fairly uniform and of standard design. The notes slant noticeably to the right with stems that are exaggerated and often begin on the wrong side of the note head ($\mathcal{q}$ $\mathcal{q}$). The notes frequently spill over into the following measure. Sixteenth notes have separately formed flags, with the exception of those in *Gegrüsset seist du* ($\mathcal{E}$ vs. $\mathcal{L}$).

In the Dresden collection, four manuscripts seem to be written by the same hand.

Herr, nun lässest Du deinen Diener (parts)
Gelobet sei der Herr (earlier version, parts)
Der Herr ist Nahe (parts)
Einsamkeit, o stilles Wesen (parts)

Each of these works exists as a set of performing parts with title page. All except *Gelobet sei der Herr* bear a monogram that appears to be "J.S.," although construction of the design apparently required the "S" to be written first: (⟨symbol⟩). The handwriting of these manuscripts is generally angular and very firm, although not flambuoyant. Another noteworthy feature is the bar lines, which are only partial, frequently intersecting only one or two staff lines.

Another five manuscripts of the Dresden collection are characterized by a much more flowing writing style. This group includes

> *Lass dichs nicht irren* (score)
> *Es naheten aber zu Jesu* (score)
> *Mag auch ein Blinder* (score)
> *Der Segen des Herrn* (parts)
> *Gelobet sei der Herr* (later version, parts).

Added to the works in this hand are certain sections of *Lobe den Herrn*. The mixture of writing styles in this manuscript poses some interesting questions, and a more detailed examination will follow below.

In addition to the flowing handwriting, the script in these manuscripts is characterized by the sixteenth note written: (⟨symbol⟩), a C clef (⟨symbol⟩), a G clef (⟨symbol⟩) or (G), F clef (⟨symbol⟩), and half notes with descending stems: (⟨symbol⟩). Although *Gelobet sei der Herr* appears to fit with the others in every respect, the C clef (with one exception) is different, usually appearing thus: (⟨symbol⟩).[7]

The two works not accounted for thus far are *Ach, was soll ich Sünder machen* and *Heilig ist Gott der Herr*. Both are from the Berlin group. The former is characterized by eighth notes with a leftward curling flag if the stem points down (⟨symbol⟩), but a straight flag to the right if the stem points up: (⟨symbol⟩). The sixteenth note's flag always turns to the right (⟨symbol⟩). All stems, whether up or down, are placed on the right side of the note head. This is true of half notes and quarter notes as well. Bass clefs employ the vertical double bar (⟨symbol⟩), G clefs look like G's, and C clefs are square (⟨symbol⟩).

Heilig ist Gott der Herr is in a particularly flambuoyant hand. Loops on letters are deep and note stems are long. A fast writing speed is indicated by such factors as descending stems on the right side of the note head made without lifting the pen after formation of the note head (⟨symbol⟩) and ascending stems made in a descending direction (2 motions) but missing the note head (⟨symbol⟩). The G clef also suggests haste for it combines the clef with the flat sign in one unbroken motion (♭). Nevertheless, this manuscript shows greater care in a number of repects. Figures in the continuo part and the bowings of the string parts are more complete, and instrumental doublings, although omitted as in the other manuscripts, are clearly specified with designations such as "con canto," "unison," etc.

Accuracy of Sources

Because there is only one known source in each case for most of these compositions, and almost all of the sources are clearly not autographs, judging the accuracy of the manuscripts in question is difficult. Of the extant works, only two have more than one version, namely *Gelobet sei der Herr, der Gott Israel* and *Einsamkeit, o stilles Wesen*. If the Berlin version of the latter is indeed an autograph, it would, of course, become normative for that work. Since this now appears doubtful, however, the two can only be judged on their relative merits. Actually the differences between the two are minor, the Berlin score having a few more figures in the continuo, more accidentals, etc. There are some text differences, however. These will be discussed in our study of revisions.

In the case of *Gelobet sei der Herr, der Gott Israel*, Dresden manuscript #504 appears to be more accurate than #509. This fact is already seen in their titles. Although the texts of both compositions begin "Gelobet sei der Herr, der Gott Israel," the title page of manuscript #509 truncates this to "Gelobet sei Gott."[8] The numerous other variants of #509 involve mostly accidentals or individual notes. Some of these are convincing, others are not. In general, then, manuscript #504 would seem to be the more reliable source.

Although it is difficult to judge a manuscript's accuracy if only one version of it exists, certain aspects can nevertheless be evaluated. These include correspondence between voice or instrumental parts and their instrumental doublings, numerical totals of rhythms within a measure vis-a-vis the given meter, the degree of consonance (particularly at cadences), consistency in the use of accidentals, and the synchronization of parts when rearranged into score format.

When evaluated according to the above set of criteria, the sets of parts copied by "J.S." (including *Gelobet sei der Herr*, which lacks this monogram) are mostly free of error. Two notable exceptions occur in *Herr, nun lässest Du deinen Diener*. The soprano part at the end of the first chorus does not synchronize properly with the other parts, and the "violin concerto" part (written in a different hand) is riddled with errors.

The other manuscripts are less accurate but still mostly free of errors, although the five cantatas earlier described as being written in a flowing hand (*Lass dichs nicht irren, Es naheten, Mag auch, Der Segen, Gelobet*), even though they are neater than the others, are not as accurate. The three scores in this group (*Lass dichs, Es naheten* and *Mag auch*) present an additional element of imprecision by omitting key signatures much of the time.

Chronology

Only four compositions are dated, and all four are early works:[9]

Einsamkeit, o stilles Wesen:	second day of Easter, 1709
Der Herr ist Nahe:	third day of Easter, 1709
Herr, nun lässest Du:	Feast of Mary's Purification (February 2), 1714[10]
Gelobet sei der Herr:	Feast of St. John the Baptist (June 24), 1707[11]

Nevertheless, certain stylistic differences between the compositions do have chronological implications. Of the four early works just listed, all contain da capo arias.[12] Since only two of the other compositions contain da capo arias,[13] we are inclined to conclude that these undated works are earlier works still.[14]

Another change in Heinichen's style is documented in the composer's treatise, where he himself tells us that thick contrapuntal textures characterized his early works.

> Was it not the opinion of the best contrapuntists in the past that one recognizes a learned composer more easily by his two-, three, and four-voiced compositions than by his excessive (use of) overladen contrapuntal combinations, where it is impossible by their nature to observe the purest rules of composition? Why should the strength of noble music consist of laborious school craft? Yes, if one wants to work and work, achievements of all kinds are possible in theatrical music as well as in the strictest

church style. I recall that in my previous Leipzig operas I was working laboriously on arias in six, seven, and up to eight real parts; however, today I would write over most of them: *sed cui bono*. True art is found elsewhere than on paper.[15]

Three works are written for more than four parts. *Meine Seele erhebet den Herrn* is written for double choir (SATB/SATB), but even the infrequent tutti sections never have more than four independent vocal parts. *Gegrüsset seist du* is à 5 (SSATB), and *Es lebet Jesus* is à 6 (SSATTB). This last work does have some truly thick polyphony in which not only the vocal but also the instrumental parts participate.[16] The presence of a da capo aria (which, however, is fully written out, despite the fact that the manuscript is a score) suggests that this work may not have been written quite as early as some of the others, but its thick texture, nevertheless, indicates it was probably written during Heinichen's Leipzig period.

Compared with the Masses, which we know to have been written at the end of Heinichen's life, we find these German church compositions to be old-fashioned in a number of respects. The musical phrases are often still constructed according to the procedures of Baroque *Fortspinnung*. In the Masses, however, the patterns of classical periodicity are much more prominent. For this reason, the musical phrases in the German church compositions are also less symmetrical than those in the Masses.[17]

The concertante technique found in these works also suggests that they were written in the earlier part of Heinichen's life. The instrumental parts frequently simply echo the voices in a sectional, through-composed structure that presents the text phrase by phrase. Some works do have instrumental ritornelli, but not yet the three-part type found in the Masses.[18]

Finally, at least two works strike one as being particularly early works. Both *Lass dichs* and *Mag auch* contain awkward writing that suggests Heinichen was just beginning to learn his craft. These two compositions are also the only ones containing examples of the strophic aria, a form that was quickly becoming obsolete.

Revisions

A close study of the manuscripts reveals a few interesting additions or revisions. In *Herr, nun lässest Du*, the most obvious addition is a continuo part designated *continuo transpos*. It is written a tone lower than the prevailing key of the other parts and only includes certain movements. The handwriting of this part is characterized by an accentuated backhand and, therefore, contrasts sharply with the rest of the manuscript. Another addition to this cantata is the "violino concerto" part. It simply reinforces the violin part in three of the movements. It has been hastily written and is full of mistakes. Finally, the alto part of the duet "Weg, O Welt" has been rewritten in the soprano clef and inserted after the regular soprano part. Apparently the duet was performed by two sopranos on some occasion.

The most immediately striking addition in *Lobe den Herrn* is the chorale that has been squeezed into the space at the bottom of each of the two violin parts. A closer examination of the soprano, alto, bass, viola, and continuo parts reveals that there, too, a chorale has been added by a different copyist. The most obvious difference between the two writing styles is the manner in which the C clefs are formed. Whereas the first copyist wrote his C clefs thus: (⑂), the copyist who added the chorale wrote them thus: (⑂♭). Furthermore, the entire tenor part, including the chorale, was apparently written by this person, as was all of the oboe 1, oboe 2, bassone, and the chalcedono parts.[19] Since the woodwinds form an integral part of the orchestration (most notably in the two main choruses and in the alto aria), the most plausible conclusion is that two copyists worked simultaneously on the manuscript. The chorale was then added by the second copyist, probably not long after the original work was done.

One further complication exists in this cantata. An extra chorale tune without text is found on page 37 of the manuscript (between the bassone and chalcedono parts). It was written by the second copyist and appears to be a version of "Der güldnen Sonne Lauf und Pracht." In all likelihood, it was being suggested as an alternate chorale.

Only two of Heinichen's works have more than one manuscript source each. In the case of *Einsamkeit, o stilles Wesen*, one manuscript is a score, the other a set of parts. As indicated earlier, the musical differences between the two versions are minor, being restricted mainly to a few accidentals. Part of the text in the bass aria differs however. The parts have:

Ich will künftig disputieren,
Jesus soll die Thesis sein,
Diesen will ich nur allein
Stets in meinem Munde führen.

The score however has a more conventional rendering:

Ich will meinen Jesum loben,
Jesus soll mein Jesus sein,
Diesen will ich nur allein
Stets in meinem Munde führen.

Since the score version does not rhyme the first and fourth lines, and since it is also much less imaginative than its counterpart (although perhaps aesthetically superior), it is likely that the score is a later version than the set of parts and represents a desire to modify a somewhat awkward text.[20]

There are two manuscript sources for *Gelobet sei der Herr, der Gott Israels*. Both are sets of performing parts and belong to the Dresden collection. They carry library designations MUS 2398-E-504 and MUS 2398-E-509. In general, manuscript #504 is a more complete version than its counterpart. It has separately written oboe parts, whereas #509 combines them with the violin parts. It has choral ripieno parts while #509 has none. It also has extra bass parts, which, although usually identical with each other, are different from the continuo bass. Both versions end with the rubric "Gelobet Da capo," but in #509 the chorale "Nun lob mein Seel" has been added. In some parts the addition involved squeezing the chorale into the space left at the bottom of the page. Only in the viola 1 and violone parts has the "Da Capo" rubric been crossed out. Nevertheless, the intention to sing the chorale as an alternative to repeating the opening chorus seems clear.

In #504 the continuo consists of two parts, one marked "organo" and one marked "continuo". Both are in F major and are, therefore, nontransposing. Number 509 likewise has two continuo parts. One is in F and marked "violone"; the other is in Eb and marked "organo L. violone". The latter does not include the chorale, which was added in the other parts. Since there is still some space left at the bottom of the page, this omission suggests that the chorale had been added at a later time and for a performance that did not require the transposed organ part.

One unique feature of #509 is the inclusion of an extra violin 1 part. Since the other two violin parts are combined with their oboe counterparts, the existence of this extra part may indicate that extra string players were used on a particular occasion. On the other hand, it may simply indicate that on some occasion the oboe 1 and violin 1 players had to be physically separated.

We may summarize our study of the sources of Heinichen's fifteen German choral church works with the following generalizations. Of the seventeen sources, all are manuscripts. Ten are scores, the others are sets of performing parts. Apparently none are autographs but rather the work of six or more copyists. Only four manuscripts are dated. The dates identify these four as early compositions, yet, of all the works, they display the most progressive style characteristics. For this reason, we judge most of the other works to have been written at least as early as these. Although some of the compositions have been revised somewhat, in most cases the revisions appear to reflect changing performance situations and do not significantly alter the profiles of these works.

Chapter 4. Notes

1. P. 48.

2. See Günter Hausswald's list in "Heinichen," *Die Musik in Geschichte und Gegenwart*, vol. 6 (1957), col. 49.

3. *Bettmeister*

4. Fürstenau, *Beiträge*, p. 144.

5. For Hausswald's description of Heinichen's handwriting, see Hausswald, *Instrumentalwerke*, p. 28.

6. Wolfgang Horn's findings were shared with this author by letter. For an example of another Heinichen autograph see the facsimile pages reproduced in Horn's edition of Heinichen's *Magnificat in A* (Stuttgart: Carus-Verlag 40.951/01, 1986), p. 43.

7. The exception occurs at the end of the soprano part where a clef resembling those characteristic of the other cantatas in this group can be found.

8. On the other hand, since each stanza of the ode forming the heart of this libretto begins "Gelobet sei Gott!" the copyist may have chosen to call the entire cantata by that title.

9. *Warum toben die Heiden* is dated on the bottom of the last page with this inscription: "S.D.G. 1715. *pridie diei viridium*." The reference to green may refer to the changing of liturgical color. Green has traditionally been used "from the octave of Epiphany to Septuagesima, and between Trinity and Advent except festivals and their octaves and Ember day." See Walter Alison Phillips, "Vestments," *Encyclopaedia Brittanica* (London: William Benton, 1959), 23:111. The Lutheran Church generally kept or reinstated the traditional liturgical colors. See E. Hertzsch, "Farben," *Die Religion in Geschichte und Gegenwart*, 3d ed., edited by Kurt Galling (Tübingen: J.C.B. Mohr (Paul Siebeck), 1957-1965), vol. 2, col. 875.

10. Since Heinichen was reportedly in Italy in 1714, it is probable that this work was actually written earlier, and performed by someone else in 1714. See chapter 6.

11. The third digit is not clear. The date could be 1717. Both Hausswald and Schmitz date this work 1723, a date probably taken from the second Dresden manuscript (Mus. 2398-E-509). See Hausswald, "Heinichen," col. 49, and Eberhard Schmitz, "Die Messen J.D. Heinichens" (Ph.D. dissertation, University of Hamburg, 1967), p. 212.

12. The da capo aria in *Gelobet* has its da capo written out.

13. *Meine Seele erhebet den Herrn* and *Es lebet Jesus unser Hort*

14. It should be noted however, that the Masses (which are late works) do not use da capo form. See Schmitz, p. 155.

15. Heinichen, p. 29, trans. in Buelow, "Johann David Heinichen's Der General-Bass in der Composition" (Ph.D. dissertation, New York University, 1961), p. 578.

16. See chapter 9.

17. See chapters 9, 12. *Heilig* is an exception. The periodic phrase structure and Alberti bass both suggest this work was written later than the others.

18. Heinichen apparently learned the new techniques and styles from Vivaldi during his Italian stay. See chapter 9.

19. For identification of these instruments, see chapter 6.

20. For a further discussion, see chapter 5.

5.
The Liturgical and Theological Context

Liturgical Specifications

Terms Used in Liturgies

Although the frequency of church services varied from city to city in Saxon Germany, there were generally many in every church, every week. This was especially true in Dresden and even more so in Leipzig. In both these centers, citizens could attend preaching and prayer services on any day of the week.[1] In its specifications regarding the type of vocal music to be sung during these services, the contemporary literature uses the terms *Figuralmusik* or *figuraliter* (contrapuntal music; polyphonically),[2] *choraliter* (monophonically),[3] and *Music* (concerted music). The term *Kantate* is, of course, not used.[4] That the terms *Music* and *musiciren* referred only to concerted music is emphasized by Stiller:

> *Music* and *musiciren* in worship services were in those days always understood as the presentation of contrapuntal music accompanied by obligato instruments.[5]

The term motet was apparently not used for such concerted pieces for Bach, in his letter to the city council of Leipzig dated August 15, 1736, writes concerning the role of the choristers singing at the New Church, that they "have nothing to sing but motets and chorales, and have nothing to do with other *Concert Musique*, since the latter is taken care of by the organist."[6] Similarly, the *Leipziger Kirchen-Andachten* differentiates between *Music* and motet: "at Communion there is, first *Music* or a motet, then hymns are sung,"[7] and Christoph Sicul differentiates between a *concerto* and a motet: "a concerto or motet is performed."[8] In Leipzig, most of the motets were, in fact, taken from the *Florilegium Portense*, a motet collection of late sixteenth- and early seventeenth-century motets by German and Italian composers. Almost all of these motets are Latin, and most are for eight voices.[9]

Although the liturgies of Lutheran services varied in their details, they were usually based on Luther's *German Mass and Order of Service* of 1526.

> While Luther's prescriptions formed the invariable basis of the
> Evangelical liturgy, local churches were encouraged to develop
> particular uses.[10]

In many ways, this liturgy resembled the old Catholic one, since Luther only
intended to correct the abuses, as he himself declared:

> In the first place we assert, it is not now, nor has it ever been,
> in our mind to abolish entirely the whole formal cultus of God,
> but to cleanse that which is in use...[11]

As a whole, the liturgy for the main service was divided into three
parts:
1. Entrance section dominated entirely be prayer and thanksgiving[12]
2. Service of the Word (Pulpit Service)[13]
3. Service of the Sacrament[14]
Thus, the liturgy traditionally had two high points: the sermon and Holy
Communion.[15] Later, under the influence of Rationalism, "there was evidence
of a tendency to separate the celebration of Holy Communion from the
actual main service of the congregation and to conduct it in an attached
separate service for communicants only."[16]

Although Luther intended the publication of his *German Mass and
Order of Service* to end the confusion that had resulted from the "clamor for
German Masses and services,"[17] it was not his intent to legislate all of the
details.

> It was not my thought that all Germany must immediately adopt
> our Wittenberg Order...but it would be well if, in every jurisdic-
> tion, public worship were uniform...[18]

Thus, certain liturgical details varied from city to city. There were even a few
local variations in the pericopes.[19] Since Leipzig and its environs were the
most likely locations to have seen the initial performances of Heinichen's
cantatas,[20] the liturgies of this city are of particular interest to this study.

The Leipzig liturgy exhibited a strong adherence to the traditions of the
Lutheran reformation.

In the liturgical practice in Leipzig at the time of Johann Sebastian Bach there was still a definite dependence, even to the smallest details, on the worship practice of Reformation times.[21]

That some of the liturgical details were unique is indicated by the fact that Bach found it necessary to outline the liturgy for the main service of the First Sunday in Advent on the inside cover of his cantata BWV 61, even after a half year in office.[22] Bach's confusion may have been caused by the ambivalence of the Leipzig authorities.

In Leipzig no other Sunday in the church year had such a conflicting significance as this Advent Sunday did, which, on the one hand, was counted among the special festivals, but on the other, did not show that special hallmark of the festival service: the Latin Preface.[23]

The Leipzig Liturgy

As was true elsewhere, in Leipzig the morning service on Sundays and feast days was the single most important service.[24] The liturgy for these days "basically remained the same for all Sundays and festivals."[25] Contrapuntal music was performed at a number of points during this service. In chronological order, these occasions were:

1. **The Introit Motet.** This motet was usually one from the *Florilegium Portense*.[26] On special festivals it was replaced with Latin hymns sung in parts by the choir.[27] In seasons of penitence it was replaced with chant.[28]

2. **The Kyrie and Gloria.** On high festivals and high Sundays the Kyrie and Gloria were "performed in concerted settings."[29] In less important services and when the second choir was singing, the Gloria intonation was followed by the Gloria hymn *Allein Gott in der Höh sei Ehr* sung by choir and congregation.[30] On days of penitence and mourning, both *Et in terra* and *Allein Gott in der Höh* would be sung, but monophonically.[31]

3. **Hauptmusik.** The chief music of the service was performed between the Gospel and the Sermon.[32] Its purpose was to proclaim the Word, and in this

it followed Luther, "who not only credited music with the capability of interpreting and concertizing the Word of God, but also designated this as its commission."[33] It was introduced with an organ prelude[34] and was then usually performed by voices and instruments. "According to the time schedules in Lorenz Mizler's *Musikalische Bibliothek* (IV, 5, 108) the cantata was to last no longer than thirty-five minutes in summer and twenty-five minutes in winter."[35] It was frequently in two parts, the second part being performed after the sermon.[36]

In Leipzig, such concerted music was normally performed only by the first choir of the St. Thomas School, which alternated between the St. Nicholas and St. Thomas Churches from Sunday to Sunday.[37] Meanwhile the second choir would perform much simpler music (presumably motets)[38] in the alternate church. On high festivals, the choirs would already switch for the afternoon (Vespers) service so that the first choir could present its cantata in both churches.[39] On such festivals the second choir might also perform concerted music but of a much simpler kind. Bach himself wrote:

> The concerted church pieces that are performed by the Kantorei, which are mostly of my composition, are incomparably harder and more intricate than those that are sung by the second Kantorei (and this only on feast days), so that I must be chiefly guided, in the choice of the same, by the *capacité* of those who are to perform them.[40]

Although it was normal practice to print the librettos of the cantatas for the congregation in booklet form, none exist for compositions performed by the second choir. This "leads to the conclusion that the text of these compositions must have been comprehensible by itself and that they were substantially shorter in performance time than the works presented by the first Kantorei".[41] In any case, the shortage of instrumentalists of which Bach had complained signifies that the second chorus could not have performed concerted music very often.[42]

4. Music after the Sermon. Frequently the Pulpit Service was concluded with more concerted music. This might be the second part of a double cantata or even the second part of a cantata that did not have an obvious two-part structure.

Not infrequently, only two or three movements would be offered
in the first part of the cantata and...this first section could often
be concluded with an aria, and thus not necessarily with a
chorale or a movement by a participating choir.[43]

That two-section cantatas were performed also on ordinary Sundays is
demonstrated by the fact that Bach wrote a number of such works for
ordinary Sundays: BWV 17, 20, 35, 39, and 45.[44] On some days, notably
apostles' days, a motet was sung after the sermon.[45]

5. Communion. Polyphonic music was also performed during Communion. On
festival days, this included the "polyphonic presentation of the Sanctus."[46] The
notes by the sexton of St. Thomas "show that [this] practice was observed on
all first and second holidays of the three great festivals of the church year
as well as on all special festivals of the church year that were placed on the
same level with these high festivals."[47]

During the Distribution, more vocal music was performed. On ordinary
Sundays, this consisted of motets. On festival days, concerted music was
presented; frequently such concerted music consisted of movements from
cantatas.

Selected parts of cantatas were also used as music for the
Sacrament on certain Sundays and festivals. While it cannot be
shown to what extent the first and second Kantoreien would sing
motets and even present contrapuntal instrumental music during
the Distribution, there was always special music for the Sacrament
at Communion on Sundays in both churches. On ordinary
Sundays this would mean only certain motets, but on festival days
there would also be *Music*...[48]

It seems one can safely assume that in the selection of this music
Bach not infrequently gave consideration not only to the well-
known motets but also to movements of his own taken from his
cantatas.[49]

Polyphonic music was also presented at services other than the
Hauptgottesdienst. Chief of these was the Vespers service on important
Sundays and festivals in the two main Leipzig churches (St. Thomas and St.

Nicholas), as well as the New Church.[50] The printed texts, which always indicated the place of performance in Leipzig, show "that on festivals the cantata presented in one of the two churches was then sung in the other church at Vespers on the same day."[51] In the New Church concerted music was performed only occasionally in any event, the performers being "the organist of the church and...singers and instrumentalists available to him for that purpose."[52] These singers and instrumentalists were students and members of the Collegium Musicum.[53]

All Vespers services included a motet and the Magnificat. In times of penitence, this motet was replaced by a monophonic Psalm.[54] The Magnificat was sung in German on ordinary Sundays, in Latin on high festivals.[55] The German versions were apparently mostly monophonic ones, while the Latin settings included instruments.[56] After 1714 these Latin setting were replaced more and more by the German version.[57] As for weekday Vespers services, "the presentation of contrapuntal music in weekday services is affirmed only for Saturday Vesper services at St. Thomas."[58] This music consisted of several motets.[59]

A number of other public functions also included contrapuntal music. Motets and cantatas were performed at full bridal Masses.[60] Such works are sometimes identified by their inclusion of hymns customarily sung at weddings. There were only four of these: *Was Gott tut, das ist wohlgetan, In allen meinen Taten, Sei Lob und Ehr dem höchsten Gut,* and *Nun danket alle Gott.*[61] As Stiller points out,

> These are the same hymns about which Johann Sebastian Bach composed cantatas that significantly lack application to a worship service and in the new chronology of Bach's cantata offerings (cf. Dürr, *Chronologie)* cannot be assigned to a specific Sunday of the year. These are cantatas BWV 97, 100, 117, 192...It must be concluded that Bach composed these cantatas for weddings, although that does not preclude a later use of these works in Sunday services.[62]

Despite the reduction of contrapuntal music considered appropriate during times of penitence and mourning, motets and even concerted music "that the bereaved would request and suitably remunerate"[63] might also be performed at funerals or memorial services. Thus, Dürr mentions a memorial service on February 6, 1727, in honor of Johann Christoph von Ponickau,[64] which included a performance of a cantata entitled *Ich lasse dich nicht, du segnest mich denn*. Since the text (which was printed as part of the memorial sermon) matches that of Bach's cantata BWV 157, it may indeed have been Bach's composition that was performed on the occasion.[65] Cantatas may also have been performed at deathbeds of prominent citizens.[66]

Liturgies in other Cities

Although we have been speaking here of the Leipzig liturgy and customs, the practice in other cities was apparently similar. Thus, the Weissenfels liturgy, which, we are told, was based on the Dresden one,[67] specifies contrapuntal and/or concerted music at almost identical places within the liturgy. On ordinary Sundays and apostle days, for instance, concerted music ("ein Stück Musiciret") was performed both before and after the sermon.[68] Unlike the Leipzig practice, however, introits were not sung on ordinary Sundays. Instead, a Psalm from Becker's Psalter was sung.[69] Festival days, on the other hand, followed the usual Sunday order but added a choral introit.[70]

On the three chief festivals (Christmas, Easter, and Pentecost), the morning liturgy included only one item of concerted music, and that came after the sermon.[71] In the afternoon services of these days, however, the usual two opportunities returned.[72] The same format prevailed in the afternoon services on ordinary Sundays.[73]

The Vesper service on the evening preceding one of the three chief festivals, as well as the Vesper service of the third day of such a festival was celebrated as a *Musikalische Vesper* and had no less than three opportunities for concerted music (*Musik*) in addition to the Magnificat.[74] Concerted music was also performed at confessional Vespers (*Beicht Vesper*) whenever the prince was present.[75]

In Leipzig, Weissenfels, and elsewhere, no contrapuntal music was performed during Lent or Advent, with the exception of the first Advent Sunday, and it was customary everywhere to stop the music during times of state mourning.[76] That these periods could be numerous and lengthy can be seen from Seiffert's list of such enforced "holidays" at the court of Weissenfels just after the turn of the century:[77]

In 1701/2, from Trinity 18 to Mary's Purification
In 1703, from Reminiscere to Trinity 6
In 1704, from Trinity 7 to Trinity 13
In 1705, from Trinity 2 to Trinity 6
In 1706, from February 7 to Easter
In 1711, from Rogate to Pentecost

Interaction between Lutheran Theology and the Cantata Genre

Church Music as Proclamation

According to orthodox Lutheranism, "the chief and greatest aim of any Service is to preach and teach God's Word."[78] The *Hauptmusik* of the Lutheran service was invariably linked to the pericopes and, hence, to the sermon of the day. One of the main reasons that the cantata genre developed as fully as it did was that it was regarded as a significant medium for the proclamation, amplification, and interpretation of the Word.

> The sermon music (all the way to Bach's cantatas) was able to appear as a dominating second legitimate form of the Sermon in the Lutheran service because it had the same goal as the Sermon spoken from the pulpit, namely to practice the interpretation of the Word of God.[79]

The orthodox theologians were, therefore, keenly interested in and supportive of the genre. Indeed, most of the cantata librettists were clergymen "who took the substance of their poetry from their sermons for Sundays and festival days."[80] A few composers wrote their own texts,[81] but usually they availed themselves of librettos written by others. Every city had any number of theologians, court poets, school-masters, and officials who were writing cantata texts,[82] and composers usually did not need to look far afield for their texts. On the other hand, the more popular poets often published their works as general devotional literature, thus making these texts available to composers who were not personally acquainted with them.[83]

After 1700 the cantata librettos were often published, and copies were given to the congregation for use during the service. In some cases, text cycles for an entire church year were published and sold as devotional literature for private meditation.[84] Some of these publications even contained pictures for the edification of the worshipers. One such cycle of poetry was published by the Darmstadt court poet Lichtenberg, who wrote in his preface,

> In the texts [you will find] pictures,[85] charming engravings interspersed, so that those who do not wish to read the words during the musical performance can occupy themselves with an examination of these etchings.[86]

Mysticism and Pietism

One of the most striking elements in cantata texts of this time is the emphasis on the mystical union between Christ (symbolized as the bridegroom) and the Christian believer (symbolized as the bride). This doctrine had already been clearly delineated by such seventeenth-century theologians as Abraham Calovius (1612-1686), John Andrew Quenstedt (1617-1688), and David Hollaz (1646-1713).[87] Of this marriage, Calovius wrote,

> The espousal of Christ with believers is that which He eternally marries Himself to believers through faith, so that they become one spirit, and by His power communicates to them, as to His spiritual bride, intimate and enduring love, all His blessings and all His glory, so as to finally lead them to His home, and dwell with them in His celestial and eternal kingdom.[88]

This union was understood to occur not merely between the corporate body of believers and Christ but between the individual Christian and Christ. Thus, Calovius could write:

> The mystical union of Christ with the believer is a true and real and most intimate conjunction of the divine and human nature of the theanthropic Christ with a regenerate man.[89]

Despite this clear teaching by seventeenth-century theologians of a personal mystical union between Christ and the believer, it was not until the eighteenth century that the doctrine gained a strong foothold within Lutheran orthodoxy.[90] Frequently, this increased emphasis on a subjective spiritual fervor is attributed to Pietism. Such a view holds many of Bach's texts to be pietistic. Thus, Kretzschmar writes, "Bach used a heavy preponderance of pietistic texts in his compositions,"[91] and Buszin writes, "We find marked indications of the influence of Pietism in the sacred choral music of J.S. Bach."[92] Others vehemently argue that a lively piety developed from a reform movement within the orthodox church and was independent of Pietism.

> In [Pietism's] place independent measures toward a permanent improvement of piety were taken. Only the entire lively surge of strength of Lutheran orthodoxy in its late period is able to shed the proper light on this phenomenon. We cannot emphasize it strongly enough that by itself neither Pietism nor rationalism was able to contribute anything decisive to the intensification of public worship life...[93]

Ulrich Siegele echoes this distinction between orthodox piety and Pietism: "Piety and Pietism are not always and necessarily identical; there is a genuine piety of Lutheran orthodoxy."[94] As for Bach's mystic cantata texts, Stiller writes of them, "In reality, however, all these texts are to be attributed to the mysticism that gained a foothold at just this time of later Lutheran orthodoxy."[95] According to Stiller, much of the personal, subjective language in these texts is to be understood in the collective sense:

> Even a text that at first glance strikes tones that are altogether too subjectivistic, such as that of Cantata BWV 49 which presents a single dialogue between Christ and "the soul," does not find its final explanation in a purely individual interpretation. "Soul" frequently does not denote the individual soul, but the church... In Bach's age this mode of expression was still current according to which the statement was individual but the intention collective.[96]

Attempts to identify the origins of mystic sentiments in the cantata texts are compounded by the fact that "we can distinguish within the broader term 'Pietism' between a practical impulse toward ecclesiastical and pedagogical reform and a devotional impulse inclined to mysticism."[97] On both counts,

Pietist writers usually considered themselves reformers standing in the tradition of Luther.[98] Regarding the tendency to mysticism Stoeffler writes,

> We know, of course, that [Luther] progressively grew away from mysticism, but the mystical tradition within Lutheranism could always point to the fact that in the beginning he felt and wrote differently. It is for this reason that books on mystical piety by such men as Tauler, à Kempis, and the author of the German Theology were always found in Lutheran homes.[99]

That Pietists emphasized a vital inner spiritual life is undisputed. Philip Spener (1635-1705), considered the "central symbol of Pietism,"[100] had "little natural inclination for mysticism in his preoccupation with practical Christianity,"[101] yet wrote:

> One should therefore emphasize that the divine means of Word and sacrament are concerned with the inner man. Hence it is not enough that we hear the Word with our outward ear, but we must let it penetrate to our heart, so that we may hear the Holy Spirit speak there, that is, with vibrant emotion and comfort feel the sealing of the Spirit and the power of the Word."[102]

Because of this emphasis on sincerity, Pietism had a great distrust of the traditions and rituals of the institutional church. Their preference was for simple, unadorned worship services. That this teaching posed a grave threat to the sophisticated music of Lutheran orthodoxy is clear from the writings of Christian Gerber, a student of Spener,[103] who protested particularly strongly against concerted music in the worship service. In an attempt to show that his argument is consistent with Luther's teaching, he writes,

> Luther desires an altogether different kind of church music than we have today: "The whole crowd should sing along," he says. But among us the whole crowd cannot sing along, for a text is being presented musically that is not familiar to the congregation, and also, the congregation cannot understand the words because of the clangor of the instruments...On the other hand, when a familiar hymn is sung and instruments are used with it, the whole

crowd can sing along and praise and glorify God together with the instruments.[104]

Gerber also cites Spener's teacher Johann Konrad Dannhauer (1603-1666) as rejecting "the current custom that voices and instruments are combined in performance...because the words sung in this way can obviously not be understood by anyone while the instruments rumble and bluster."[105] Furthermore, Gerber thought the cantors had too much authority, behaving "as if command and control in the church and in the service belonged to them."[106] His wish to curtail their activities is explicit:

> One could wish that these lordly cantors and choir directors would listen to the memoirs of Christian teachers and curb their musical presentations. For there are certainly many Christian people who lament when they have to listen to so loud and long a musical performance and nevertheless only rarely understand a word, but never achieve a complete understanding of it, much less derive benefit and edification from it.[107]

Gottfried Vockerodt, another Pietist critic of the church music abuse in the 1690s,[108] wrote of the cantors,

> They take up their profession with the intention of thereby fulfilling their lusts, enjoying the good life, achieving riches, praise, and human favor...through wonder and esteem for their art they become insolent to the point of looking down on other profession in comparison to theirs.[109]

In view of Pietism's threat to the rich liturgical traditions, it is small wonder that some writers have tried to make a sharp distinction between pietistic mysticism and the mysticism of Lutheran orthodoxy. Others have acknowledged a link between the two movements while recognizing Pietism's threat to church music. According to Leo Schrade,

> Pietism must have repelled Bach because of its denial of artistic music while it still attracted him for personal religious reasons.[110]

Whatever the link between the revival of piety within the orthodox Lutheran church and Pietism, it is clear that by the turn of the century, the term "Pietist" was a pejorative one.[111] Antipietist sentiment was especially strong at the University of Leipzig, "which, in close fraternal relation with Wittenberg, constituted the universally recognized bastion of Lutheran Orthodoxy."[112] In Berlin, however, the religious policy of the House of Hohenzollern

> ...was a policy not only of religious toleration, but of trying to use religion as a cohesive force within the state. Thus the power of the state was exercised consistently on the side of the most irenical elements within both the Reformed and the Lutheran confessions.[113]

How this policy operated can be seen clearly in the political measures undertaken by Elector Frederick III to rebuild the city of Halle after the ravages of the Black Death (1682) and two major fires (1683 and 1684).[114] After these disasters, the town was economically and socially bankrupt.[115] The political measures undertaken by Elector Frederick III are recounted by Stoeffler:

> In the hope of saving the town from complete ruin Elector Frederick III, who had acquired the duchy of Magdeburg in 1680, opened it to Huguenot refugees in 1685...These were industrious, capable people, who quickly introduced new life into Halle's sagging economy and in the process of doing so, achieved a measure of economic well-being. The result was that they were bitterly resented, both because of their relative wealth and because of their Reformed Faith, by the original members of the community...It was under these circumstances that the elector decided to open the fourth university within his domain at Halle ...The chief theological objective of this new seat of learning was to be that of fostering among the prospective clergy of the land the newer trends in the self-understanding of Protestantism which tended to regard religion primarily as a quality of life rather than a dogmatic system...[116]

Of the theologians active in Halle, the most influential was August Hermann Francke (1663-1727), a disciple of Spener, who had been driven out of Leipzig in 1690. An alumnus of the University of Leipzig,[117] Francke had returned to Leipzig in 1689 to give a series of lectures. Students by the hundreds came to hear him, while totally neglecting the other theological lectures.[118] When Francke was forced to leave Leipzig "because of the determined opposition of Johann Benedict Carpzon II (1639-1699), professor of theology at Leipzig, and his orthodox friends,"[119] he moved to Erfurt for a time, then through Spener's influence, was appointed to the University of Halle.[120]

Francke proved to be as popular in Halle as he had been in Leipzig, and Halle soon became the center for training pietistic pastors. The main emphases for which Francke and his colleague Joachim Justus Breithaupt (1658-1732)[121] fought were "the right to hold conventicles in a home without the presence of a pastor, the right to preach 'active' faith, and the need for the spiritual illumination of a theologian (or pastor)."[122] These teachings were met with the "immediate and vigorous opposition of Orthodoxy,"[123] and because the ruling house of Prussia sided with the Pietists, the controversy quickly became a political one, pitting the town fathers, as well as the local consistory, who sided with the orthodox theologians against the Prussian government.[124] Soon thereafter, Frederick III ruled that the clergy of Halle were not to speak publicly against Francke and that all grievances had to be brought before the consistory in Berlin. "In this way the local authorities in both church and state were effectively circumvented, and the way to the rapid development of Pietism in Halle was at least initially assured."[125]

Saxony, with the University of Leipzig as one of its focal points, remained the "major bastion of rigid Orthodoxy."[126] At first, Spener had received a sympathetic hearing from the nobility, and for this reason Johann Georg III had called him to Dresden in 1686.[127] Spener had little influence there, however, and by 1691 was already in Berlin.[128] Some theologians at the University of Leipzig were indeed sympathetic to pietistic ideas, although they did not wish to align themselves politically with Pietism. These included Johannes Olearius (1639-1713), his son, Gottfried Olearius (1672-1715), Christian Friedrich Börner (1683-1753), and Johann Gottlob Pfeiffer (1668-1740). Adam Rechenberg (1642-1721), a son-in-law of Spener, was "more resolutely on the side of the Spener-Halle axis."[129] The most ruthless opponent of Pietism at the University of Leipzig, on the other hand, was Johann Carpzov II (1639-1699).

As the controversy raged in the first part of the eighteenth century, several Leipzig clergymen were dismissed from office on account of their leanings toward Pietism.[130] Because of a fear of a break in political relations with Prussia, however,

> ...a promulgation on August 20, 1727, inspired by the Saxon government, forbid all writing against Pietism. On Sept 8 this was read to the faculties...On the practical level it accomplished that the persecution of people touched by the Spener-Halle spirit became impossible, though it remained equally impossible to call into being a popular pietistic movement in Saxony.[131]

In view of the foregoing, we conclude that what Orthodoxy primarily opposed was not Pietism's mystic emphasis, but the social and political power inherent in the individualism of pietistic theology. This conclusion is supported by Stoeffler:

> It is interesting to find that almost all the polemical missives thrown at the Pietists by the defenders of Orthodoxy were motivated by the fear that these people might somehow upset the applecart by departing from traditional systems and commonly accepted values.[132]

Mysticism, as such, was accepted, even by many of the theologians at the conservative University of Leipzig, provided that it was not aligned politically with the Pietist movement. As for the mystical sentiments in the cantata texts of the time, they could only come from the pens of orthodox theologians because the cantata genre itself was inimical to the Pietist.

> In point of fact, among the writers of Bach's texts, so far as they have hitherto been identified, there was not one Pietist; nor indeed could there have been, since to them all the new church cantatas were a sinful abomination.[133]

Lutheran Theology and Operatic Style

Thus far we have examined the interaction between Lutheran theology and the cantata librettos, with special regard to their emphasis on mystical union. Just as striking as the pervasive subjectivism of their texts, however, is the cantata's whole-hearted adoption of operatic style. It is noteworthy

> ...that throughout Bach's 27-year tenure in Leipzig not a single case is on record in which the charge of secularization was brought by the Consistory of the clergy against the cantor's compositions for the church.[134]

This is not to say that the development went unchallenged. Indeed, a "bitter literary war broke out along the whole line, which declared itself in endless paper missiles on both sides."[135] The opponents to the new developments included primarily Pietists[136] (some of whose objections we noted above), "certain musicians of the old stamp,"[137] and laymen who, like the Pietists, were interested in correcting abuses in church music.[138] The orthodox theologians, however, accepted the theatrical forms as legitimate if dedicated to ·the service of God.

> The new style was in no way understood to be a phenomenon of secularization in the areas of Germany that were under the control of Lutheranism. It is worth noting that the musicians and the musical theorists of the seventeenth and eighteenth centuries who lived within the range of the evangelical Lutheran Kantorei tradition did not know the distinction between *stilus ecclesiasticus* and *stilus theatralis*, so that in Germany we can speak of a "monism of style" as one of the "main characteristics of the Lutheran tradition" as opposed to the development in Italy, which was definitely dominated by a "dualism of style."[139]

> The acceptance and use of the new musical forms such as recitative and aria in German Lutheran church music in no way represent a secularization of church music to begin with, for according to Lutheran thinking everything finally depended on the answer to a much more fundamental question, namely whether or not these new musical forms presenting themselves

could become "vessels and bearers of ecclesiastical proclamation" and "ecclesiastical confession."[140]

Erdman Neumeister, who, we must remember, was a leading theologian himself, answered this question in the affirmative:

> I have already said that a cantata has the appearance of a piece taken out of an opera, and it might almost be supposed that many would be vexed in spirit and ask how sacred music and opera can be reconciled, any more that Christ and Belial, or light and darkness. And therefore it might be said I should have done better to choose some other form. But I will not strive to justify myself in this matter till first I am answered: Why certain other spiritual songs are not done away with which are of the same *genus versuum* as worldly, nay, often profane songs? Why the *instrumenta musica* are not broken which we hear in churches today, and which only yesterday were performed upon for the luxury of worldly pleasure? And hence, whether this kind of poetry, though it has borrowed its model from theatrical verse, may not be sanctified by being dedicated to the service of God? Whether the Apostle's words may not be applied to this case, as it is written in I. Cor. xiv. 7; I. Tim. iv. 5; Phil. i. 18, and whether such an application is not a sufficient answer on my part?[141]

In the theology of orthodox Lutheranism, then, the sacred-secular antithesis had no place. Some modern writers find this perspective hard to grasp. Thus, for instance, J.A. Westrup concludes that the reason Neumeister began incorporating "tutti" movements in his later text cycles may have been that he realized he had "gone too far" with the incorporation of operatic style into church music.[142] The implication, of course, is that Neumeister was secularizing the cantata. In his argument against a close relationship between text and music in Bach's cantatas, Westrup cites cases where Bach adapted secular material for his church cantatas. In his discussion of such parodies,[143] Westrup repeatedly fails to distinguish the two separate procedural aspects involved in his examples: 1) the use of the same musical material for texts with apparently differing affects, and, 2) the reuse of musical material with secular origins in a sacred composition. The first aspect may, of course, be used in defense of the argument (that Bach's musical settings do not necessarily grow out of their texts). The second aspect, however, has no bearing on the argument, given the fact that the sacred-secular antithesis was foreign to the theology of Lutheran orthodoxy.

Of this matter Stiller writes,

Only from the viewpoint of this basic frame of mind of Lutheran-ism, which did not as yet know the modern dismemberment of all being into what is "secular" and what is "sacred" and consequently in the field of music did not as yet undertake a distinction between the "secular" and the "sacred," can the much-discussed problem of the parody also be explained sensibly. The musician of that time who composed in this Lutheran frame of mind did not think he was contributing to a secularization of church music when he appropriated for worship purposes works that he had previously composed for occasions not associated with the church and then reworked more or less extensively for this purpose.[144]

Heinichen's Works

Having examined both the liturgical specifications for concerted music and the interaction between Lutheran theology and the cantata genre, we now turn to Heinichen's works themselves.

Liturgical Designations

Eight of the works have liturgical designations on their title pages or, if there is no title page, on the first page of music.

Herr, nun lässest Du	Mary's Purification
Einsamkeit	second day of Easter or at anytime[145]
Der Herr ist nahe	third day of Easter[146]
Gelobet sei der Herr	Feast of St. John the Baptist
Lass dichs nicht irren	first Sunday after Trinity
Es naheten aber zu Jesu	third Sunday after Trinity

Mag auch ein Blinder　　　　　fourth Sunday after Trinity
Der Segen des Herrn　　　　　fifth Sunday after Trinity

In comparing the scriptural texts of the libretti with the standard pericopes,[147] we find that, in each case, the libretti are either part of the Gospel for that Sunday or are related in some way to the Gospel lesson. Thus, for example, *Lass dichs nicht irren* does not actually incorporate the Gospel lesson of the day[148] but presents, instead, two Psalm texts that relate to the theme,[149] while *Es naheten aber zu Jesu* incorporates the first nine of the ten verses contained in the lesson.[150]

The other seven works have no liturgical designations. Two have texts specific enough to make their relation to the church calendar clear, despite the fact that neither incorporate literal Scripture passages. The focus of *Es lebet Jesus unser Hort* is Christ's victory over death, a sentiment closely aligned to the Gospel for the first day of Easter.[151] *Gegrüsset seist du* presents (in rhymed verse) the appearance of the angel Gabriel to Mary and was, therefore, likely intended for the Feast of the Annunciation, since the Gospel for that day is the scriptural passage on which this text is based.[152]

Meine Seele erhebet den Herrn is based on an abbreviated version of the German Magnificat, incorporating Luke 1:46-47, 49, 52-53, 55. It may have been intended for the Feast of Mary's Visitation (which has the complete passage as its Gospel) or as Vespers music on one of the chief festivals. According to Stiller, in 1714 "the Latin Magnificat was supplanted more and more by the German version" in Leipzig.[153] This setting omits key verses, however, and, ostensibly, would therefore be more suitable for the Feast Day service, since on that day the entire passage would be read in the Gospel lesson. Furthermore, after the opening chorus, the subsequent verses of scripture are set as relatively inconsequential recitatives. Much more prominent are the arias (with non-Scriptural texts) that alternate with these recitatives. This emphasis on reflective texts is, of course, a primary characteristic of "sermon music," a fact that would lead us to conclude this work was intended as the *Hauptmusik* for the Feast of Mary's Visitation. For the same reason, it can legitimately be called a cantata.

Lobe den Herrn and *Gott ist unsere Zuversicht* are both Psalm cantatas, although the latter is almost too short to be called a cantata.[154] The former alternates literal verses from Psalm 103 with rhymed paraphrases, the latter uses Psalm 46:2-8 for its text. In both cases a specific *de tempore* designation is not possible to determine. Similarly, the chorale cantata *Ach was soll ich*

Sünder machen interpolates no other texts, making it difficult to establish its intended place in the church year.

Heilig ist Gott der Herr is almost certainly communion music. Not only is its text the German version of the Sanctus but it appears in a manuscript containing other settings of the Sanctus, including another German version by Schieferdecker (no first name given) and Latin settings by Rathgeber, Cesare, and Heinichen himself.[155] As communion music, this work cannot be called a cantata in the usual sense of the term.

Text Sources

None of the manuscripts identify the source of their librettos, and attempts to identify the poets have thus far proven unfruitful.[156] To be sure, it is possible that Heinichen furnished these texts himself.[157] One of the most important cantata librettists of the time was Erdmann Neumeister (1671-1756), who worked at the court of Weissenfels from 1704 to 1706.[158] Since Heinichen moved to Weissenfels in 1705, and the court composer Johann Philipp Krieger had been using Neumeister's poetry for his cantatas as early as 1702,[159] Heinichen must have known Neumeister's work. It is surprising, therefore, that he apparently did not use any of Neumeister's cantata texts.[160]

Text Types

Of the fifteen works under discussion, five have texts consisting only of Scripture (literal, or paraphrased in rhyme), and/or chorale stanzas: *Der Segen*,[161] *Lobe den Herrn, Ach was soll ich Sünder machen, Gott ist unsere Zuversicht*, and *Heilig*. In addition to these, *Gegrüsset seist du* is, with the exception of the final chorus, entirely a paraphrase of Scripture.[162] From a theological perspective, this gives these works a highly conservative, orthodox appearance. Even in the compositions with freely composed texts, the mood is usually didactic or confessional. A moralizing tone is particularly strong in *Lass dichs, Es naheten*, and *Mag auch*, the three works that are similar in so many other ways.[163] At times, the results seem mawkish. One such example occurs in *Lass dichs nicht irren*:[164]

Poor Lazarus has left behind many brethren
Who must cringe like dogs
And to make matters worse, receive but empty words.
It is no different here;
He who is poor must endure it,
But can content himself with his lot
And be of good cheer.
Although the rich already receive their reward
In this life,
There God will exchange his poverty for riches.
They are transient and last but a short time.
Let the rich delight himself in his possessions.
In the end, it will still be reported
That he died and was buried.
Even though this happen with the greatest pomp,
He who is calm and disregards it
Will be content.

Although *Es lebet* is unique in that it uses no Scripture (not even paraphrased Scripture) or chorale texts, it avoids individualism and subjectivism, choosing, rather, a corporate and confessional perspective. Even in the alto aria, which speaks of the spiritual benefits inherent in Christ's victory over death, this tone is not abandoned.

These are the fruits of Thy victory
That we may appear before Thy judgement seat
Enamored with Thy favor.
Grace and Life are the gifts
That can fully revive us,
That Thy resurrection affords.

Only in three works does one find any of the subjectivism and individualism associated with the doctrine of mystical union that became prominent in cantata texts during the course of the eighteenth century. In *Der Herr ist nahe* these subjective expressions are limited to a few phrases:

Christ is risen, free of chains and bonds,
And has brought us delight.[165]

We now enter into a thousand joys,
Out of suffering, into Pleasure's canopy.[166]

In *Einsamkeit*, we find Christ addressed personally and intimately.

When dark shadows frighten me
Gracious Jesus, be my light
Let thy wings my cover be,
When the light of day has failed.
So let Satan rage,
A destined end awaits him.
Jesus will be my protection
And I remain unharmed.[167]

The intensity of the believer's emotional attachment to Christ is made explicitly clear in the opening soprano aria:

O solitude, thou essence of silence,
If my Jesus does not kiss me
I have chosen death,
For I constantly yearn for Him.
I am completely forsaken by Him,
I consider my times,
If I cannot embrace Him
Then all is vanity.

The same cantata contains a bass aria that was later revised.[168] As we concluded in chapter 4, the earlier version was apparently the one we find in the parts:

I will now argue my case,
Jesus shall be my thesis.

A revised version is found in the other source (score). It is more subjective, and its first phrase parallels the closing expression of the earlier alto aria:

I will praise my Jesus,
Jesus shall be my Jesus.

The most outspoken expressions of love for Christ occur in the two bass arias of *Herr, nun lässest Du*. The context of the cantata is Mary's visit to the temple,[169] and both arias are presumably to be understood as amplifications of the Nunc Dimittis text that is sung by the elderly Simeon as he takes the child in his arms.

> O precious One, satisfy me!
> I take Thee, Savior, in my arms,
> With desire I clasp Thee
> To my loving breast,
> And warm myself.

> My eyesight, no matter how much before old age it fail,
> Has now seen Thy salvation.
> How blessed is he, who, ere he dies,
> Kisses and embraces Jesus.

If some of the texts strike the modern reader as overly sentimental and others as too moralistic, he may be reminded that their primary function was to assist in the proclamation of the Word. For this reason, poets of cantata texts were more interested in theological persuasiveness than in beauty. Neumeister expresses this sentiment in the foreword to his publication of 1704:

> In this style I have preferred to retain biblical and theological modes of expression. For it seems to me that a magnificent ornamentation of language in human artistry and wisdom can impede the spirit and charm in sacred poetry as greatly as it may promote both in political verse.[170]

Chapter 5. Notes

1. Christian Gerber, *Historie der Kirchen-Cermonien in Sachsen* (Dresden and Leipzig, 1732), cited in Stiller, p. 55.

2. This could include the four-part rendering of a chorale by the choir. See Stiller pp. 60, 86, 90.

3. Stiller, pp. 89, 125.

4. See chapter 1.

5. Stiller, p. 75.

6. Hans T. David and Arthur Mendel, eds., *The Bach Reader*, revised edition (New York: W.W. Norton and Company, Inc., 1966), p. 140.

7. J.F. Leibniz, ed., *Leipziger Kirchen-Andachten: Darinnen der Erste Theil, Das Gebetbuch oder die Ordnung des gantzen öffentlichen Gottes-Dienstes durchs ganze Jahr... Der Ander Theil, Das Gesangbuch...* (Leipzig, 1694), quoted in Stiller, p. 82.

8. Christoph Ernst Sicul, *Neo annalium Lipsiensium Continuatio II: Oder des mit 1715ten Jahre Neuangegangenen Leipziger Jahrbuchs Dritte Probe* (Leipzig, 1717) cited in Stiller, p. 82.

9. Erhard Bodenschatz, a cantor at Schulpforta, compiled this motet collection and published it in 1603. He revised it in 1618 and added another volume in 1621. In total, the collection contained 271 motets of some 89 composers (26 motets are anonymous). See Otto Riemer, "Florilegium Portense," *Die Musik in Geschichte und Gegenwart*, 16 vols. (Kassel: Bärenreiter Verlag, 1949-1979), vol. 4 (1955), cols. 429-432. See also Stiller, p. 86.

10. Charles Sanford Terry, *Joh. Seb. Bach, Cantata Texts Sacred and Secular With a Reconstruction of the Leipzig Liturgy of his Period* (London, 1926), p. 19. Luther's liturgy with preface is reproduced in Bard Thompson, *Liturgies of the Western Church* (Philadelphia: Fortress Press, 1982), pp. 123-137.

11. Martin Luther, *Formulae Missae et Communionis* (Wittenberg, 1523), reproduced and translated by Thompson, *Liturgies*, p. 107.

12. Stiller, p. 120.

13. Stiller, pp. 120-125.

14. Stiller, pp. 125-129.

15. Sometimes the lesser churches were not allowed to serve Holy Communion as a part of their regular service. Thus, in Leipzig only St. Thomas, St. Nicholas and the New Church had this right. See Stiller, p. 129.

16. Stiller, p. 132.

17. Martin Luther, *The German Mass and Order of Service* (1526), translated by Thompson, *Liturgies*, p. 123.

18. Luther, *German Mass*, quoted in Thompson, *Liturgies*, p. 124.

19. Theodore Friedrich Dethlof Kliefoth, *Liturgische Abhandlungen*, vol. 4: *Die ursprüngliche Gottesdienst-Ordnung in den deutschen Kirchen lutherischen Bekenntnisses, ihre Destruction und Reformation*, 2nd ed. enl. (Schwerin, 1858), p. 78.

20. See chapter 6.

21. Stiller, p. 114.

22. Stiller, p. 116. A facsimile of this note is reproduced in Terry, facing p. 32.

23. Stiller, p. 275

24. The services began at seven o'clock and lasted until ten-thirty or eleven o'clock. See Stiller, pp. 49, 125.

25. Stiller, p. 129.

26. Stiller, p. 86.

27. Stiller, p. 87.

28. Stiller, p. 88.

29. Leipniz, *Leipziger Kirchen-Andachten*, Index and pp. 11-12; *Leipziger Kirchen-Staat: Das ist, Deutlicher Unterricht vom Gottes-Dienst in Leipzig* (Leipzig, 1710), pp. 5-6; Sicul, *Neo annalium*, p. 569. Quoted in Stiller, p. 88.

30. Stiller, p. 118.

31. Stiller, p. 89.

32. In most churches the cantata was performed in the morning service but there were some exceptions to this rule. Thus, for instance, Graupner regularly performed cantatas in the afternoon services at the court in Darmstadt. See Friedrich Noack, *Christoph Graupners Kirchenmusiken, Ein Beitrag zur Geschichte der Musik am landgräflichen Hofe zu Darmstadt* (Leipzig: Breitkopf & Härtel, 1916), p. 14.

33. Oskar Söhngen, "Bach und die Liturgie," *Der Kirchenmusiker* (1950), p. 172, quoted in Stiller, p. 156.

34. Stiller, p. 91.

35. Stiller, p. 80.

36. Stiller, pp. 80-81.

37. Stiller, pp. 75-76.

38. See Stiller, p. 86.

39. Stiller, pp. 50, 51, 79.

40. David & Mendel, *Bach Reader*, pp. 140-141.

41. Stiller, p. 80.

42. Stiller, p. 78.

43. Stiller, p. 81.

44. See Stiller, p. 125.

45. Leipniz, *Leipziger Kirchen-Andachten*, p. 86, and other sources cited by Stiller, p. 81.

46. Stiller, pp. 125-126.

47. Stiller, p. 86.

48. Stiller, p. 82.

49. Stiller, p. 85.

50. Stiller, p. 76.

51. Stiller, p. 79.

52. Stiller, p. 91.

53. Stiller, p. 91.

54. Stiller, p. 92.

55. Stiller, p. 92.

56. Stiller, p. 93.

57. Stiller, pp. 93, 118.

58. Stiller, p. 93.

59. Stiller, p. 93.

60. Less elaborate weddings, called quarter weddings or half bridal Masses, included no contrapuntal music. See Stiller, p. 94.

61. Stiller, p. 94.

62. Stiller, p. 94.

63. Stiller, p. 94.

64. Actual death occurred on October 31, 1726.

65. Dürr, *Die Kantaten*, 2:618.

66. Arnold Schering, *J.S. Bach und das Musikleben im 18. Jahrhundert* (Leipzig, 1941), p. 54; Arnold Schering, *Johann Sebastian Bachs Leipziger Kirchenmusik* (Leipzig, 1936), p. 13 ff., cited by Stiller, p. 95.

67. Max Seiffert, foreword to "Johann Philipp Krieger," vol. 53/54 (1916) of *Denkmäler Deutscher Tonkunst* (Leipzig: Breitkopf & Härtel 1892-1931), p. LXI. Seiffert reproduces the liturgical specifications.

68. Seiffert, p. LXV.

69. Seiffert, p. LXV.

70. Seiffert, p. LXV.

71. Seiffert, p. LXV.

72. Seiffert, p. LXVI.

73. Seiffert, p. LXVI.

74. Seiffert, pp. LXIV, LXV.

75. Seiffert, p. LXVIII.

76. Feder, col. 583.

77. Seiffert, p. LXXVI. Additional recesses for other reasons are also given by Seiffert. For times of mourning in Weissenfels during the late 1600's see p. LXII.

78. Martin Luther, *The German Mass and Order of Service* quoted in Thompson, *Liturgies*, p. 129.

79. Stiller, p. 151. See also chapter 2.

80. Paul Friedrich Brausch, "Die Kantate: Ein Beitrag zur Geschichte der deutschen Dichtungsgattung" (dissertation, University of Heidelberg, 1921) quoted in Stiller, p. 143.

81. Composers who wrote their own librettos include Johann Fasch, Gottfried Stölzel, Johann Telemann, and Petrus Wockenfuss, and, perhaps, J.S. Bach. See Feder, col. 583.

82. Feder, col. 583.

83. Feder, col. 583.

84. Feder, col. 583, Seiffert, p. LXXVI; Terry, *Bach's Cantata Texts*, pp. 30-31; Stiller, p. 79.

85. *Sinnbilder*

86. Friedrich Noack, "Christoph Graupner als Kirchen Komponist," supplement to *Denkmäler Deutscher Tonkunst* LI-LII (Leipzig: Breitkopf & Härtel, 1926), p. 12, trans. by M. Unger.

87. See quotations in Heinrich Schmid: *Doctrinal Theology of the Evangelical Church*, trans. Charles Hay and Henry E. Jacobs, 3d edition, revised (Minneapolis: Augsburg Publishing House, 1961), pp. 480-486.

88. Quoted in Schmid, p. 483.

89. Quoted in Schmid, pp. 482-483.

90. Stiller, p. 99.

91. H. Kretzschmar, *Bachkolleg: Vorlesungen über J.S. Bach* (Leipzig, 1922) p. 34, quoted in Stiller, p. 99.

92. Walter E. Buszin, "Criteria of Church Music in the Seventeenth and Eighteenth Centuries," *Festschrift Theodore Hoelty-Nickel: a Collection of Essays on Church Music* (Valparaiso, Indiana, 1967), p. 16. See also Dürr, *Die Kantaten*, 1:27.

93. Stiller, pp. 102, 103.

94. Ulrich Siegele, "Bachs Ort in Orthodoxie und Aufklärung," *Musik und Kirche* 51(1981):11, quoted in Joyce Irwin, "German Pietists and Church Music in the Baroque Age," *Church History* 54 (1985):30.

95. Stiller, p. 99.

96. Stiller, p. 152.

97. Irwin, p. 39.

98. F. Ernest Stoeffler, *The Rise of Evangelical Pietism* (Leiden: E.J. Brill, 1971), pp. 233-239.

99. Stoeffler, pp. 192-193.

100. Stoeffler, *Rise of Pietism*, p. 229.

101. Dale Brown, *Understanding Pietism* (Grand Rapids: William B. Eerdmans Publishing Co., 1978), p. 18.

102. Philip Jacob Spener, *Pia Desideria*, trans. and edited with intro. by Theodore G. Tappert (Philadelphia: Fortress Press, 1964), p. 117.

103. Stiller, p. 146.

104. C. Gerber, *Historie*, p. 290, quoted in Stiller, p. 148.

105. C. Gerber, *Historie*, p. 282, quoted in Stiller, p. 146.

106. Quoted in Stiller, p. 147.

107. C. Gerber, *Historie*, p. 289, quoted in Stiller, p. 147.

108. Joyce Irwin, "German Pietists and Church Music in the Baroque Age," *Church History* 54 (1985), p. 36.

109. Gottfried Vockerodt, *Missbrauch der freyen Künste, insonderheit Der Music* (Frankfurt, 1697), pp. 29-30, quoted in Irwin, p. 37.

110. Leo Schrade, "Bach: The Conflict Between the Sacred and the Secular," *De Scientia Musicae Studia atque Orationes*, ed. Ernst Lichtenhahn (Bern, 1967), pp. 441, 442 quoted in Irwin, p. 29.

111. As a pejorative term, it even appears in some of Neumeister's cantata texts. See examples in Spitta, *Bach*, 1:479 and Brausch, Appendix, #4. Orthodoxy had not always been hostile to Pietism. At first Pietism enjoyed almost unlimited approval in Leipzig and Dresden. See Stiller, p. 101.

112. F. Ernest Stoeffler, *German Pietism during the Eighteenth Century* (Leiden: E.J. Brill, 1973), p. 4.

113. Stoeffler, *German Pietism*, p. 40.

114. Stoeffler, *German Pietism*, p. 41.

115. Of ca. 200 houses, 37 were "establishments of prostitution." Stoeffler, *German Pietism*, p. 42.

116. Stoeffler, *German Pietism*, p. 42.

117. Stoeffler, *German Pietism*, p. 4.

118. Stoeffler, *German Pietism*, p. 6.

119. Stoeffler, *German Pietism*, p. 7.

120. Ibid. The initial appointment was as professor of oriental studies. Francke's interest in theology was practical rather than polemical.

121. Breithaupt was the first professor of theology to be appointed to the faculty. He was succeeded in 1709 by Joachim Lange (1670-1744). See Stoeffler, *German Pietism*, pp. 42-43.

122. Stoeffler, *German Pietism*, p. 61.

123. Stoeffler, *German Pietism*, p. 59.

124. Stoeffler, *German Pietism*, pp. 59-60.

125. Stoeffler, *German Pietism*, p. 60.

126. Stoeffler, *German Pietism*, p. 79.

127. Stoeffler, *German Pietism*, p. 79.

128. Stoeffler, *German Pietism*, p. 71.

129. Stoeffler, *German Pietism*, p. 79.

130. Stiller, p. 100.

131. Stoeffler, *German Pietism*, p. 80.

132. Stoeffler, *German Pietism*, p. 52.

133. Spitta, *Bach*, 1:366.

134. Friedrich Smend, *Bach in Köthen* (Berlin, 1951), p. 138 quoted in Stiller, p. 149.

135. Spitta, *Bach*, 1:479.

136. Spitta, *Bach*, 1:479.

137. Spitta, *Bach*, 1:480.

138. Ibid.

139. Stiller, p. 143. Citations from "Johann Sebastian Bach," vol. 170 of *Wege der Forschung*, ed. Walter Blankenburg (Darmstadt, 1970), pp. 273, 281.

140. Stiller, p. 143. Citations from Smend, *Bach in Köthen*, p. 139.

141. Erdmann Neumeister, *Geistliche Cantaten statt einer Kirchenmusik* (Weissenfels, 1704) quoted in Spitta, *Bach*, I:478, 479.

142. Westrup, *Bach's Cantatas*, p. 6.

143. Westrup, *Bach's Cantatas*, pp. 7, 17-18, 22-23, 43-44.

144. Stiller, p. 149.

145. The designation reads "Ad Fer. 2 Pasch. e per ogni tempo." By comparison, we note that Bach marked two cantatas (BWV 21 and 51) "in ogni tempo." See Dürr, *Kantaten* 2:625.

146. According to Stiller, only Leipzig still observed three celebration days for the chief festivals. See Stiller, p. 106.

147. See Kliefoth, pp. 55-78; Ernst Ranke, *Der Fortbestand des herkömmlichen Perikopenkreises von geschichtlichem und praktisch-theologischem Standpunct aus* (Gotha, 1859), pp. 127-137; Terry, *Bach's Cantata Texts*.

148. Luke 16:19-31.

149. Ps. 49:17-18: "For when he dieth he shall carry nothing away..." Ps. 37:37: "...behold the upright: for the end of that man is peace."

150. Luke 15:1-10.

151. Mark 16:1-8.

152. Luke 1:26-38.

153. Stiller, p. 118.

154. Duration: ca. ten minutes. This work also does not have distinct movements. See chapter 7.

155. Berlin MS. No. 30221.

156. For a survey of cantata librettists see Paul Friedrich Brausch, chapter 4.

157. See earlier discussion.

158. Tagliavini, col. 1401.

159. Snyder, p. 154.

160. None of Heinichen's librettos appear in any of the eight cantata cycles contained in *Fünfffache Kirchen-Andachten* (Leipzig, 1716/17) and *Fortgesetzte Fünfffache Kirchen-Andachten* (Hamburg, 1726); collections that combine Neumeister's previous publications. The last volume of the series, *Dritten Theil der fünfffachen Kirchen-Andachten* (Hamburg, 1752) was not available to the writer, but is not applicable since Heinichen had died long since.

161. We include *Der Segen* in this category despite the poetic text of the alto solo, for that text appears to loosely paraphrase Ps. 127:1-2.

162. *Gott ist unsere Zuversicht* and *Heilig* contain only Scripture; *Ach was soll ich* contains only chorale stanzas. No chorales are found in *Einsamkeit, Meine Seele, Gegrüsset, Gott ist unsere Zuversicht* and *Heilig*. While no chorale is contained in the early version of *Gelobet sei der Herr*, one is added in the later version.

163. See later chapters.

164. For a further discussion of the recitative in this cantata see chapter 10.

165. Bass aria.

166. Alto aria.

167. Tenor aria.

168. See chapter 4.

169. Luke 2:22-32.

170. Quoted in Seiffert, p. LXXVI, trans. M. Unger.

6.
Performance Practice

The Geographical Origins of Heinichen's Cantatas

To examine the specific conditions under which Heinichen's German church compositions were performed, we must first determine the locations of their performance. Unfortunately, this task proves to be a difficult one. None of the manuscripts identify any geographical locations, and only four of the manuscripts carry dates. (All are sets of performing parts.) These are presumably the dates when these works were performed.

> *Einsamkeit, o stilles Wesen*: second[1] day of Easter, 1709, 1714, 1719.
> *Der Herr ist nahe*: third day of Easter, 1709, 1722.
> *Herr, nun lässest Du*: Feast of Mary's Purification (February 2), 1714, 1720, 1722, 1723, 1729, 1734.
> *Gelobet sei der Herr*: Feast of St. John the Baptist (June 24), 1707,[2] 1723,[3] 1724.

If we note the first performance date given for each composition, we see that all of these works (with the possible exception of *Gelobet sei der Herr*) were first performed before Heinichen became *Kapellmeister* in Dresden. As we will see from the case of *Herr, nun lässest Du*, some of these performances may well have occured under the direction of musicians other than Heinichen and, therefore, in unidentifiable locations. Nevertheless, matching Heinichen's geographical locations with the earliest performing dates on the manuscripts gives us at least one set of possible performance locations. Unfortunately, Heinichen's movements before he arrived in Dresden are not precisely known. They can only be circumscribed by the following known events.

1705/6-1709:	Heinichen lived in Weissenfels. No specific documentation could be found by Seibel.[4]
Easter, 1709:	Heinichen's opera *Mario*[5] and *Carneval von Venedig*[6] were performed during the Easter Festival in Leipzig.

June, 1709:	Heinichen's opera *Olimpia vendicata* was performed during the Festival of St. Peter and St. Paul the Apostles (June 29), in Naumburg.[7]
1709:	Heinichen was hired by Duke Moritz Wilhelm of Zeitz.[8]
Dec. 5, 1709:	*Carneval* was repeated at the centennial celebrations of the University of Leipzig.[9]
1710:	Heinichen's opera *Der glückliche Liebeswechsel* was performed in Naumburg under the patronage of Duke Wilhelm.[10]
July 9, 1710:	Heinichen requested a release from his position and a letter of recommendation from the duke so that he could make a tour of German courts and their musical establishments. The letter of recommendation was sent by Duke Wilhelm to Duke Anton Ulrich of Braunwchweig and Lüneburg, where Heinichen apparently intended to attend the wedding celebrations of Prince August Wilhelm.[11]
1710:	Heinichen arrived in Venice.[12]

Since the two Easter cantatas are both dated 1709, they were likely written and performed in Leipzig, for it was exactly at Easter that Heinichen's two operas were being premiered at the Leipzig opera theater.[13] Perhaps the cantatas were performed at the St. Thomas or St. Nikolas churches, whose establishments were still under the direction of Heinichen's former teacher, Johann Kuhnau. There is no evidence, however, to indicate that the two men were close friends after Heinichen left the St. Thomas school; in fact, his involvement with Telemann and the operatic circles of Leipzig while a student at the University might well have created a certain degree of estrangement between the two men.[14] In any case, Kuhnau apparently rarely performed cantatas by other composers.[15] Perhaps these two cantatas were performed at the New Church, whose musical life, since Telemann's departure in 1704, had been directed by Melchior Hoffmann.[16]

The earliest date on the title page of *Herr, nun lässest Du* is 1714, which places it in the middle of his Italian residency, which lasted from 1710 to 1717.[17] Since a performance in Italy of this Lutheran church music seems impossible,[18] it is likely that it was actually written earlier and that it was simply copied and performed by someone else in 1714.[19] One factor that argues in favor of such a conclusion is that this manuscript appears to have been copied by the same person who wrote out the two Easter cantatas. The title pages of each of the three cantatas bear the monogram "JS." Unfortunately, attempts to identify the copyist have proven inconclusive.[20]

Although the earlier manuscript version of *Gelobet sei der Herr* (Dresden MS. 2398-E-504) lacks the monogram of the above three cantatas, it, too, seems to have been copied by "J.S." Since the date of this manuscript could be either June 1707 or 1717, this cantata came from either Heinichen's Weissenfels or Dresden periods respectively.[21] Its identification with the other three cantatas would make the Weissenfels/Leipzig area a more likely location. Its older style would support this conclusion.[22]

All of the dated compositions, then, are relatively early works, and, with the possible exception of *Gelobet sei der Herr*, they were composed and presumably performed first in locations other than Dresden. However, the dates on the title pages indicate that all of them were performed more than once, with at least one performance in each case falling into Heinichen's Dresden period. If these performances took place, in fact, under Heinichen's own direction, they would then have occured in the Protestant chapel of the Dresden court.

As for the undated compositions, all of them could have been performed by Heinichen in a variety of locations and performance situations. The most probable locations are the two courts at which Heinichen held appointments: the court of Duke Moritz Wilhelm at Zeitz, where Heinichen was chapel master for a brief period before travelling to Italy, and, of course, the court of August the Strong at Dresden, where he worked from 1717 to the end of his life.[23]

Unfortunately, records providing information about the court at Zeitz during this period have been largely destroyed.[24] We do know that Heinichen's association with the court of Zeitz lasted only about a year[25] and that the demand for his services during these years were primarily based on the success of his operas. Perhaps his churchly duties at Zeitz were minimal. By contrast, Heinichen's tenure at the court in Dresden was much more significant.

Since 1697, when August the Strong converted to Roman Catholicism, two chapels had existed at the Dresden court: a Protestant one and a Catholic one. The conversion of August the Strong had occurred in May, 1697, while the elector was in Vienna, and was apparently politically motivated; it made him a more suitable candidate for the Polish crown, which was subsequently bestowed on him in September of that year.[26] His wife, however, remained Protestant. Her influence on court life was probably minimal because she spent little time in Dresden.[27]

The king reorganized his musical establishments into two chapels in June of that year. Presumably in anticipation of this reorganization, all court servants had already been dismissed the previous April. The Catholic organization was entitled the "Royal Polish and Electoral Saxon Chapel" (*Königlich Polnische und Churfürstlich Sächsische Kapelle*) and was also called *Kammermusik*. The Protestant musical establishment was named the "Protestant court church music" (*protestantische Hofkirchenmusik*).[28] Most of the previously employed musicians were rehired for the Protestant chapel; a few were rehired for the Catholic one.[29] Johann Schmidt was made the chapel master of both institutions, although he was helped in the Catholic chapel by Ruzisky.[30] The twelve choir boys were divided equally between the two institutions.[31] The instrumental forces for the Protestant chapel at this time included two organists, two violinists, two violists, and one violonist.[32] The orchestra of the Catholic chapel, on the other hand, was significantly larger and included two organists, one theorboist, five violinists, six oboists, three bassoonists, three trumpeters, and one drummer.[33] In addition, six unspecified instrumentalists are listed on the roster. According to a roster of 1711, the orchestra by this time numbered thirty-five, including five violinists, six violists, three cellists, one bassist, three flautists, three oboists, three bassoonists, two horn players, two organists, a theorboist, and a lutenist.[34] Payroll records also indicate that additional trumpeters and drummers were hired on occasion.[35]

At first, the Catholic services were held discreetly in a private room of the palace.[36] Since the king spent most of his time in Poland during these years, there was little need for elaborate Catholic services in Dresden. The musicians, too, were gone much of the time, accompanying the king on this trips to Crackow and Warsaw.[37] In 1699, however, the king took his first major step toward the public establishment of Catholic worship services in Dresden by rededicating the Protestant church in the castle at Moritzburg for Catholic worship. The services began there at Christmas of that year.

By 1708 the need for a Catholic church at the Dresden residence itself had become apparent, due to the influx of Poles, French, and Italians. Accordingly, the old opera house "am Taschenberge" was remodelled as a Roman Catholic chapel. It was dedicated April 5, 1708.[38]

The crown prince and his wife (after their marriage in 1719) were especially supportive of the Catholic services, and in 1720 the latter was instrumental in procurring a Silbermann portative organ for the chapel.[39] As time passed, the number of Catholic services increased, and the responsibilities of the musicians likewise grew.[40]

Meanwhile, the Protestant establishment had decreased in size and importance. Already in 1698 the musical forces had been reduced to one or two organists, two cantors, and six choir boys,[41] and in the regular services the music consisted only of chorales.[42]

Whenever the king was in residence, however,[43] the Catholic chapel musicians would occasionally play at the Lutheran services, allowing the chapel master Schmidt to perform more elaborate music.[44] This presumably included cantatas.

In 1717 a new chamber orchestra called the "Polish orchestra" (*polnische Kapelle*) or the "small chamber music" (*kleine Kammermusik*) was formed to accompany the king to Poland instead of the larger ochestra (*grossen Kammermusik*). This group was placed under the leadership of Giovanni Alberto Ristori (1692-1753) and consisted of five violins, one oboe, two horns, three bassoons, and one double bass.[45] One musician to begin his career in this orchestra was Johann Quantz (1697-1773), presumably as an oboist.[46] The formation of this chamber group apparently left the larger orchestra free to remain in Dresden all year.

When Heinichen came to Dresden in 1717, he was apparently only in charge of the Catholic chapel, until Schmidt's death in 1728, when he assumed responsibility for the Protestant chapel as well.[47] Since Heinichen only survived Schmidt by one year,[48] his health was probably quite poor by this time, and his involvement during this last year may well have been minimal.

The obvious problem for us is that Heinichen's cantatas could only have been performed in the Protestant chapel, which was apparently outside his musical jurisdiction. Furthermore, the Protestant chapel had no instrumental resources of its own; it could only borrow the services of the Catholic chapel musicians when they were available. As for the relationship between the two men, it seems to have been characterized by a certain amount of rivalry, for Quantz writes in his autobiography:

> The chapel master Schmidt promised to teach me counterpoint, but kept procrastinating so that nothing came of it. I did not dare to speak to the chapel master Heinichen about it for fear of

offending the former, particularly since they were not the best of friends.[49]

That Heinichen in no way considered Schmidt his superior is made clear by his own statement:

> May no one misinterpret it as blameworthy ambition, if, at the close of this work I remind them that in more than one previous treatise, the abuse has been proceeding that, in naming the two German Dresden chapel masters Schmidt and Heinichen, the former has been given the title of chief chapel master. Since on no occasion has the latter allowed himself to be subordinated to the chief chapel master, and the former (to speak nothing of other reasons) has not even once pretended it, and has often openly declared this: therefore one wished herewith to disabuse good friends of their notion.[50]

In practice, however, a certain amount of collaboration probably took place between the two men, and the jurisdiction of the two chapels was likely not as clear-cut as it would at first appear. This view is supported by a roster of musicians for the *Kapell- und Kammermusik* (i.e., the Catholic chapel musicians), which lists both Schmidt and Heinichen as chapel masters.[51] Furthermore, Hiller writes that by the time Heinichen was hired, Schmidt was composing little or nothing.[52] Since at least eight of the performances indicated on the title pages of Heinichen's manuscripts occurred during Heinichen's Dresden years,[53] these works were probably performed in the Protestant chapel, under either Schmidt's or Heinichen's direction.[54] The other works, being undated, might also have been performed in Dresden with the same performance forces.

When Heinichen arrived in Dresden, he encountered one of the finest and largest musical establishments in Europe. A roster of 1719 lists the following orchestral personnel.[55] The dates indicate the times of residency in Dresden.[56]

Chapel masters: Schmidt and Heinichen
Concert master: J.B. Volumier (1709-1728)[57]
Chamber composer and chamber violinist: Francesco Maria Veracini
    (1717-1722)[58]

Chamber composer and chamber organist: Christian Petzold
   1697-1733)[59]
Organist: Johann Wolfgang Schmidt (copyist since 1709, organist since
   1719)[60]
Pantaleonist: Pantaleon Hebenstreit (1714-1750)[61]
Theorboists: Silvius Leopold Weiss (1718-1759)[62] and Francesco Arigoni
   (already mentioned in roster of 1697)[63]
Viola da gambist: Gottfried Bentley (already mentioned in roster of
   1709)[64]
Seven violinists. Included in the seven was Johann Georg Pisendel
   (1712-1728)[65]
Five violists
Five cellists. Three were French, two Italian.
Three contrabassists. Two of these were Gerolamo Personelli (1717-
   until after 1720)[66] and Johann Dismas Zelenka (1710-1745)[67]
Two flautists. One of these was Pierre Gabriel Buffardin (1715 to
   retirement in 1749)[68]
Five oboists. Two of these were Francois Le Riche (1699 to at least
   1733)[69] and Johann Christian Richter (already mentioned in roster
   of 1709, to 1744)[70]
Two natural horn players. These were presumably Johann Adalbert
   Fischer and Franz Adam Samm who had been hired in 1711.[71]
Three bassoonists
One copyist
One keyboard tuner
One servant

The double bass player Personelli was hired upon Lotti's request.
Another bass player requested by Lotti was Angelo Gaggi.[72] Gaggi, however,
left Dresden after his one-year contract (1717-1718) expired.[73]

The famous flautist Johann Joachim Quantz had already been hired as
an oboist in 1718[74] so was probably included in the five listed above. After
travels that took him away from Dresden (1724-1727),[75] he was hired as a
flautist in 1727 and remained at the Dresden court until he left for the court
of King Fredrick II (Berlin) in 1741.[76] In 1719 the famous gambist Ernst
Christian Hesse was also hired (March to October, 1719).[77]

In addition to the above instrumentalists, chapel masters at Dresden
also had the court trumpeters and drummers available to them. In 1709 the

records lists one chief trumpeter (*Oberhoftrompeter*), twelve court trumpeters, and one drummer.[78] By 1736 this had increased to thirteen trumpeters, two drummers, two trumpet students, and one drum student.[79] The court also employed sixteen bagpipers[80] and ten hunting pipers.[81] Frequently the court also drew on the wind players (oboes, bassoons, natural horns, and fifes[82]) and a dozen drummers.[83] For particularly grand celebrations, even these forces were insufficient, and more players were imported. Thus, for the Carneval of 1695, 150 extra musicians were hired, mostly violinists, violists, bass players, shawm players, cymbalists and lutenists.[84]

Singers of the court during Heinichen's time included most notably, the newly hired Italian opera troupe under the direction of Antonio Lotti.[85]

Female Singers:
>Santa Stella Lotti, soprano (Sept. 1, 1717 - 1719)[86]
>Margherita Catterina Zani called "Marucini," soprano (Sept. 1, 1717 - Sept. 1, 1718)[87]
>Livia Constantini called "La Polacchina," soprano (1717 - 1719)[88]
>Lucia Gaggi called "Bavarini," wife of the bass player, contralto (Sept. 1, 1717 - Sept. 1, 1718)[89]
>Margherita Durastanti (April, 1719, - February 1, 1720)[90]
>Maria Antonia Laurenti called "Coralli," (April, 1719 - February 1, 1720)[91]
>Vittoria Tesi, contralto (April, 1719 - February 1, 1720)[92]
>Madelaine de Salvay (1719 - February 1, 1720)[93]
>Johanne Eleonore Hesse (March to October, 1719)[94]

Male Singers:
>Francesco Bernardi called "Senesino," soprano (Sept. 1, 1717 - February 1, 1720)[95]
>Matteo Berselli, soprano (Sept. 1, 1717 - February 1, 1720)[96]
>Cajetano Bernstadt, alto (Sept. 1, 1717 - Sept. 1, 1718)[97]
>Guiseppe Maria Boschi, alto (1717/18 - February 1, 1720)[98]
>Francesco Guicciardi, tenor (Sept. 1, 1717 - February 1, 1720)[99]
>Lucrezio Borsari, bass (1717/18 - 1719)[100]

The Italian singers, besides appearing in Dresden appearances, also accompanied the king on trips to Poland.[101] To what extent the opera singers participated in the church services is not clear. That they were hired with some church duties in mind can be seen from a disposition of August the Strong which states "qui peut servir a l'opera et pour l'eglise..."[102] In any case, they were all dismissed in February, 1720, after the oft-quoted altercation involving Senesino, Berselli, and Heinichen.[103]

In addition to the opera singers, there were also singers assigned to the chapels themselves. Although all singers had been dismissed in 1707 due to a shortage of funds caused by the Northern War,[104] at least the Catholic organization was immediately reestablished by the hiring of two sopranos, two altos, one tenor, one bass, four instrumentalists (of which two were violinists), one organist, and a musical director.[105] These musicians lived with the clerics and probably performed the services during the week as well as the vocal part of the music during Sundays and Feast days, when the court orchestra played.[106] According to markings on the manuscripts of Heinichen's Masses, this choir was enlarged with court members having some vocal ability and outside soloists, including some female singers.[107] The number of resident singers however, remained unchanged until 1771.[108]

The situation in the Protestant chapel is less clear. According to Fürstenau, although all of the choir boys lived with Schmidt until his death in 1728, only six of them sang in the Protestant chapel (already since 1699). The rest of the choir was made up of singers not belonging to the chapel establishment (*Kapelle*). The adult singers had already been dismissed in 1698.[109]

By 1724 the Italian singers were missed so greatly by the crown prince and his wife that arrangements were made to have young singers trained in Venice.[110] They finally arrived in Dresden in 1730.[111]

In the meantime (April 1725), other singers were hired:[112]

Female Singers:
> Margherita Ermini, soprano (1725-1765)
> Ludowica Seyfried, soprano (1725-1732)

Male Singers:
> Andrea Ruota, soprano (1725-1731)
> Nicolo Pozzi called "Nicolini," alto (1725-1758)
> Matteo Luchini, tenor (1725-1731)
> Cosinio Ermini, bass (1725-1745)

These singers belonged to the "Royal Chapel and Chamber" and, at first, apparently spent much of their time performing chamber and church music.[113]

In summary, it is clear that although the personnel tended to change, the musical establishment at the Dresden court was a large and distinguished one. However, because the musical requirements at the court were so diverse and because the operatic and theatrical performances largely overshadowed music-making in the church, it is difficult to determine the extent to which the musicians were available for church services, especially in the Protestant chapel.

Conclusions Drawn from the Manuscript Sources

Certain information regarding the performance practice of Heinichen's compositions can be gained from the manuscripts themselves, especially those that are sets of performing parts. Five of these have title pages, of which three indicate flexibility in the number of performing parts.[114] These title pages read as follows:

> *Einsamkeit, o stilles Wesen* (Dresden Ms. 2398-E-508)
> à 7. 8. ò 12. 2 Violini, Viola, Fagoto [sic], 4 Voci, 4 Voci in Rip., con Continuo à doppio.

> *Der Herr ist nahe*
> 8 ò 12. 2 Violini, Viola, Fagoto [sic], C.A.T.B. 4 Voci a Rip con Continuo a doppio

> *Gelobet sei der Herr* (Dresden Ms. 2398-E-504)
> â 9 ô 12. 2 Violini, 2 Viole, Fagoto [sic] ô Violone.
> 2 Hautbois ⎫
>   ⎬ B. al piac.
> Bassone ⎭
> C.A.T.B, 4 Voci in Ripieno con Continuo a doppio

In the case of *Einsamkeit*, the main choice appears to be whether or not to use the ripieno parts. The bassoon and double continuo parts are apparently counted as one, even though they would require three players. If the work is to be performed with only seven parts, it is probably the viola that is to be dropped, for its material is the least indispensible.

In *Der Herr ist nahe*, the variable factor is again the ripieno vocal parts. Once again the bassoon and double continuo parts are counted as one.

In *Gelobet* the choices are also fairly clear. Performing with nine parts would include four string parts, bass (*fagoto* [sic][115] or violone plus continuo), and four voice parts. The two *hautbois* and the *bassone* are clearly marked as the optional parts. Whether or not the ripieno parts would be included if these woodwinds were not, is not stated. There seems to be no reason to exclude them if the extra singers are available.

The double continuo parts mentioned on the title pages of the above three cantatas are, in most cases, identical to each other,[116] and in all three cases they are continuous. These instruments' participation is in no way linked to the presence or absence of vocal ripieno parts.

Two other compositions have multiple continuo parts as well. *Herr, nun lässest Du* has three figured continuo parts: two marked "continuo," and one, in a completely different hand, marked "continuo transpos." This part was probably added later, for even the notation on the title page, which reads "Basso per il Org. in triplo," is written in such a way that the words "in triplo" could easily have been added later.[117] That the other two continuo parts were also intended for organ is clear from the "org. solo" markings found on both parts at the beginning of the bass solo "Mein Augenlight." Both of these continuo parts are present in every movement except the opening sonata, in which only one participates. The transposed organ part on the other hand, includes only some of the movements (mainly the choral ones) indicating that it was added to the other two and did not replace them.

Although Heinichen's scores do not identify the continuo instrument(s) (with the one exception noted below), the parts almost always designate at least one part "organo." It is therefore reasonable to assume that, as Bach did in Leipzig, Heinichen normally relied on the organ as the standard continuo instrument.[118] One exception to this rule is *Heilig ist der Herr*, a score which carried this designation: "a 4. Voci, 2 hautbois, 2 violini, Fagotto et Cembalo." The actual continuo line is, as in the other scores, undesignated.

The other work with two figured continuo parts is *Lobe den Herrn*. One part is marked "continuo," the other part is marked "Chalcedono," which is apparently a German corruption of "colascione."[119] The colascione was a fretted string instrument of Middle Eastern origin and was known in Italy during the seventeenth and eighteenth centuries. It usually had two or three strings, which were played by plucking, and a long neck.[120]

That the German version of the colascione was very different from the Italian model has recently been demonstrated by Donald Gill.[121] Instead of two or three strings, the German instrument had six and was therefore well-suited for playing the thorough-bass.[122] Heinichen probably learned to appreciate the instrument from Telemann, who used it in many of his church cantatas.[123] The chalcedono part in Heinichen's cantata reveals that it was capable of fast passagework (thirty-second notes in the bass recitative) and octave leaps. The presence of figures indicates that chords were also possible. On the other hand, the clef changes present in the other continuo part, are absent here, probably because doubling the bass was impossible.[124]

As for the actual realization of the continuo parts, Heinichen's exhaustive treatment of the subject can only be touched upon here. He emphasizes a full-voiced, chordal style that does not distract with embellishments or contrapuntal imitation.[125] In fact, the only suitable places for embellishment, according to Heinichen, are those where the thorough-bass plays alone.[126] His caution against elaborate accompaniments is very clear:

> An accompanist, however, is not usually expected to find the place for such elaborated "themata," "inventiones," or "variationes" of a composer and, by imitating the same, to encroach upon the other (instrumental) parts dedicated to this task. Such arts the amateur can better utilize in (extemporizing) preludes; this is where they really belong.[127]

The continuo player may double the bass in octaves, except on occasions where a C or G clef replaces the usual bass clef. Parts marked "tasto solo" must be played as single lines, and passages where two parts are written one over the other must be played without additional notes.[128]

In the performance of Heinichen's church works, the continuo group may well have included the violone as standard practice, doubling the continuo line at the lower octave and, in this way, giving the bass line greater strength. This practice would clarify those musical passages in which the vocal bass dips below the instrumental bass and generally give the composition a more solid foundation. We know that Bach used the violone in this way, retaining it even in treble arias that do not require such a strong bass.[129] Of Heinichen's six compositions for which we have performing parts, only the three mentioned above actually specify the violone, however. In the case of *Gelobet sei der Herr*, which exists in two versions (both are sets of performing parts), the earlier one[130] designates the part "Violone ouero Fagoto." It doubles the *bassoun* part[131] rather than the continuo bass. In the later version of this cantata,[132] the violone part doubles the continuo bass since there is no *bassoun* part. The single continuo part in this version is marked "organo L. violone." Since it is doubtful that two violoni would play, this designation may simply indicate that the two parts are identical.

If the violone were also used in the performance of the other three cantatas to which we have performing parts[133] (even though no separate violone parts are included), the violonist must have read from another player's music, perhaps sharing music with the "fagottist." The remaining nine cantatas survive only as scores and carry no indication as to the number of players playing the bass part.

The violoncello is never mentioned.[134] However, some undesignated parts in the scores of *Gegrüsset seist du* and *Ach, was soll ich Sünder machen* (II) were probably intended for cello. They are written in the bass clef and sound in consort with other undesignated parts whose clefs suggest violins and violas. In both works, these parts are not the same as the continuo bass, and another cello may well have played that part. In Heinichen's more elaborately scored compositions, however, bassoons (*fagotti* rather than *bassoni*) frequently play the continuo line, and it is possible that they replaced the cello in the continuo group. On the other hand, just as it has often been assumed that an unmentioned bassoonist read from the cello part,[135] so the reverse may be true. Heinichen's own statements seem to imply that cellos were not always used or, on the other hand, that they might replace the basses, for in a discussion regarding methods to enhance melodic lines through the use of instrumental unisons, he indicates that, on occasion, the basses were too obtrusive and should be replaced by bassetti (i.e. cellos).[136]

Four of Heinichen's compositions have vocal ripieno parts: *Herr, nun lässest Du, Gelobet, Der Herr ist nahe*, and *Einsamkeit*.[137] Neither *Gelobet* nor *Einsamkeit* have "soli/tutti" markings in the concertino parts; the ripieno parts reinforce the vocal lines without warning. In the other two cantatas, "soli/tutti" or "soli/Cap." markings are to be found[138] but the terms are not used consistently. In the bass part of *Der Herr ist nahe*, for instance, there are none at all. In *Herr, nun lässest Du*, the alto part has a "Cap" marking in the fifth movement, when all ripieno parts are silent. The other three vocal parts, although participating, have no markings at all. Since this manuscript uses all three terms: "soli," "Cap," and "tutti," one wonders whether a three-way division were possible, in which the term "Capella" referred to a smaller group than the "tutti." There are no other indicators to suggest such a view, however, and since the usual meanings of the two terms are identical, one must conclude that the designation in the alto part is an error.

Whether or not the soloists were members of the choir or were imported (opera) singers, as they were in the Catholic chapel,[139] they apparently sang along with the others in the choral movements. This view is supported by the markings in *Meine Seele erhebet den Herrn*. Here the soprano duet (presumably sung by two soloists) is marked "S Chor 1" and "S Chor 2."[140]

The total number of singers at Heinichen's disposal would have had to be at least twelve for a cantata like *Herr, nun lässest Du*, (four soloists plus eight in the "Kapelle") and at least sixteen for the cantata *Meine Seele erhebet den Herrn* (eight in each choir including the soloists). The six-part cantata *Es lebet Jesus unser Hort* would require a minimum of twelve singers.

Since most of Heinichen's works have no "soli/tutti" markings, a systematic division of the four-part vocal movements into solo and choral passages is unwarranted, although some solo passages within concertante movements that are accompanied only by continuo may well have been performed soloistically.[141] We can quite safely assume, however, that S.A.T.B. movements were sung by a chorus, while arias were sung by soloists.[142]

Certain conclusions regarding the performance practice of Heinichen's church compositions can also be drawn from the transpositions of the instruments used. Whenever oboes or *bassoni* appear in the performing parts, they are usually written a major second or minor third higher than the vocal, string, and continuo parts.[143] This situation suggests that the high organ pitch (*Chor-Ton*) was used as the standard, and the lower-pitched woodwinds (which were either in *Cammer-Ton* or *tief Cammer-Ton*) were then transposed up by the required interval.

Regarding the tunings and pitches in use during this time, Arthur Mendel writes that, although organ pitch varied from city to city, until the late eighteenth century, it was normally called *Chor-Ton*.[144] *Cammer-Ton* was then defined as a major second or minor third below *Chor-Ton*.[145]

From a notational perspective, the composer's two options can then be pictured thus:

Option 1

Chor-Ton: organ, strings (tuned to the organ), voices, trumpets[146]

Cammer-Ton: woodwinds (treated as transposing instruments)

Option 2

Chor-Ton: organ, trumpets (treated as transposing instruments)

Cammer-Ton: woodwinds, strings (tuned to the woodwinds), voices

In Leipzig, Johann Kuhnau switched to *Cammer-Ton* as the standard pitch (option 2) soon after beginning his tenure as the director of church music (c. 1701).[147] Bach, too, switched to this system after coming to Leipzig.[148] Since Heinichen's usual practice still follows the earlier tradition, it is possible that the works in question were not originally performed in Leipzig, or at least that the performance associated with these extant parts took place outside Leipzig. On the other hand, Kuhnau admitted the that the new practice was resisted by the continuo players because it required them to play in more difficult keys.[149] For this reason we may suppose that not all composers in Leipzig immediately abandoned the older system.

In the late (1723) version of *Gelobet sei der Herr* Heinichen does switch to *Cammer-Ton* (option 2). Here the oboe, string, and voice parts are in the original key of F major, while the continuo part is in Eb. Since the Dresden court had also abandoned *Chor-Ton* as the pitch standard by 1709,[150] and many of the new organs, including Silbermann's Dresden organ of 1722, were being built to *Cammer-Ton*,[151] it is clear that Heinichen was following the prevailing notational practices by this time.

In *Es lebet Jesus unser Hort*, all of the wind parts (*clarini, trombe, hautbois, traverso*) are notated in the same key as the strings, chorus and continuo. Since trumpets were usually pitched in the higher *Chor-Ton* (hence also called the *Cornett-Ton*),[152] transposition would be required either way; the trumpets and organ would need to have transposed parts if the choir and strings were in the lower pitch (*Cammer-Ton*) of the woodwinds; the woodwinds would need transposed parts if the choir and strings were in the higher pitch (*Chor-Ton* or *Cornett-Ton*) of the trumpets and organ. The simplest explanation for the nontranposed parts is that the manuscript, being a score, does not reflect the actual performance situation.

A similar situation is found in the score *Heilig ist der Herr*, where parts for the oboes, *fagotto*, choir, and continuo are all written in the same key.

In this case, the organ may not have played at all, however, for the title specifies *cembalo*.

We have already seen that the three organ parts in *Herr, nun lässest Du* were apparently intended to be used simultaneously, since the transposed organ part contains only certain movements of the work. Since the *hautbois* and *bassone* are already transposed up a minor third (implying *tief Cammer-Ton*), the rest of the performers must have played in the *Chor-Ton* of the other two organ parts. The transposed organ part must then have been in a still higher tuning, since it is notated a major second **below** the others.

Two works have both *bassone* and *fagotto*[153] parts. In both cases (*Herr, nun lässest Du* and the earlier version of *Gelobet sei der Herr*), the *fagotto* part is notated at the same pitch as the other parts, while the *bassone* is notated at a higher pitch (a minor third and major second higher, respectively). In the one composition with only a *bassone* part (*Lobe den Herrn*), the *bassone*, like the oboes, is transposed up a major second. Since both instruments are apparently bassoons, one wonders about their differences. Likely the *fagotto* was of German origin, hence the higher pitch, while the *bassone* was of non-German origin and therefore employed the lower pitch characteristic of France and at least parts of Italy.[154]

In view of the fact that the *bassone* usually plays or rests in time with the oboes while the *fagotto* plays more or less continuously with the continuo bass,[155] it is likely that Heinichen intended both instruments to play in the two works that have both *bassone* and *fagotto* parts. This conclusion is further supported by the fact that these parts were apparently written by the same copyist and even at the same time. If the two parts had been occasioned by performances in different places or at different times, we would expect not only that they would be identical to each other but also that they would show some variation in writing style (a different hand, greater haste, etc.). That more than one bassoon should be used is not surprising; the bassoon was a very popular instrument in the orchestra of eighteenth-century Europe.[156] It is also likely that the timbre of the *bassone* matched that of the oboes more closely than did that of the *fagotto*; this would explain why we never find their roles reversed.

Chapter 6. Notes

1. The title page of Dresden MS. 2398-E-508 reads: "Ad Fer 2. Pasch. e per ogni tempo." However, the digit appears to have been corrected to read "2", and the notation on the lower portion of the title page reads,
"Fer. 1. Paschat.   1709
                     1714
                     1719."
The title on the score contained in Berlin MS. 30210 states: "Feria Paschat: 2dâ."

2. The third digit is unclear. The date could be 1707 or 1717.

3. 1723 is the date on Dresden MS. 2398-E-509. All of the other dates appear on MS. 2398-E-504.

4. Seibel, p. 10. See also Arno Werner, *Städtische und fürstliche Musikpflege in Weissenfels bis zum Ende des 18. Jahrh.* (Leipzig: Breitkopf & Härtel, 1911).

5. Seibel, p. 31.

6. Seibel, p. 30.

7. Seibel, p. 35.

8. Seibel, p. 12.

9. Seibel, p. 11. This 300th anniversary was celebrated for three days. See Rudolf Eller, "Leipzig: II. Vom Westfälischen Frieden bis zum Ausgang des 18. Jh.," *Die Musik in Geschichte und Gegenwart* (Bärenreiter: Kassel, 1949-1979), vol. 8, col. 547.

10. Seibel, p. 36.

11. Seibel, p. 14.

12. Seibel, p. 15.

13. This is also Seibel's conclusion. Seibel, p. 48.

14. Martin Ruhnke, "Telemann," *New Grove*, vol. 18, col. 648.

15. Kuhnau and Graupner were exceptional Kapellmeister in that they performed mostly their own works. See Friedrich Wilhelm Riedel, "Johann Kuhnau," *Die Musik in Geschichte und Gegenwart*, vol. 7, col. 1880.

16. Eller, col. 548.

17. The Italian troupe left Venice on September 5, 1717. Heinichen may have left Venice in spring, or even at the beginning of the year. See chapter 3.

18. The assumption that Heinichen had no opportunity to perform Protestant works between 1710 and 1717 is undermined by one important fact, however. The manuscript score of the solo cantata *Warum toben die Heiden* is clearly marked as an autograph composed in "1715. *pridie diei viridium*." As we have shown in chapter 4, this manuscript is likely **not** an autograph at all. Since this writer has not had the opportunity to examine other autograph scores of Heinichen, it is necessary, at least, to acknowledge the discrepancy.

Even the remotest possiblity that the designation is correct leads one to speculate how this work might then have originated. Perhaps Heinichen composed it with no performance in view or perhaps he composed it for a private gathering. To be sure, a private performance of this cantata, whose orchestration requires only violin and continuo (including bassoon) would be much easier to arrange than that of a cantata as fully orchestrated as *Herr, nun lässest Du*. Many unanswered questions still remain regarding Heinichen's activities during his stay in Italy. Perhaps Heinichen actually made two trips to Italy. We are told that Prince Leopold of Cöthen tried to hire him during this time (Seibel, p. 16). However, since the Venetian performances of his operas *Le passioni per troppo amore* and *Mario* occured in 1713, he must have stayed in Italy at least until that year. (According to Hiller, there were numerous performances of these operas. See Hiller, p. 16.) Then, at the end of 1713, the German composer Gottfried Heinrich Stölzel travelled to Italy and visited Heinichen for some time (Mattheson, *Ehrenpforte*, p. 345). It seems unlikely that Heinichen would have returned to Germany by the Feast of Purification (February 2, 1714) to perform *Herr, nun lässest Du*. If this were possible, however, Heinichen could then have written and performed the solo cantata *Warum toben die Heiden* in 1715 while in Germany and could have returned to Italy in the spring of 1716. We do know that in October of that year he was in Venice, for in that month his Serenata in honor of the crown prince of Saxony was performed.

19. With the notable exceptions of Graupner and Telemann, most music directors performed cantatas composed by others. Thus, for instance, Krieger's record indicates that he performed a solo cantata by Heinichen in Weissenfels on St. Michael's Day, 1711. (See Seiffert, p. LVI.) Since Seiffert does not list subsequent performances of any of the works in his reproduction of the catalogue, we do not know if this work was ever performed again by Krieger or his son. No further performances are listed by Werner either. See Werner, *Weissenfels*, pp. 139, 145.

20. Some contemporaries of Heinichen's whose names have these initials include his former classmate Johann Christian Schieferdecker who was in Lübeck since 1704, his former classmate Johann David Schieferdecker who became a Superintendent in Weissenfels (see Seibel, p. 6; Werner, *Weissenfels*, p. 34; Seiffert, p. LXXVIII), and Johann Wolfgang Schmidt, who was copyist at the court in Dresden from at least 1709 (Fürstenau, *Geschichte*, 2:51). Of course, the Kapellmeister in Dresden at this time could also be considered, Johann Christoph Schmidt. Although one might expect the copyist to be a student or some other person of subordinate rank, the handwriting of these manuscripts is firm and angular, suggesting a fairly mature musician.

21. If the correct date of *Gelobet* is, in fact, June 1717, this cantata was probably written in Dresden. Although the Italian opera troupe hired by Prince Friedrich left Venice for Dresden on Sept. 5, 1717, the fact that Mattheson had already requested Heinichen's biography for his book *Grundlage einer Ehren-Pforte* in February of that year leads Seibel to the conclusion that Heinichen was already in Dresden by this time. See Seibel, p. 20 and Mattheson, *Das beschützte Orchestre* (Hamburg, 1707), introduction. See also our chapter 3.

22. Whereas the other three cantatas incorporate da capo arias, *Gelobet* is a *Spruchoden-kantate* and its arias employ no da capos.

23. No cantata could have been performed at the court of Weissenfels because Krieger's exhaustive record lists only the solo cantata performed on St. Michael's Day 1711. See Seiffert, p. LVI and Arno Werner, *Weissenfels*, pp. 139, 145.

24. According to Werner, the court diaries for 1709 and 1710 are missing. See Werner, *Zeitz*, p. 81. See also Seibel, p. 15; Günther Kraft, "Zeitz," *Die Musik in Geschichte und Gegenwart*, vol. 14, col. 1191.

25. According to Seibel, Heinichen was hired after the performance in Naumburg of his opera *Olimpia vendicata*. This happened in June of 1709. He resigned his position July 9, 1710. Since a period of state mourning was no doubt declared after the death of the crown prince on February 10, 1710, Heinichen had probably been idle since then. See chapter 3.

26. Fürstenau, *Geschichte*, 2:12; Irmgard Becker-Glauch, "August der Starke," *Die Musik in Geschichte und Gegenwart*, vol. 1, col. 841. The confusion that one frequently encounters over the titles of August the Strong and his son arises from that fact that August the Strong was called Friedrich August I as Elector of Saxony, and Friedrich August II as King of Poland. His son was then Friedrich August II as Elector of Saxony, and Friedrich August III as King of Poland.

27. Becker-Glauch, "Dresden, Von den Anfängen bis zum Tode Augusts der Starken," *Die Musik in Geschichte und Gegenwart*, vol. 3, col 764, and Fürstenau, *Geschichte*, 2:6.

28. Fürstenau, *Geschichte*, 2:13.

29. Fürstenau, *Geschichte*, 2:13, 18.

30. Fürstenau, *Geschichte*, 2:18.

31. Becker-Glauch, "Dresden," col. 763; Fürstenau, *Beiträge*, p. 112.

32. Fürstenau, *Geschichte*, 2:14.

33. Fürstenau, *Geschichte*, 2:19.

34. Fürstenau, *Beiträge*, pp. 113-115.

35. Fürstenau, *Geschichte*, 2:19.

36. Fürstenau, *Geschichte*, 2:20.

37. Fürstenau, *Geschichte*, 2:20.

38. Fürstenau, *Geschichte*, 2:34.

39. Fürstenau, *Geschichte*, 2:39.

40. Fürstenau, *Geschichte*, 2:39.

41. Fürstenau, *Geschichte*, 2:16.

42. Fürstenau, *Geschichte*, 2:16.

43. Especially from 1709 on, the king spent more time in Dresden than previously. He would normally leave for Poland in August of each year, returning in December or January. Sometimes he would be gone until Easter. See Fürstenau, *Geschichte*, 2:43.

44. Fürstenau's phrase "ausnahmsweise öfters" seems to imply that normally the orchestra played in the Protestant chapel at widely-spaced intervals; during some periods, more often. See Fürstenau, *Geschichte*, 2:17.

45. Fürstenau, *Geschichte*, 2:120.

46. Quantz later switched to the flute. See Fürstenau, *Geschichte*, 2:120; Fritz Bose, "Quantz, Johann Joachim," *Die Musik in Geschichte und Gegenwart*, vol. 10, col. 1797.

47. The responsibility of housing the choir boys, which had also been Schmidt's, was taken over by Pantaleon Hebenstreit. See Fürstenau, *Geschichte*, 2:17.

48. Schmidt died on April 13, 1728; Heinichen on July 16, 1729.

49. Friedrich Wilhelm Marpurg, "Herrn Johann Joachim Quantzens Lebenslauf von ihm selbst entworfen," *Historisch-kritische Beyträge zur Aufnahme der Musik* (Berlin, 1755), I:210, trans. by M. Unger.

50. Heinichen, *General-Bass*, p. 960; translated by M. Unger.

51. Fürstenau, *Geschichte*, 2:134.

52. Hiller, p. 222.

53. The last performance of *Herr, nun lässest Du* occurred in 1734, hence after Heinichen's death.

54. Of course it is possible that these performances occured elsewhere under the direction of some chapel master who had procurred the music for his own use.

55. The musicians of the Polish orchestra were apparently in addition to these. For a reproduction of the roster, see Hill, pp. 912-914. A salary list of musicians in 1720 is reproduced on pp. 915-917. See also Fürstenau, *Beiträge*, pp. 123-124. Singers were not listed in these rosters because their pay came out of the opera budget. See Fürstenau, *Beiträge*, p. 124.

56. These have been added by this writer and are individually documented.

57. Fürstenau, *Geschichte*, 2:65. In *Beiträge*, Fürstenau gives the date 1706. See p. 115.

58. Fürstenau, *Geschichte*, 2:106, 112.

59. Fürstenau, *Geschichte*, 2:65-66.

60. Fürstenau, *Geschichte*, 2:51, 134.

61. Alfred Berner, "Hebenstreit," *Die Musik in Geschichte und Gegenwart*, vol. 6, col. 4.

62. Fürstenau, *Geschichte*, 2:126, 127. In *Beiträge*, Fürstenau gives the date 1715. See p. 116.

63. Fürstenau, *Geschichte*, 2:19.

64. Fürstenau, *Geschichte*, 2:50.

65. Fürstenau, *Geschichte*, 2:84, 87.

66. Fürstenau, *Geschichte*, 2:105, 154.

67. Fürstenau, *Geschichte*, 2:71, 76.

68. Fürstenau, *Geschichte*, 2:95.

69. Fürstenau, *Geschichte*, 2:66.

70. Fürstenau, *Geschichte*, 2:50, 66.

71. Fürstenau, *Geschichte*, 2:58.

72. Fürstenau, *Geschichte*, 2:113.

73. Fürstenau, *Geschichte*, 2:126.

74. Bose, "Quantz," col. 1797.

75. Ibid.

76. Fürstenau, *Geschichte*, 2:164, 165.

77. Fürstenau, *Geschichte*, 2:133.

78. Fürstenau, *Geschichte*, 2:57, 58.

79. Fürstenau, *Geschichte*, 2:58.

80. *Bockpfeife*. See Fürstenau, *Geschichte*, 2:67.

81. *Jagtpfeifer*. Fürstenau, *Geschichte*, 2:67.

82. *Querpfeifer*. Fürstenau, *Geschichte*, 2:68.

83. Fürstenau, *Geschichte*, 2:68.

84. Fürstenau, *Geschichte*, 2:69.

85. Fürstenau, *Geschichte*, 2:105. See also chart in Becker-Glauch, *Bedeutung*, pp. 24-25. She indicates initial contracts began on October 1, 1717 rather than Sept. 1, 1717. See also Hill's salary roster, Hill, pp. 904 ff.

86. Fürstenau, *Geschichte*, 2:105, 149.

87. Fürstenau, *Geschichte*, 2:105, 126.

88. Fürstenau, *Geschichte*, 2:26.

89. Fürstenau, *Geschichte*, 2:105, 126.

90. Fürstenau, *Geschichte*, 2:133, 154.

91. Fürstenau, *Geschichte*, 2:133, 154.

92. Fürstenau, *Geschichte*, 2:133, 154.

93. Fürstenau, *Geschichte*, 2:133, 154.

94. Fürstenau, *Geschichte*, 2:133.

95. Fürstenau, *Geschichte*, 2:105, 154. At a one-year salary of 7000 Taler, Senesino was the highest paid singer. He received almost six times as much as Heinichen.

96. Fürstenau, *Geschichte*, 2:105, 154.

97. Fürstenau, *Geschichte*, 2:105, 126.

98. Fürstenau, *Geschichte*, 2:105, 154.

99. Fürstenau, *Geschichte*, 2:105, 154.

100. Fürstenau, *Geschichte*, 2:105, 149.

101. Fürstenau, *Geschichte*, 2:119.

102. Quoted in Becker-Glauch, *Bedeutung*, p. 26. See also Fürstenau, *Beiträge*, p. 124.

103. Fürstenau, *Geschichte*, 2:153.

104. Fürstenau, *Geschichte*, 2:33.

105. Fürstenau, *Geschichte*, 2:35, 36.

106. Fürstenau, *Geschichte*, 2:38.

107. Schmitz, pp. 13, 224.

108. Schmitz, p. 13.

109. Fürstenau, *Beiträge*, p. 112, Fürstenau, *Geschichte*, 2:16-17.

110. Fürstenau, *Geschichte*, 2:160. The reason for choosing young singers was to avoid high salaries.

111. Fürstenau, *Geschichte*, 2:165.

112. Fürstenau, *Geschichte*, 2:160-161.

113. Fürstenau, *Geschichte*, 2:161.

114. Of course, the number of parts is not equivalent to the number within the ensemble. Regarding the question of balance, Quantz suggests the following relationships between instruments:
for 4 violins: 1 viola, 1 cello, 1 violone of medium size
for 6 violins: same as above plus a bassoon
for 8 violins: 2 violas, 2 cellos, 2 violone (1 medium size, 1 somewhat larger), 2 oboes, 2 flutes and 2 bassoons

for 10 violins: same as above plus an additional cello

for 12 violins: 3 violas, 4 cellos, 2 violone, 3 bassoons, 4 oboes, 4 flutes, and, if it is an orchestra, an additional harpsichord, plus a theorbo.

Natural horns could be used with either large or small ensembles. See Johann Joachim Quantz, *On Playing the Flute*, trans. Edward R. Reilly (London: Faber and Faber, 1966), p. 214.

115. The difference between a *fagoto* [sic] and a *bassone* appears to be mainly a matter of transposition. Furthermore, their roles are somewhat different; the *fagoto* usually plays with the continuo bass instruments, the *bassone* in consort with the oboes. See later discussion.

116. A possible exception occurs in *Einsamkeit* which has only one figured part. It is marked "organo." However, a part for violone (not mentioned as such in the title page and perhaps the second part meant) is included. It is identical to the organo part except for a few spots in choral sections where both the vocal bass and the violone are silent while the organo part continues.

117. The second violin part was also likely added later. The title page reads "Violino a doppio" and once again the handwriting as well as the off-center position of the words "à doppio" indicate that they could have been added later. The handwriting of the second violin part is completely different from the rest of the manuscript, although also clearly different from the transposed organ part. Thus these two parts, although both added at a later time, were not written by the same person, and hence not necessarily at the same time.

118. Dürr, *Die Kantaten*, 1:69.

119. Curt Sachs, *Handbuch der Musikinstrumentenkunde* (Leipzig, 1930; reprint ed., Hildesheim: Georg Olms, 1967), p. 228.

120. Ian Harwood, "Colascione," *New Grove*, 4:523-524.

121. Donald Gill, "Colascione," *The New Grove Dictionary of Musical Instruments*, 3 vols., ed. Stanley Sadie (London: MacMillan, 1984), 1:434-436.

122. It was different from the theorbo, however.

123. Gill, "Colascione," p. 435.

124. Clef changes signalled a keyboard player to stop doubling the bass. See Buelow, *Thorough-Bass*, p. 191.

125. Buelow, *Thorough-Bass*, pp. 195-199.

126. Buelow, *Thorough-Bass*, p. 195.

127. Heinichen, *General-Bass*, p. 516, trans. by Buelow, *Thorough-Bass*, p. 193. Concerning the types of embellishments played by the "other parts," we may rely on Quantz's extensive instructions. Particularly significant is his differentiation between French and Italian styles of ornamentation, and his instructions regarding playing an *adagio* movement. See Quantz, *Flute*, chapter 14. See also chapter 18 for a comparison of French and Italian style.

128. Buelow, *Thorough-Bass*, p. 191.

129. Dürr, *Die Kantaten*, 1:68.

130. Dresden MS. 2398-E-504

131. The part itself is marked "bassoun," the title page reads "bassone."

132. Dresden MS. 2398-E-509

133. The three other works that have surviving performance parts are *Herr, nun lässest Du*, *Lobe den Herrn*, and *Der Herr ist nahe*.

134. Violoncelli do appear in the scores of Heinichen's Masses. See Schmitz, p. 12.

135. Dürr, *Die Kantaten*, 1:68.

136. Heinichen, *General-Bass*, pp. 60, 61

137. These are the four sets of parts copied by "J.S."

138. *Der Herr* uses "soli" and "Cap," *Herr, nun lässest Du* uses "soli," "Cap," and "tutti."

139. Schmitz, pp. 13, 224.

140. In Leipzig, the soloists were always part of the choir. See Stiller, p. 151.

141. For example, the duets in *Meine Seele erhebet den Herrn*, mvt. I. Treiber suggests that, in imitative movements with homophonic introductions, the introductions were performed as tuttis, the contrapuntal sections as solos in the manner of an Italian concerto. Fritz Treiber, "Die thüringisch-sächsische Kirchenkantate zur Zeit des jungen J.S. Bach (etwa 1700 - 1723)," *Archiv für Musikforschung II* (1937): 145.

142. Dürr, *Die Kantaten*, 1:67.

143. *Herr, nun lässest Du, Gelobet sei der Herr* (early version), *Lobe den Herrn*.

144. Mendel found two basic types of organ pitches, a semitone apart. See Arthur Mendel, "Pitch in Western Music since 1500, a Reexamination," *Acta Musicologica* 50 (1978), pp. 73-75.

145. Mendel believes that, although his survey of North German organs showed about equal samples of high and low *Chor-Ton*, one type must have been more prevalent during the eighteenth century in order for contemporary writers like Quantz and Agricola to write as if there were only one standard. By a series of deductions Mendel concludes that this standard was the higher type, and that *Cammer-Ton* and *tief Cammer-Ton* were defined in relation only to it. See Mendel, "Pitch since 1500," pp. 74, 77.

146. *Chor-Ton* was also called *Cornett-Ton*. See later discussion.

147. Mendel, "Pitch since 1500," pp. 13, 73.

148. Mendel, "Pitch since 1500," p. 73.

149. Mendel, "Pitch since 1500," p. 13.

150. Fürstenau, *Geschichte*, 2:51.

151. Quantz, *Flute*, pp. 267-269; Arthur Mendel, "On the Pitches in Use in Bach's Time," *Musical Quarterly*, XLI (1955): 468, 471.

152. Arnold Schering, *Johann Sebastian Bach's Leipziger Kirchenmusik*, 3d ed. (Wiesbaden: Breitkopf und Härtel, 1968), p. 58; Mendel, "Pitches," p. 338.

153. Usually spelled "fagoto" in the manuscripts

154. Quantz, *Flute*, pp. 267-269. In attempting to determine the absolute values of the various tunings, Arthur Mendel rejected statistical findings by the nineteenth-century researcher Alexander J. Ellis and concluded that only *A-Cammer-Ton* and the Roman and Parisian tunings were actually lower than our present system, while the Venetian and Lombardic tunings, as well as the German *Chor-Ton* were actually higher than ours. His conclusions have, at least in part, been contradicted by recent statistical research that corroborates the more generally held view of lower eighteenth century pitch values. See Arthur Mendel, "Pitch since 1500," pp. 74, 76, and J.K. Rhodes, W.R. Thomas, "Pitch. 2. Baroque Chamber Pitch, Ellis and Praetorius," *New Grove*, 14:781-782.

155. In *Gelobet sei der Herr*, both parts basically double the continuo. In *Heilig*, there is no *bassone* part and the *fagotto* plays with the oboes/violins rather than doubling the continuo.

156. See Walter Kolneder, "Fagott," *Die Musik in Geschichte und Gegenwart*, vol. 3, col. 1725.

7.
Large-Scale Structure

As we have seen in our earlier discussion of terminology, the Lutheran church cantata of the seventeenth and eighteenth centuries was never a well-defined genre. In retrospect, we tend to call those works cantatas that have:
1. Orchestral material that is independent of the voices at least some of the time
2. Moderate length (often Bach's twenty to thirty-minute cantatas are taken as the norm)
3. Relatively independent movements
4. A libretto related to the liturgical lessons and often consisting of a compilation of texts taken from a variety of sources[1]
5. Recitatives

These last two characteristics are typical mainly of the eighteenth-century cantata. Older analogues of the genre almost never contain recitatives and, furthermore, are not always linked to the lessons.[2]

Sectionalization

From a structural perspective, the cantata's most salient feature is its sectionalization into relatively independent movements.[3] The factors that contribute to this sense of sectionalization are numerous and varied, but all relate to a stopping and renewing of the musical momentum. Where this happens the sections have, on the one hand, sufficient length and unity to appear complete in themselves. On the other hand, such sections contrast sufficiently with the surrounding material to appear separate and distinct. This can be accomplished through a change of tonality, orchestration, texture, tempo, or meter. For the purposes of this discussion, the term "section" will be used for musical units that tend to follow one another without much cessation of musical momentum, the term "movement" for those units that have sufficient independence to suggest a pause before the following material is commenced.[4]

Most of Heinichen's works consist of seven to ten reasonably independent units. The length and complexity of these units varies from fully developed movements, such as da capo arias, to short interjections or responses in a contrasting tempo and orchestration. As one would expect, it is the longer works that have the more fully developed inner movements. One of these is *Herr, nun lässest Du*, a cantata of about thirty minutes duration. After a fifty-four measure opening sonata, a fifty-nine measure choral movement follows. The longest movements, however, are the two da capo arias comprising 136 and 159 measures respectively.

Toward the other end of the spectrum is the seven-minute work, *Der Segen des Herrn*. Composed entirely in the key of G minor, this work consists of seven short sections that are connected but nevertheless differentiated by the juxtaposition of contrasting texts, orchestrations (including the alternation of choral and solo sections), and often also meters and tempi. Because the work is designated for the fifth Sunday after Trinity, we know that it was intended as "sermon music" (*Hauptmusik*), and its heterogenous textual origins underscore this liturgical function. Its structure and length more closely resemble that of the motet, however. We can only conclude that it is a transitional form between the motet and cantata.[5]

Another work of this type is *Gott ist unsere Zuversicht* which, although slightly longer, likewise comprises a series of connected sections. In this case, short solo statements accompanied usually only by continuo alternate with equally short choral sections accompanied by strings. The text consists entirely of successive verses from Psalm 42, with each section comprising one verse. Other than the alteration between solo and tutti, minimal contrast distinguishes the sections: of eleven sections, only three do not begin in G minor. Three (including the substantial opening chorus) are in triple meter; the rest, however, are all in common meter. Between sections, indications that the musical momentum should stop are seldom to be found. However, a fermata ends VII, and double bar lines end VIII, IX, and X. Whether such a short work with such minimal sectionalization should be called a cantata is debatable. Like *Der Segen*, this work appears to be a transitional form.

Earlier we observed that *Heilig ist der Herr* is almost certainly communion music and should not be called a cantata.[6] Its overall structure, too, supports this conclusion. Most significant is its brevity; at three and one-half minutes it is far too short to be called a cantata. The text is divided into only two sections the way the Sanctus text usually is: "Heilig ist der Herr Zebaoth" and "Alle Lande sind seiner Ehren [sic] voll." Both sections are for choir and instruments; there are no solo sections at all.

Of Heinichen's other works, most are about fifteen to twenty minutes long and have clearly defined movements, although many of the movements are not as fully developed as those in *Herr, nun lässest Du*. The movements range in length from a few measures to over a hundred and often end with a double bar line, fermata, or rest, suggesting a stop of musical momentum. Often a clear change of texture, orchestration, and tempo signals the beginning of a new movement, although tonality and meter may remain unchanged. In a few cases, however, sections with clearly contrasting characters flow directly one into the other. Such joining of movements can be found in *Lass dichs nicht irren*, where two recitatives move directly into strophic arias. In the first instance, a tenor recitative is followed by a strophic aria in which the first strophe is sung by the tenor, the second by the soprano. In the second instance, an alto recitative is followed by a two-strophe aria in which the alto sings both strophes. Two similar combinations occur in *Mag auch ein Blinder*. The first instance employs tenor and soprano voices in a pattern identical to the one above. The second instance is likewise similar to its counterpart in *Lass dichs nicht irren*, differing only in its addition of the bass voice to both recitative and aria.[7]

Whether or not any two successive sections in Heinichen's work are truly independent of each other, the literary contrasts between successive textual units invariably produce changes of rhythm, texture, meter, etc., and, hence, a certain degree of sectionalization. As a result, longer, independent movements often contain several, semi-independent, sections within their span. In general, sectionalization tends to be greater where texts with contrasting origins are juxtaposed for the purpose of theological interpretation and exegesis,[8] a procedure that was of fundamental importance to the church cantata and underscores its liturgical *raison d'être*. Even in cases where the textual units have the same origin (such as successive verses of Scripture), however, contrast, and hence a sectionalized structure, results from a motetlike procedure whereby successive phrases of text are each given a distinctive musical gesture.

Although the whole of Heinichen's short works like *Der Segen des Herrn* and *Gott ist unsere Zuversicht* consist of such brief sections, the longer works often contain such contrasting sections within the span of their individual movements whenever a contrasting text element is introduced. To the extent that individual movements are internally sectionalized in this way they imitate the motet style and may, therefore, be regarded as old-fashioned for as the motet evolved into the cantata, while the degree of contrast between the sections increased, these sections themselves achieved greater thematic unity.[9]

In *Herr, nun lässest Du*, a soprano and alto duet, "Weg o Welt," begins a sequence of contrasting musical sections. The duet itself ends with a codetta of six measures in a contrasting 6/8 meter. Then, while the tutti sopranos begin a chorale, the lower voices continue with textual and melodic material derived from the duet just completed. A short choral fugato follows. Because the choral material is related to the preceding duet and because the tonality remains unchanged, these disparate sections should probably be regarded as one unit rather than as two separate movements, despite the double bar lines at the end of the duet and before the choral fugato.[10]

A codetta similar to the one at the end of the duet just mentioned occurs at the end of the duet in *Gelobet sei der Herr*. In this case, an anapestic couplet is set in 6/8 meter for chorus and, thus, extends the movement by sixteen measures.

In *Ach, was soll ich Sünder machen*, the alto solo divides into two clearly contrasting parts. This two-part structure was, no doubt, suggested by the form of the chorale stanza, whose six lines end with a rhyming couplet. It seems that Heinichen decided to emphasize the sentiments of these last two lines, for he makes the second section disparately long (forty-seven measures as compared with the previous twelve), obstinately repeating one bit of melody in what is apparently intended as a picture of tenacious Christian committment.[11]

Within choral movements, too, sectionalization is frequent. Often a homophonic, mottolike opening is followed by a contrapuntal section. This second section may simply extend the previous text or, if the text is longer, move on to the next phrase of text. The technique is similar to that found in motets of the period.

Architecture

In general, the overall structures of all these compositions fall into two broad categories:

1.	(sonata)	chorus	soli	chorus		
2.	(sonata)	chorus	soli	chorus	soli	chorus

These two architectural plans are closely related to the types of texts chosen for the libretto. In the first plan, the heart of the libretto consists of a series of metrically identical poetic strophes (an ode).[12] These are assigned to alternating solo voices, which present a new musical setting for each stanza of text. Choral movements then frame this complex; the first chorus is invariably a setting of a scriptural text, the second is usually a chorale. Because the ode forms the heart of this plan, such works are really elaborated ode cantatas.[13]

In the second plan, the libretto consists of a mixture of texts, which, although related in theme, have unrelated origins. Bible verses, single strophes of poems, and chorale texts are combined to form cantatas of a type sometimes called "mixed cantatas."[14] Since convention suggested certain relationships between types of texts and musical forms,[15] the decisions made in compiling such librettos greatly affected the architecture of the cantata as a whole, as well as the structure and type of the individual movements. It would, therefore, be helpful to know whether the compilations were made by the composer himself or someone working in close collaboration with him, for, in that case, we could assume that Heinichen's musical concerns influenced the literary choices. Unfortunately, we have not been able to determine the authors of any of these librettos.

Perhaps because the mixing of diverse texts tends to fragment the structure, Heinichen not only framed these works with choral pillars, but placed an additional choral movement in the center of each work. This, too, was a conventional procedure and was probably anticipated by the librettist when he chose to place a scriptural text in the center of his work. In Heinichen's settings, the first of the three choral movements is usually a full-scale setting of a scriptural passage (*dictum*),[16] the second is another setting of Scripture, and the third, a chorale. Between these choral pillars, solo arias present a series of poetic commentaries.

Only a relatively few of Heinichen's works follow the first architectural plan. In *Der Herr ist nahe*, four strophes are set as four contrasting arias (a soprano aria is followed by bass, alto, and tenor) and framed with choral movements: a Psalm setting at the beginning, and a chorale setting at the end.

Es lebet Jesus is built on a similar plan, although the opening choral movement has a poetic rather than scriptural text, and two of the arias are duets. In addition, the bass aria ends à 4.

In a sense, the chorale cantata *Ach was soll ich Sünder machen* can also be considered an ode cantata, for despite the fact that the strophic poem in this case is indeed a chorale, the chorale tune itself appears infrequently. It can be found in its complete form only in the tenor aria and in the closing chorus. The first movement introduces a few phrases of the chorale as an instrumental cantus firmus (there are seven measures in total) but does not use the chorale melody in any other way. In the other movements, no traces of the chorale tune are discernable. The architectural plan of *Ach was soll ich Sünder machen* is like that of the other ode cantatas: a series of solos is framed with choral movements.

Gelobet sei der Herr uses four stanzas of (presumably the same) poem but sets the third one for chorus. This produces a symmetrical plan with a chorus standing in the center. Thus, despite the fact that it is an ode cantata, it falls into our second architectural category.

A far larger number of Heinichen's works follow the second architectural pattern: *Herr, nun lässest Du, Lass dichs nicht irren, Es naheten aber zu Jesu, Mag auch ein Blinder, Gelobet sei der Herr, Lobe den Herrn,* and *Einsamkeit, o stilles Wesen.* This last composition departs slightly from the general plan. It begins (after the sonata) with a soprano solo instead of the usual chorus.[17] A choral movements then follows. The suitability of this reversed order is made clear by an examination of the sentiments expressed in the texts; the emphasis on individuality in the opening text clearly calls for a solo setting, while the response of corporate faith logically requires a choral setting.

Solo:

> O solitude, thou essence of silence,
> If my Jesus does not kiss me,
> I have chosen death,
> For I constantly yearn for Him.
> I am completely forsaken by Him,
> I consider my times,
> If I cannot embrace Him
> Then all is vanity.

Chorus:

> The Lord is near to all who call on Him,
> To all who call on Him in truth.

In the Psalm cantata *Lobe den Herrn*, the division of the central text (Ps. 103:11-12) into two movements, each containing one verse, represents a curious departure from Heinichen's normal procedure. Placed in the middle of the cantata, these two verses would normally together form the basis for the central choral pillar.[18] Instead, Heinichen sets the first of the two verses chorally, the second as a very short, five-measure recitative.

Why Heinichen chose not to combine the two verses in one choral movement is unclear, since the two verses parallel each other in their images and are similar in affect.

Vs. 11

> For high as the heavens are above the earth
> So great is His lovingkindness toward those who fear Him.

Vs. 12

> As far as the east is from the west,
> So far has He removed our transgressions from us.[19]

Despite the parallel imagery, Heinichen apparently believed it would be difficult to unify the movement if the texts were joined.

Even given Heinichen's decision to set verse 12 as a separate movement, we wonder why he chose to set it as a brief recitative rather than as a full scale aria. The reason may well lie in the effect the additional aria would have had on the architectural shape of the work. As it now stands, the two arias in the first half of the cantata are balanced by two arias in the second half. The recitative is relatively unobtrusive and upsets the architectural balance of the cantata far less than an aria setting would.

Another reason may be related to the fact that a full-scale aria setting would conventionally require a rhymed poem for its text. If Heinichen received the libretto in its present form, such a text would have had to be newly composed. An overview of the cantata's libretto shows that it alternates scriptural verses with poetic strophes of identical structure. These rhymed texts are, in fact, paraphrases of the intervening Psalm verses:

1. Sonata
2. Chorus (Ps. 103:1-3)
3. Soprano Aria (paraphrase of Ps. 103:4-6)

4. Alto Aria (paraphrase of Ps. 103:8-10)
5. Chorus (Ps. 103:11)
6. Bass Recitative (Ps. 103:12)
7. Bass Aria (paraphrase of Ps. 103:13)
8. Tenor Aria (paraphrase 0f Ps. 103:14-16)
9. Chorus (Ps. 103:17)
10. Chorale

If Heinichen actually compiled the libretto himself (selecting stanzas from an ode that paraphrased the Psalm and alternating these with literal scripture), the ode from which he was drawing the aria texts may have combined verse 12 with the previous one, thus making the strophe unusable. In this case, however, Heinichen's decision to separate the two verses would represent a conscious rejection of the poet's decision to link the two verses.

Heinichen could, of course, have chosen to omit verse 12 altogether, especially since verse 7 is also omitted from the libretto. When we compare the two verses, however, we find that verse 7, with its specific historical references, has a more limited appeal than verse 12.

Vs. 7

> He hath made known his ways to Moses,
> His acts to the sons of Israel.

Vs. 12

> As far as the east is from the west,
> So far has He removed our transgressions from us.

By setting verse 12 as a recitative, Heinichen was able to include a crucial verse with only a slight loss of structural balance.

A few of Heinichen's works fit neither of our architectural categories. Earlier we noted that *Heilig ist der Herr* comprises only two sections, both for chorus. In *Gegrüsset seist du*, the dialogue between Mary and the angel Gabriel is set as a series of alternating arias. A single chorus (not a chorale) ends the cantata. *Meine Seele erhebet den Herrn*, on the other hand, begins with a chorus but has no other choral movements at all. It is hard to believe that this cantata could end without a tutti movement. It seems more likely that a chorale originally ended the work but has since been lost. *Gott ist unsere Zuversicht* begins with a substantial section for chorus (fifty-five measures), then alternates short choral and solo sections (usually ten to twenty measures in length) in an almost continuous fabric.

Although scriptural texts normally become the bases for choral movements, the scriptural passages in a few of Heinichen's works with mixed texts are longer than what can easily be accommodated in one movement. They are then divided into parts, the first segment being presented in the opening chorus and the rest of them in a series of solos that are separated by other solo movements. In *Es naheten aber zu Jesu*, this plan produces a series of alternating recitatives and arias. The scriptural text, which in this case is narrative, is presented in the recitatives, a few verses at a time, and arias are inserted as commentaries in between. A similar plan is followed in *Meine Seele erhebet den Herrn*, where parts of the Magnificat text, set as tenor recitatives, are alternated with reflective duets.[20]

Symmetry

In some of Heinichen's compositions, entire movements are repeated, giving these works a certain degree of symmetry. One of these is *Gelobet sei der Herr*, where both the first and fourth stanzas of the ode are given to the soprano, who simply repeats her first aria with the new set of words. The cyclical element, which is thus introduced, is further strengthened by repeating the opening chorus at the end of the work.

Sonata	Chorus	S: vs. 1	B: vs. 2	Chorus: vs. 3
-	A	B	C	D

S: vs. 4	Duet (A/T)&Chorus	Chorus
B	E	A

Fig. 1. Symmetry in *Gelobet sei der Herr*

Repetitions of whole movements are to be found in some of the other works as well. In *Es naheten aber zu Jesu*, two stanzas of the chorale, *Werde munter mein Gemüte* are sung, the first at the midpoint of the cantata, the second at the very end. In this way the chorale is used to divide the cantata into two equal parts, which are quite similar when seen from a textural perspective. Textually, each half presents a parable; the first, the parable of the lost sheep, the second, the parable of the lost coin. In each case, an arioso presenting the parable is followed by an aria identifying the Christian believer with the lost article ("Ich bin das verlorne Schaf... Ich bin der verlorne Groschen"). The other musical parallels are less obvious, although at least two are immediately striking. The sixteenth-note triplets used to set the word "murret" in the bass aria reappear in the parallel tenor aria as a laughing figure ("lachen") and the ariosos that follow both end in triple meter for the text "rejoice with me."

1. Sonata and Chorus
2. Bass Aria: ("murret")
3. T/B Arioso: (parable) C-3/4
4. Sop. Aria: ("Ich bin das Schaf")
5. Chorale

6. Bass Recit.
7. Tenor Aria: ("lachen")
8. Bass Arioso: (parable) C-3/4
9. Alto Aria: ("Ich bin der Groschen")
10. Chorale

Fig. 2. Symmetry in *Es naheten aber zu Jesu*

Several of Heinichen's cantatas use a chorale tune as a unifying element, although none is a strict chorale-cantata in the sense that each movement is in some way related to the chorale tune. In *Herr, nun lässest Du*, the chorale *Freu dich sehr, o meine Seele* first appears as a cantus firmus in the second half of the sinfonia. It appears again at the end of the duet (the spot mentioned above) and then ends the work in a version using triple meter.[21] In *Einsamkeit, o stilles Wesen*, what appears to be a chorale tune[22] is introduced in the sonata, then immediately presented again in a simple setting for soprano and basso continuo. While *Ach was soll ich Sünder machen* uses the chorale text throughout, the tune appears in its complete form in only two movements.[23] The first three phrases of the chorale can also be found as an instrumental cantus firmus in the opening chorus.[24] In some of Heinichen's compositions, musical themes other than chorale tunes serve to unify the overall structure. Examples of this cyclical procedure can be found in *Gegrüsset seist du*, where a melody from the first movement reappears in the final chorus,[25] and in *Lass dichs nicht irren*, where the violin obbligato of the first movement likewise reappears in the last.

The Individual Works: Overall Structure Chart

(Showing total number of measures, tonality, meter, tempo, text type, poetic meter, line length, rhyme scheme. Unspecified tempi are indicated with a hyphen)

1. *Herr, nun lässest Du* (Dresden #500) duration: 29 min.

    1. Sonata: 54 mm., AM, C, adagio-allegro

    2. Chorus: 59 mm., AM, C, (-)
       Luke 2:29

6.	9.	6.	9.	6.	7.	6.	7.	11.	6.	8.	
A	B	C	D	A	D	C	E	E	F	F	

7.	8.	7.	6.	6.	6.	7.	6.	7.	10.	8.	.4
G	H	G	I	I	J	K	L	K	M	N	M

    3. Bass Aria (D.C.): 136 mm., AM, 3/2-C, -adagio
       iambic

6.	4.	7.	6.	6.	7.
A	A	B	C	C	B

    4. Tenor Aria (D.C.): 159 mm., Bm-DM, 3/4, adagio-presto
       iambic

7.	6.	7.	6.	6.	7.	6.
A	B	A	B	C	C	B

    5. Chorus: 57 mm., AM, C, (-)
       Luke 2:30-32

    6. Bass Aria: 25 mm., DM-Am, C, -adagio e p
       iambic

4.	8.	7.	4.	5.	3.	7.
A	A	B	C	D	C	B

7a. Soprano & Alto Duet: 39 mm., AM, C-6/8, (-)
   trochaic
   7.   8.   8.   7.   7.   7.
   A   B   B   A   C   C

7b. Chorus: 46 mm., AM, C, (-)
   above text + chorale

8. Chorus: 98 mm., AM, 3/4, vivace
   Chorale ("Freu dich sehr, o meine Seele")

2. *Lass dichs nicht irren* (Dresden #501) duration: 13 min.

1. Chorus: 54 mm., DM, C, (-)
   Ps. 49:17-18

2. Tenor Recit: 24 mm., Bm-DM, C, (-)
   iambic

3. Tenor/Soprano Aria: 35 mm., DM, C, (-)
   trochaic
   4.   4.   7.   8.   8.   7.   (2 stanzas)
   A   A   B   C   C   B

4. Chorus: 32 mm., DM, 3/4, (-)
   Ps. 37:37

5. Alto Arioso: 11 mm., Bm-AM, C, (-)
   iambic
   9.   8.   8.   9.   8.   10.
   A   B   B   A   C   C

6. Alto Aria: 27 mm., AM, C, (-)
   trochaic
   7.   8.   8.   7.   7.   (2 stanzas)
   D   E   E   D   D

7. Bass Recit.: 6 mm., DM, C, (-)
   iambic
   11.   13.   8.   8.
   A   A   B   B

8. Chorus: 26 mm., DM, C, (-)
   Chorale (from: "Sag was hilft alle Welt")

3. *Es naheten aber zu Jesu* (Dresden #502) duration: 20 min.

   1. Chorus: 27 mm., GM, C, (-)
      Luke 15:1, 2

   2. Bass Aria: 34 mm., Em, C, (-)
      iambic
      6.   7.   6.   7.   7.   5.   6.   6.
      A   B   C   B   D   E   F   E

   3. Tenor/Bass Arioso: 41 mm., GM, C-3/4, (-)
      Luke 15:3-6

   4. Soprano Aria: 34 mm., GM, C, (-)
      trochaic
      7.   8.   8.   (7.7.)*   (2 stanzas)
      A   B   B   (CC)*
      *(text of last two lines is missing)

   5. Soli/Chorus: 30 mm., GM, C, (-)
      Chorale (from: "Werde munter mein Gemüte")

   6. Bass Arioso: 10 mm., GM, C, (-)
      Luke 15:7

7. Tenor Aria: 32 mm., DM, C, (-)
    trochaic
    8.   8.   8.   8.   8.   7.   7.   8.   8.
    A*   B   B   A   B   C   C   A   A*
    *(last line is a repetition of first line)

8. Bass Recit.: 26 mm., DM-GM, C-3/4, (-)
    Luke 15:8, 9

9. Alto Aria: 80 mm., GM, 3/4-C-3/4, (-)
    trochaic
    8.   7.   7.   8.   8.   (2 stanzas)
    A*   B   B   A   A*
    *(last line is a repetition of first line)

10. Soli/Chorus:
    Chorale (from: "Werde munter mein Gemüte")
    (repeats movement #5, subsequent verse)

4. Mag auch ein Blinder (Dresden #503) duration: 13 min.

1. Chorus: 48 mm., Am, C, adagio-vivace
    Luke 6:39

2. Tenor Recit.: 14 mm., CM, C, (-)
    iambic
    10. 9.   7.   8.   9.   6.   6.   8.   7.
    A   B   B   A   C   D   D   E   E

3. Tenor/Soprano Aria: 45 mm., CM, C, (-)
    trochaic
    7.   7.   8.   8.   7.   7.   7.   (2 stanzas)
    A   B   C   C   B   A   A

4. Chorus: 29 mm., Am, C, allegro
    Luke 6:42b

5. Alto/Bass Recit.: 11 mm., CM-Am, C, (-)
   iambic

7.	6.	6.	9.	7.	9.	6.	8.	8.	8.
A	B	B	A	C	C	D	D	E	E

6. Alto/Bass Aria: 103 mm., Am, 3/4, (-)
   trochaic

7.	8.	8.	7.	7.
A	B	B	A	A

7. Chorus: 25 mm., Am, C, (-)
   Chorale (from: "Allein zu dir Herr Jesu Christ")

5. *Gelobet sei der Herr* (Dresden #504 & #509) duration: 15 min.

1. Sonata: 14 mm., FM, C, (-)

2. Chorus: 39 mm., FM, C, (-)
   Luke 1:68,69

3. Soprano Aria (D.C.): 78 mm., BbM-Gm-BbM, 3/4, adagio
   anapestic

11.	11.	11.	11.	11.	(Stanza #1 & 4)
A	B	B	A	A	

4. Bass Aria: 31 mm., FM, C, prestissimo
   anapestic

11.	11.	10.	11.	11.	(Stanza #2)
A	B	B	A	A	

5. Chorus: 21 mm., FM, 12/8, prestissimo
   anapestic

11.	11.	11.	11.	11.	(Stanza #3)
A	B	B	A	A	

6. Soprano Aria
   repeat #3 (stanza #4)

7. Alto & Tenor Duet: 19 mm., Gm, C, adagio
    iambic
    6.   7.   7.   6.
    A   B   B   A

Chorus: 16 mm., BbM-FM, 6/8, (-)
    anapestic
    12.   12.
    C   C

8. Chorus
    #2 repeated or chorale: ("Nun lob mein Seel")

6. Der Segen des Herrn (Dresden #505) duration: 7 min.

*(1.) Sonata: 18 mm., Gm, 3/2, (-)

(2.) Chorus: 21 mm., Gm, C, vivace
    Prov. 10:22

(3.) Alto Solo: 16 mm., Gm, C, adagio
    iambic
    8.   8.   9.   9.
    A   A   B   B

(4.) Chorus: 11 mm., Gm, C, (-)
    Ps. 115:12

(5.) Tenor Solo: 49 mm., Gm, 3/4, (-)
    Matt. 6:33

(6.) Chorus: 13 mm., Gm, C, (-)
    Chorale (from: "Warum betrübst du dich mein Herz")

(7.) Chorus: 50 mm., Gm, ¢, (-)
    1 Tim. 4:8
  * sections rather than real movements

7. *Lobe den Herrn* (Dresden #506) duration: 21 min.

1. Sonata: 21 mm., BbM, C, -adagio

2. Chorus: 77 mm., BbM, C, -adagio-allegro-adagio
   Ps. 103:1-3

3. Soprano Aria: 42 mm., Gm, C, (-)
   paraphrase of Ps. 103:4-6
   trochaic

8.	8.	8.	7.	8.	7.	7.	8.	7.	7.
A	B	A	B	C	D	D	C	E	E

4. Alto Aria: 41 mm., FM, 6/8, (-)
   paraphrase of Ps. 103:8-10
   trochaic

8.	7.	8.	7.	8.	7.	7.	8.	7.	7.
A	B	A	B	C	D	D	C	E	E

5. Chorus: 41 mm., BbM, C, adagio
   Ps. 103:11

6. Bass Recit.: 5 mm., EbM-Cm, C, (-)
   Ps. 103:12

7. Bass Aria: 36 mm., Cm, C, vivace
   paraphrase of Ps. 103:13
   trochaic

8.	7.	8.	7.	8.	7.	7.	8.	7.	7.
A	B	A	B	C	D	D	C	E	E

8. Tenor Aria: 17 mm., BbM, C, (-)
   paraphrase of Ps. 103:14-16
   trochaic

8.	7.	8.	7.	8.	7.	7.	8.	7.	7.
A	B	A	B	C	D	D	C	E	E

    9. Chorus: 42 mm., BbM, C, -allegro-adagio
        Ps. 103:17

  10. Chorus: 36 mm., BbM, 3/2, (-)
        Chorale (from: "Nun lob mein Seel")

8. *Der Herr ist nahe* (Dresden #507) duration: 18 min.

    1. Sonata: 20 mm., Dm, C, (-)

    2. Chorus: 50 mm., Dm, C, (-)
        Ps. 34:19

    3. Soprano Aria (D.C.): 129 mm., Dm-FM-Dm, 3/4, adagio
        trochaic/iambic

8.	8.	7.	9.	5.	7.
A	A	B	C	C	B

    4. Bass Aria: 32 mm., FM, C, (-)
        trochaic/iambic

8.	8.	7.	9.	5.	7.
A	A	B	C	C	B

    5. Alto Aria: 87 mm., BbM, 3/8, (-)
        trochaic/iambic

8.	8.	7.	11.	5.	7.
A	A	B	C	C	B

    6. Tenor Aria: 54 mm., FM, 3/4, molto adagio
        trochaic/iambic

8.	8.	7.	9.	5.	7.
A	A	B	C	C	B

    7. Chorus: 80 mm., Dm, 3/2, (-)
        Chorale (from: "Jesu meine Freude")

9. *Einsamkeit, o stilles Wesen* (Dresden #508, Berlin Ms. #30210)
duration: 17 min.

1. Sonata: 33 mm., FM, C, (-)

2. Soprano Aria: 21 mm., FM, C, (-)
   trochaic

8.	7.	8.	7.	8.	7.	8.	7.
A	B	A	B	C	D	C	D

3. Chorus: 24 mm., FM, C, (-)
   Ps. 145:18

4. Alto Aria (D.C.): 43 mm., CM-FM-CM, C, (-)
   trochaic

8.	7.	7.	8.	8.	8.
A	B	B	A	C	C

5. Chorus: 14 mm., FM, C, (-)
   Matt. 18:20

6. Bass Aria (D.C.): 59 mm., Dm-Am-Dm, C, (-)
   trochaic

8.	7.	7.	8.	8.	7.	7.	8.
A	B	B	A	C	D	D	C

7. Tenor Aria: 130 mm., FM, 3/4, adagio
   trochaic

8.	7.	8.	7.	8.	7.	8.	7.
A	B	A	B	C	D	C	D

8. Chorus: 33 mm., FM, C, -adagio
   Is. 65:24

10. *Ach was soll ich Sünder machen* (Berlin Ms. #30210) duration: 19 min.

    1. Sonata: 38 mm., Em-GM-Em, C-3/4-C-3/4, -adagio-adagio

    2. Chorus: 66 mm., Em-GM-Em, C, (-)
        Chorale (from: "Ach was soll ich Sünder machen")

    3. Bass Recit.: 10 mm., CM-BM, C, (-)
        Chorale (Verse #2)

    4. Bass Aria: 31 mm., Bm, C, (-)
        Chorale (Verse #3)

    5. Alto Aria: 59 mm., Em-GM, C-3/4, -adagio
        Chorale (Verse #4)

    6. Tenor Aria: 44 mm., Em, C, (-)
        Chorale (Verse #5)

    7. Soprano Aria: 91 mm., GM, 3/4, (-)
        Chorale (Verse #6)

    8. Chorus: 60 mm., Em, C, (-)
        Chorale (Verse #7)

11. *Meine Seele erhebet den Herrn* (Berlin Ms. #30210) duration: 15 min.

    1. Chorus: 46 mm., CM, C, (-)
        Luke 1:46, 47

    2. Soprano Duet (D.C.): 66 mm., FM-Dm-FM, C, (-)
        trochaic
        8.   7.   8.   8.   7.
        A   B   C   C   B

    3. Tenor Recit.: 5 mm., Dm, C, (-)
        Luke 1:49

4. Alto Duet: 61 mm., Dm, 6/8, affetuoso
   trochaic

8.	7.	8.	7.	8.	8.
A	B	A	B	C	C

5. Tenor Recit.: 7 mm., Dm-AM, C, (-)
   Luke 1:52, 53

6. Bass Duet (D.C.): 62 mm., CM-Am-CM, C, (-)
   trochaic

8.	7.	8.	7.
A	B	A	B

7. Tenor Recit.: 6 mm., Am-GM, C, (-)
   Luke 1:55

8. Tenor Duet: 30 mm., GM, C, (-)
   trochaic

10.	8.	8.	7.	7.
A	B	B	C	C

12. *Gegrüsset seist du holdselige Maria* (Berlin Ms. #30210) duration: 14 min.

1. Tenor Aria: 106 mm., BbM, 3/4, (-)
   anapestic/iambic

5.	12.	12.	5.	12.	12.	11.	11.
A	B	B	A	C	C	D	D

2. Soprano Aria: 79 mm., Dm-Gm, C-3/4-C, (-)
   anapestic

4.	4.	12.	12.	5.	5.	4.	4.
A	A	B	B	C	C	A	A

3. Tenor Aria: 79 mm., BbM, 3/4, (-)
   anapestic/iambic

4.	4.	12.	12.	10.	11.	6.	7.	6.	7.
A	A	B	B	C	D	E	F	G	F

4. Soprano Aria: 36 mm., BbM, C, (-)
   iambic

6.	6.	5.	5.	6.	7.	6.	7.
A	A	B	B	C	D	E	D

5. Chorus: 94 mm., BbM, C-3/4, (-)
   iambic/anapestic

4.	8.	4.	6.	6.	5.	6.	5.	6.	6.
A	B	C	B	D	E	F	E	D	D

5.	6.	5.	6.	4.	6.	4.	6.
F	G	H	G	A	B	C	B

13. *Gott ist unsere Zuversicht* (Berlin Ms. #30210) duration: 10 min.

*(1.) Chorus: 55 mm., Gm, 3/2, (-)
   Ps. 46:2

(2.) Tenor Solo: 6 mm., Gm, C, (-)
   Ps. 46:3

(3.) Chorus: 19 mm., Gm, C, (-)
   Ps. 46:4

(4.) Soprano Solo: 14 mm., Gm-BbM, C, (-)
   Ps. 46:5

(5.) Chorus: 16 mm., BbM, C, (-)
   Ps. 46:6

(6.) Alto Solo: 9 mm., BbM-Gm, C, (-)
   Ps. 46:7

(7.) Chorus: 10 mm., Gm-GM, C, (-)
   Ps. 46:8

(8.) Tenor Solo: 24 mm., Gm-GM, 3/2, (-)
Ps. 46:9

(9.) Chorus: 19 mm., Gm, C, (-)
Ps. 46:10

(10.) Bass Solo: 14 mm., BbM-GM, C, (-)
Ps. 46:11

(11.) Chorus: 12 mm., Gm-GM, C, (-)
Ps. 46:12

* sections rather than real movements

14. *Es lebet Jesus unser Hort* (Berlin Ms. #30210) duration: 14 min.

1. Sonata: 12 mm., CM, C, (-)

2. Chorus: 48 mm., CM, C-3/2, (-)
iambic
8.   8.   8.   8.
A   A   B   B

3. Bass Aria + Chorus: 41 mm., Am-CM, C-3/4-C,adagio -,-
trochaic
8.   8.   7.   8.   8.   7.
A   A   B   C   C   D

4. Tenor Duet: 81 mm., BbM, 3/4, (-) adagio-presto
trochaic
8.   8.   7.   8.   8.   7.
A   A   B   C   C   B

5. Alto Aria: 36 mm., Dm-FM, C, lento-allegro
trochaic
8.   8.   7.   8.   8.   7.
A   A   B   C   C   B

6. Soprano Duet (D.C.): 48 mm., FM, C, (-)
    trochaic

8.	8.	7.	8.	8.	7.
A	A	B	C	C	B

7. Chorus: 35 mm., CM, C, (-)
    "alleluia"

15. *Heilig ist Gott der Herr* duration: 3.5 min.

(1.) Chorus: 59 mm., FM, 2/4, (?)**
    Is. 6:3a

(2.) Chorus: 59 mm., FM, 3/4, lebhaft
    Is. 6:3b

** illegible tempo marking

Chapter 7. Notes

1. See chapter 5.

2. Krummacher, "The German Cantata," p. 707. See also chapter 1.

3. Krummacher, "The German Cantata," p. 703.

4. Zander points out that the cantata's sectionalized structure encourages the reuse of individual movements in parody settings. See Ferdinand Zander, *Die Dichter der Kantatentexte Johann Sebastian Bachs* (Ph.D. dissertation, University of Cologne, 1967), p. 5.

5. See Adrio, Forchert, "Das Vokalkonzert," col. 1566; Wolff, p. 641.

6. See chapter 5.

7. For a further discussion see chapter 10.

8. Krummacher calls these texts "illuminating tropes" and points out that they inherently embody the element of contrast. See Krummacher, "The German Cantata," p. 706.

9. Wolff, p. 641.

10. About one half of the parts have double bar lines at the first spot, slightly less than half have double bar lines at the latter spot. Only a few place them at both points.

11. This chorale stanza, like all the other stanzas, ends with the words, "meinen Jesum lass ich nicht."

12. Although we were unable to determine the source of the poem in each case, the fact that the stanzas are metrically identical leads one to believe that they are in fact stanzas of the same poem.

13. See chapter 2.

14. Feder, col. 592.

15. Scriptural passages were usually set chorally in concertante or fugal molds, strophic poetry was usually set soloistically, etc.

16. Krummacher, "The German Cantata," p. 707.

17. The aria is really a four-line song setting and could be a chorale, but we were not able to identify it.

18. The German Bible had been versified in 1586. See Kurt Galling, "Bibelübersetzungen IV. Deutsche Übersetzungen," *Die Religion in Geschichte und Gegenwart*, 3d ed., edited by Kurt Galling (Tübingen: J.C.B. Mohr (Paul Siebeck), 1957-1965), vol. 1, col. 1205.

19. New American Standard Version.

20. The emphasis on these non-scriptural texts argues that this was *Hauptmusik* rather than Vespers music. See chapter 5.

21. Bach also uses a version in triple meter in Cantata BWV 19, *Es erhub sich ein Streit.*

22. We were not able to locate it in Johannes Zahn, *Die Melodien der deutscher Evangelischen Kirchenlieder*, 6 vols. (1889; reprint ed., Hildesheim: Georg Olms, 1963).

23. The tenor aria and closing chorus.

24. Unison violins mm. 3-4, 7-8, 11-13.

25. I, mm. 39-57; V, mm. 32-44.

8.
Text Structure and Treatment

Text Structure

In most of Heinichen's German church works, the poetic structure of the rhymed texts changes from movement to movement, so that rhyme scheme and line length is constantly varied. Even the poetic meter changes at times, although, as we would expect, iambic meter is the most common.[1] Only a few works have more than one strophe of a particular pattern. Included in this group is *Lobe den Herrn*, with its four strophes in trochaic meter paraphrasing verses from Psalm 103:

#3. Soprano aria:	Ps. 103:4-6
#4. Alto aria:	Ps. 103:8-10 (verse 7 is omitted)
#7. Bass aria:	Ps. 103:13
#8. Tenor aria:	Ps. 103:14-16

Der Herr ist nahe also has a four-strophe ode as its core, as does *Es lebet Jesus* and *Gelobet sei der Herr*. This last work closes with a structurally unrelated strophe in which not only rhyme scheme and line length change but also the poetic meter. While the foregoing stanzas are built on an 11. 11. 11. 11. 11. pattern with rhyme scheme A B B A A, and are in anapestic meter, the latter strophe combines four lines of iambic meter (6.7.7.6, rhyme scheme: A B B A) with an alexandrine couplet.

Einsamkeit has an identical structure in its first and last arias,[2] and, of course, the chorale cantata, *Ach, was soll ich Sünder machen*, has the same poetic structure in all seven of its stanzas.

We have already seen that theoreticians made a definite distinction between the structure of a poem intended to be set as a recitative and one intended to be set as an aria.[3] Since none of Heinichens solo movements are actually called "recitative," and only a few are labelled "aria,"[4] and since their musical forms are not always clearly one or the other, one wonders whether these poems were written with the kind of clear distinction in mind that Neumeister outlined.[5] If one of the marks of a recitative poem is that it have at least one unrhymed line, only a few of the compositions have movements that qualify. These include *Lass dichs nicht irren* (the tenor recitative quoted above), *Meine Seele* (the three tenor recitatives), and *Gegrüsset seist du* (two arias and one chorus). Since some of the other texts disqualifed on this basis are clearly treated as recitatives, this criterion alone generally defines the form too narrowly. If, on the other hand, we admit for consideration all solo texts with iambic meter (another distinguishing mark of the recitative poem and apparently a less flexible one),[6] many more movements are eligible. Some of these, however, are clearly treated as arias. In designating the movements as recitative or aria, we have kept in mind the other characteristics distinguishing the two forms: for the aria, the presence of a central affect or moral (set lyrically with frequent word repetitions), for the recitative, greater variety of line length and rhyme scheme (set in a more declammatory fashion).[7]

Mixing meters within a single aria or recitative was frowned upon by Neumeister, who compared it to mixing hogs, sheep, goats, oxen, and cows in one herd.[8] Only a few of Heinichen's texts do this. The ode forming the textual basis for *Der Herr ist nahe* combines trochaic and iambic meters, and the first and last movements of *Gegrüsset seist du* combine iambic and anapestic meters.

Text-Music Relationships

Texts as the Source for Musical Invention

The extent to which vocal works of the Baroque period were inspired by their texts has been the subject of considerable debate. Arguments against an intimate relationship between text and music most frequently cite cases where the same music has been used for texts of contrasting character. Occasionally, they also cite examples of the same text appearing in contrasting musical settings.

J.A. Westrup uses the first type of evidence when discussing Bach's cantatas. Pointing to Bach's adaptations of secular material for some of his church cantatas he writes,

> It is obvious that this practice makes nonsense of the theory propounded by Schweitzer and other writers that Bach's music is infused with symbolism and that all his settings are intimately related to the words.[9]

He cites a number of Bach's cantata parodies to substantiate his view. In comparing the bass aria of cantata BWV 173 (*Erhöhtes Fleisch und Blut*) with its counterpart in the parent cantata BWV 173a (*Durchlauchster Leopold*), he writes,

> Whether or not we feel that the minuet rhythm is appropriate to these new words, it is impossible to argue that the music is inspired by them or in any way intimately related to them.[10]

In comparing the bass aria "Grosser Gott" in part I of the *Christmas Oratorio* with its model from cantata BWV 214, he argues that the pomp of the setting suited the original occasion (birthday celebrations for the Queen of Poland), but not the subsequent one:

> [Bach] was forgetting, however, that he was not celebrating earthly pomp but the poverty of Christ in the manger.[11]

Robert Freeman uses the second type of evidence to argue that librettos did not determine the musical choices for the composer who set them.[12] He examines two settings of the same opera libretto by Antonio Caldara (*La verita nell'inganno*) and finds no similarity of keys, modulations, meters, tempi, or accompaniments. Even the words or syllables stressed (by means of dissonances or melismas) change from one setting to the other.

Both Westrup and Freeman conclude that the *Affektenlehre* of musical theorists like Johann Mattheson were ignored by most composers.

> Many of the musical systems put forward in German treatises of the seventeenth and eighteenth centuries should be understood as attempts at theory construction rather than as descriptions of a then current musical practice.[13]

> When [theorists] talked about the way in which varying emotions could be represented in music (the so-called *Affekten-Lehre*) they were not primarily concerned with analyzing the works of their contemporaries: their purpose was to instruct composers who were inexperienced. Their teaching, to put it at its lowest, was aimed at suggesting a series of cliches which would fit a variety of situations.[14]

Heinichen himself speaks to this matter in his treatise *Der General-Bass in der Composition*. This later edition of his treatise begins with a lengthy preface in which Heinichen presents outspoken opinions about various matters, including the state of musical composition, the dangers of pedantic counterpoint, the value of experience gained through travel in acquiring good taste ("goût"), and the means by which the imagination can be stimulated when composing in the "theatrical style." In this last matter, Heinichen is remarkably explicit, as he shows the reader how musical invention must originate in some aspect of the text. His demonstration that there is more than one aspect of the text upon which a composer may base his musical ideas gives his discussion special significance, for it is this very possibility that writers like Westrup and Freeman overlook. Furthermore, although Heinichen provides only one musical example for each suggested affect, he declares that many other appropriate settings could be invented for the chosen affect.[15]

Heinichen discusses three of the sources for musical ideas at length; namely, the *antecedent*, the *concomitant*, and the *consequence* of a text.[16] In one demonstration, he examines what has happened in the preceding recitative (the *antecedent*), and then suggests three possible affects for the following aria. For each of these affects he presents an appropriate musical setting. Then he suggests three possible affects for the following aria. For each of these affects he presents an appropriate musical setting. Then he suggests three possible affects with their corresponding musical settings for the aria text itself (the *concomitant* of the text). Finally he deals with the *consequence* of another aria text which has no preceding recitative, and once again suggests three possible affects with their corresponding musical settings.

In these first nine examples, Heinichen uses texts that he considers weak in emotional content. To conclude his demonstration he turns to texts that are more stimulating to the composer and presents an additional seven examples.[17]

That so many contrasting musical settings may be used for a particular text does not at all disprove an intimate relationship between text and music. On the contrary, it demonstrates that the supply of musical possibilities generated by a single text is inexhaustible.

> If an experienced master were challenged, he could compose an aria as well as an entire opera in this manner, five or six times over, according to the possibilities of the text, and without a single aria having the slightest element in common, which is

another strong proof that the *loci topici* offer us the best path to invention and are as useful in music as in oratory.[18]

That Heinichen believed the expression of the text and its emotion to be the chief end of vocal composition as well as a never-ending challenge for the composer is clear from his own words:

> What a bottomless ocean we still have before us merely in the expression of words and the affects in music. And how delighted is the ear, if we perceive in a refined church composition or other music how a skilled virtuoso has attempted here and there to move the feelings of an audience through his "galanterie" and other expressions of the texts, and in this way [he] successfully finds the true purpose of music.[19]

On the other hand, he believed not enough effort had been made to formulate the systematic rules necessary to accomplish this task effectively. He continues,

> Nevertheless, no one has searched deeper into this beautiful musical *Rhetorica* to find good rules. What could one not write about musical taste, invention, accompaniment, and their nature, differences, and effects. But no one wants to investigate the material belonging to this lofty practice or to give even the slightest introduction to it. On the other hand, for other frequently pedantic materials cartloads of rules are devised.

Although Heinichen's treatise clearly advocates using the text as a source for musical invention and, furthermore, provides numerous practical demonstrations of this approach, it does not clearly differentiate the three principal ways that text may influence musical setting:

1. Text Declamation and Phrasing. Text rhythm, inflection, as well as punctuation typically influence musical rhythm, melodic contour, and phrase structure.

2. Expression of Words. Affect-laden words and phrases may be highlighted with appropriate rhetorical figures.

3. Expression of Affect. The affective significance evident in, or implied by, the text may suggest a particular musical expression that is then used as a unifying factor for the entire movement.

Since Heinichen was writing primarily about the emotional representation of texts, he addressed the matter of text declamation only in general terms:

> To express words with naturalness, ease, and in good taste, in such places where it occurs *a propos*, is a fine but also a difficult art. Otherwise [these attempts] sound mannered, and one can easily make oneself ridiculous with such expressions. Thus, one can find printed pieces, written by pretentious *practici* (I would rather call them *theoretici*) that could make a whole company of friends laugh without special effort. Yet it astonishes one, how such pieces without heartfelt emotion can be recited...[20]

Furthermore, in his treatise, Heinichen made little attempt to differentiate the expression of individual words or phrases from the expression of a general affect, probably because the affect is often suggested by an individual word or phrase. In this connection, when speaking of a particular uninspiring aria text, he wrote,

> What should a composer make of this? And where should he find the source of his invention? For not once in the entire aria ...is there a single word that gives the slightest opportunity for expressing a single affect.[21]

When we examine Heinichen's musical examples, we see that they primarily demonstrate the expression of a general affect, although here, too, this affect is often suggested by a particular word or phrase. By concentrating on affect rather than word painting, Heinichen placed himself alongside other progressive composers and theorists such as Quantz, who wrote,

> [Previous German composers] sought to express individual words rather than their total sense and the sentiment they contained. There were many who believed that they had done all they needed to do if, for example, they had expressed the words

heaven and hell through use of the extreme high and low registers; accordingly, much that is ludicrous used to creep in.[22]

Because Heinichen's discussion of text-music relationships confines itself to only certain aspects of the topic, we will expand the scope of our examination of Heinichen's actual practice to include all three aspects of text-music relation: text declamation and phrasing, the use of rhetorical figures to express individual words and phrases, and the expression of an overall affect within the span of a single movement.

Heinichen's Text Declamation

Although Heinichen addressed the matter of text declamation only in general terms, his contemporary, Johann Mattheson, was much more explicit in *Der Vollkommene Kapellmeister*, writing several chapters on the various aspects of this subject. In our examination of Heinichen's practice, Mattheson's statements will serve as useful points of comparison.

In his discussion of word and syllable stress, Mattheson differentiates between "accent" and "emphasis."[23] The former term applies to syllable stress, which must always fall on a metric accent or a long note. The pitch need not be raised, but should not be greatly lowered.[24] At cadences the final syllable, although weak, should fall on the down beat.[25] The term "emphasis" refers to the stress of key words by means of raised pitch. The note need not be metrically strong or of long duration.[26] Words may also be emphasized by means of a melisma or through repetition. Repetition should be minimal. Even words like "amen" and "alleluia" should be repeated no more than three or four times.[27]

In looking at the text setting of Heinichen's church compositions, we generally find evidence of a concern for the correct declamation of the words. As in Heinichen's Masses, so in these works this concern is most clearly evident in the recitatives and parlando sections of the choruses, in which accented syllables and key words are stressed with higher notes, longer durations, accented metrical possition or harmonic changes.[28]

Fig. 3. *Lobe den Herrn*, IX, mm. 38-40

In triple-meter arias, accented syllables sometimes fall on the third beat, but usually only in cases where that beat is also stressed musically (i.e., in hemiolas). Other than single hemiolas appearing at cadences, we also find double hemiolas. The following example is taken from *Der Segen des Herrn*.

Fig. 4. *Der Segen des Herrn*, mm. 82-88

The bass aria (III) of *Herr, nun lässest Du* is a sarabande in 3/2 meter and, hence, occasionally accents the second beat. Usually, this displacement of the accent occurs on the word "vergnüge:"

Fig. 5. *Herr, nun lässest Du*, III.

In measures 20 and 21, the above pattern is used as a hemiola, and is followed by an unusual measure in which the continuo bass disappears on the first beat and the two oboes enter on the second, producing two successive measures with accents on the second beat.

Fig. 6. *Herr, nun lässest Du,* III, mm. 19-21

In measure 38, although the characteristic dotted rhythm is absent, a modulatory pivot chord helps stress the second beat.

Fig. 7. *Herr, nun lässest Du,* III, mm. 37-40

In the tenor aria of the same cantata, the beat is displaced in a similar way each time the phrase "Herr, von der Welt dahin" appears. As if to reinforce the effect, Heinichen echoes the word "dahin" the last time the phrase appears, without moving the accented syllable to the strong beat.

Fig. 8. *Herr, nun lässest Du,* IV, mm. 50-52

It seems that in these examples Heinichen is more concerned with the dance-like interplay of rhythms than in a literal rendering of language inflections. The ambiguity of these passages is sometimes increased by the action of the continuo. We noticed earlier how the continuo might disappear on the final beat of what at first appeared to be a regular hemiola. A similar case occurs in the alto aria of *Ach, was soll ich Sünder machen.*

Fig. 9. *Ach, was soll ich Sünder machen,* V, mm. 13-17

The anticipation of the second syllable of the word "heute" in the above example gives the phrase a feeling of elegance, especially if it is preceded by a slight stopping of the sound. Such syllable anticipation can be found in many of Heinichen's other compositions but are especially frequent in *Der Herr ist nahe,* whose three arias in triple meter offer many opportunities to use this effect:

movement III:

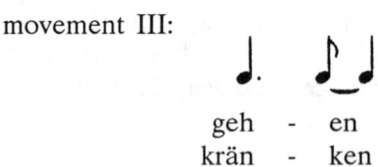

movement V:

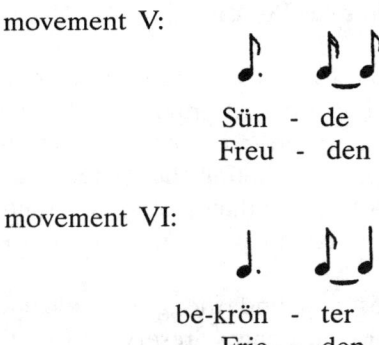

Sün - de
Freu - den

movement VI:

be-krön - ter
Frie - den

Fig. 10. Syllable anticipations in *Der Herr ist nahe*

In the tenor duet of *Es lebet Jesus unser Hort*, an anticipation of this sort appears in one voice, but not in the other, producing unsynchronized parts.

von der

Fig. 11. Unsynchronized parts in *Es lebet*, IV, mm. 47, 59

Matteson's caution regarding the excessive repetition of words is generally heeded by Heinichen, although two exceptions can be found in *Es lebet Jesus*. The bass aria has an extended section built on the repeated word "victoria" in the manner of older masters such as Heinrich Schütz,[29] while the last movement consists entirely of the repeated word "alleluia." In *Gott ist unsere Zuversicht* the word "sela" is extensively repeated on three occasions, at the end of sections III, VII, and XI.[30]

Correlation of Punctuation and Musical Phrasing

In his discussion of text setting, Johann Mattheson also concerns himself with the relationship between various types of grammatical punctuation and their musical equivalents.[31] Since punctuation essentially serves to clarify the ideas being expressed, he warns against violating the sentence structure with inappropriate musical phrasing. Admitting that poets sometimes punctuate their works incorrectly, Mattheson counsels composers to use their own judgement in such cases.[32]

In Heinichen's works we usually find the grammatical and musical pauses coinciding, with the major cadences reserved for the ends of sentences.[33] Many of the interior pauses are the result of an additive presentation of the text. Pauses occur because sentence fragments are repeated before being completed. This example occurs in *Lobe den Herrn*, VII (mm. 26-41):

lässt uns keinenfalles Spott (2x)
an den wieder Aufstand hindern (2x)
hebet, hebet väterlich, väterlich empor,
hebet väterlich empor die ihn kindlich fürchten vor,
die ihn kindlich (2x)
die ihn kindlich fürchten vor.

Sometimes this additive approach connects text phrases that should be separated by a pause, as in this example from *Gegrüsset seist du*:

lass al - le Furcht, du bist nun hoch er - freu - (et)

Fig. 12. *Gegrüsset seist du*, I, mm. 78-80

Similar examples can be found in *Der Herr ist nahe* (III, mm. 38-39), and *Einsamkeit* (VI, mm. 8-9).

According to Mattheson, the mistake most commonly made by composers is making a musical pause where there should be none. When Heinichen commits this error, he appears to be guided by the text's rhyme scheme rather than its grammatical structure. Some of the recitative in *Lass dichs nicht irren, Es naheten,* and *Mag auch ein Blinder* clearly have too many pauses. In *Lass dichs nicht irren,* the vocal line pauses twenty-one times; once in almost every measure:

> Der arme Lazarus (pause)
> hat auch viel Brüder hinterlassen, (pause)
> die vor der Reichen Tür (pause)
> sich als die Hunde müssen schmiegen, (pause) etc.

Effective pauses occur in *Gegrüsset seist du,* when Mary questions the news brought by the angel Gabriel.

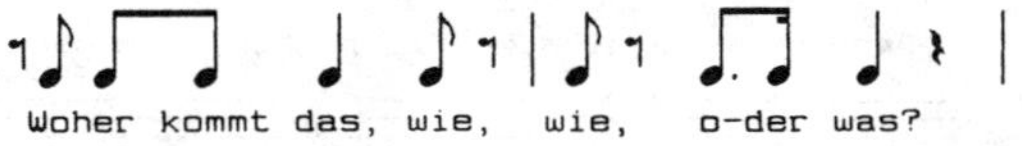

Woher kommt das, wie, wie, o-der was?

Fig. 13. *Gegrüsset seist du,* II, mm. 2-3

When this question returns after an intervening section in triple meter, the setting omits some of the pauses, and adds two repetitions of the word "wie," probably to express growing agitation.

O furcht - - same Pein, Woher kommt das,

wie, wie, wie, wie o-der was?

Fig. 14. *Gegrüsset seist du,* II, mm. 66-70

In *Gelobet sei der Herr,* V, the choir sings haltingly about its freedom from slavery. The result is a machinelike monotony that strikes one as inexplicably fitting.

Wir waren zu Sklaven des Argen ge - macht

Fig. 15. *Gelobet sei der Herr*, V

Sometimes Heinichen omits pauses that are grammatically required. Several of these occur in *Lass dichs* and *Es naheten*. In the following excerpt from *Lass dichs*, I, the two similar ideas should not only be separated by a pause, but should, according to Mattheson, also be set as similar melodic patterns.[34] Heinichen, however, relates them as subject and countersubject.

Fig. 16. *Lass dichs nicht irren*, I, mm. 19-25

Punctuation marks other than commas or periods are seldom found in Heinichen's texts. A colon is used in *Es naheten*, III, to introduce narration and is appropriately set with a rest. An exclamation point is used to express joy in the duet "Weg, O Welt!" of *Herr, nun lässest Du* and is set with a leap as suggested by Mattheson.[35] The series of questions in *Der Herr ist nahe*, III do not employ the expected rising intervals, but since these are rhetorical questions holding no real doubt, this, too, conforms to Mattheson's guidelines.[36] Although there are no parentheses as such, a parenthetical statement ("da man doch grösser tut") is contained in the text of *Mag auch*, V:

> Man weiss die kleinen Sünden, da man doch grösser tut,
> mit unbedachtem Mut an seinem Nächsten bald zu finden.

> (One finds the little sins, although committing larger ones oneself, with unthinking boldness in one's neighbor.)

Because the interpolated idea clearly contrasts with the rest of the sentence, Mattheson suggests a biplanar melody or some other means of contrasting the interpolation.[37] Heinichen accomplishes the contrast with a modulation.

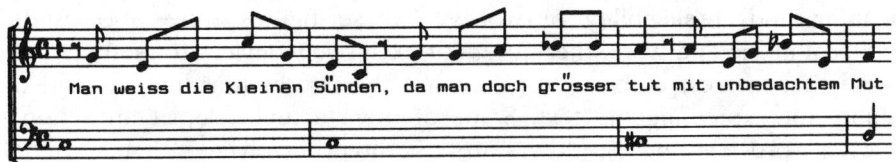

Man weiss die Kleinen Sünden, da man doch grösser tut mit unbedachtem Mut

Fig. 17. *Mag auch ein Blinder*, V, mm. 1-3

Two of Heinichen's da capo arias have A and B sections that grammatically flow one into the other: *Gelobet*, III, and *Es lebet*, VI. For this kind of grammatical structure, Mattheson suggests writing out the da capo so that a full cadence occurs only at the very end of the aria.[38] Heinichen does, in fact, write out the da capos, but only in *Es lebet* do the alterations make the closing cadence more final.

Rhetorical Figures

The most striking aspect of Heinichen's text setting, however, is the abundance of obvious rhetorical figures.[39] Despite Heinichen's lament that no systematic study of "musical rhetorica" had been made, these figures had been systematically codified and applied to music as early as 1599, when Joachim Burmeister published his *Hypomnematum Musicae*.[40] Since the context of Heinichen's statement is the excessive preoccupation with contrapuntal rules, his remarks apparently reflect the fact that many of his contemporaries used the figures without truly understanding them. This sentiment is echoed by Mattheson:

> Many will think here, we have already used such things and figures for so long without knowing what they are called or what they mean: we can hence be content, and put rhetoric aside. These seem even more ridiculous to me than *Le Bourgeois gentilhomme* of Moliere, who did not know that it was a pronoun when he said, I, you, he; or that it was an imperative when he said to his servants: 'Come here!'[41]

Although the "rhetorical orientation of Baroque music evolved out of the Renaissance preoccupation with the impact of musical styles on the meaning and intelligibility of words,"[42] these figures were also used in nonvocal music and were, therefore, not exclusively devices for setting a text. Those that interest us here, however, are the figures that have a particular affinity for expressing the text. Some of them actually depict an action or object ("word painting"[43]). Others are less direct, involving either a symbolic or psychological representation.

In Mattheson's opinion, excessive word painting was one of the greatest and most common compositional errors. He cautions his readers to use this technique modestly and discreetly, often only in the accompaniment, as if by chance.[44] Heinichen, however, uses madrigalisms freely and conspicuously. Some of the most obvious ones are the madrigalisms that show direction, number, or duration. In *Einsamkeit, o stilles Wesen*, the words "where two or three are gathered in my name" are depicted literally in a two-part (solo) counterpoint, which expands to three voices. This section is followed by a bass solo on the text "there I am in their midst."[45] Such a procedure would be fairly routine were it not for the homophonc ending in which the vocal bass no longer acts as a bass line, holding a pedal F instead, while the continuo fulfills the bass function. In this way the vocal bass is physically "in the middle."

Fig. 18. *Einsamkeit, o stilles Wesen*, V, mm. 11-14

In the preceding bass solo, the descending direction (*catabasis*) of the vocal part depicts God's involvement with man in a stereotyped way (reaching down), and the sequential restatement of this phrase (*climax* or *auxesis*) adds a degree of intensity.

In the final movement of the same cantata, the words "before they call I will answer" are set in a 1+3 texture; one part preceding the other three. First it is the soprano that precedes the others with the words "before they call," in the next phrase it is the bass (symbolizing the voice of Christ as in the previous example) that begins first, with the words "I will answer." The fact that the soprano and bass are unaccompanied at these points makes the effect even more striking, as does the trill on the bass entry.

A common method of depicting lengthy periods of time was to use long tones. An example of this happens in the final chorus of *Lobe den Herrn*, where the soprano twice holds a pedal tone on the word "eternity" (mm. 19-29). Heinichen also uses pedal tones in the alto aria of *Ach, was soll ich Sünder machen* for the text "meinen Jesum lass ich nicht" and at the end of the alto duet in *Meine Seele erhebet den Herrn* for the text "weiss nicht aufzuhören" (mm. 48-49). The persistence implied by the words in the example cited from *Ach, was soll ich Sünder machen* are further amplified by a monotonously repeated melody.

Other types of rhetorical devices do not represent the words quite so literally yet are, nevertheless, unmistakable in their intent. Melodic leaps (*exclamatio*) are often used for images of strength and are usually given to the bass voice. Thus in the bass aria of *Der Herr ist nahe*, the word "bestritten" (fought) is set as an arpeggiated figure that involves both singers and instrumentalists.

Fig. 19. *Der Herr ist nahe,* IV, mm. 13-15

A similar kind of figure appears in the bass aria of *Gelobet sei der Herr* on the words "gewaltigen Trutz" (mighty defiance). Here the figure spans an octave and a half.

Fig. 20. *Gelobet sei der Herr,* IV, mm. 13-15

In *Es naheten aber zu Jesu, exclamatio* is used as a "calling" motive on the word "rufet."

Fig. 21. *Es naheten aber zu Jesu,* VIII, m. 8

Melismas are often used to depict energy or haste. The more graphic of these consist of consecutive leaps of thirds and fourths. The bass duet of *Meine Seele erhebet den Herrn* has melismas of this type for the word "rasen" (rage),[46] and the alto aria in *Einsamkeit* uses them on the word "toben" (a synonym of "rasen").

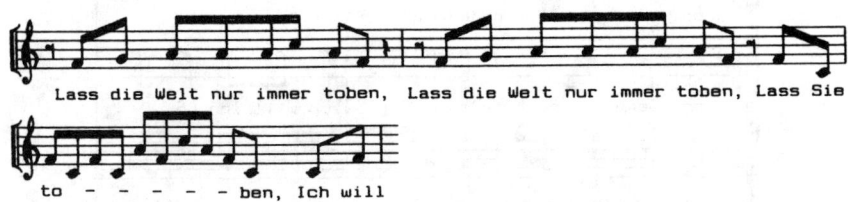

Fig. 22. *Einsamkeit, o stilles Wesen*, IV, mm. 22-24

Another example of melismas with consecutive leaps occurs on the word "Leben" in the allegro section of the alto aria in *Es lebet Jesus unser Hort*.

Heinichen also writes the traditional melismas for such words as "freuet,"[47] "eilen,"[48] "walten,"[49] "alleluia,"[50] etc. One unique use of melismas is found in the first bass aria of *Herr, nun lässest Du*. Here the significant word is "erwarmen" (to warm) and Heinichen depicts a shivering singer:

Fig. 23. *Herr, nun lässest Du*, III, mm. 68-70

Interrupted vocal lines (*suspiratio* or *tmesis*) occur on such affect laden words as "zerbrochen" and "zerschlagen" in the second movement of *Der Herr ist nahe*, depicting both the emotional and literal meanings of "brokenness." In the last movement of *Einsamkeit*, Heinichen interrupts the word "hören" in three voices, as if the singers are stopping their activity in order to listen. All the instruments stop as well, and only the vocal bass (perhaps again symbolizing Christ) sings through the eighth note rest.[51]

Fig. 24. *Einsamkeit, o stilles Wesen*, VIII, mm. 28-30

The two expositions of the fughetta that precedes the above example,[52] both present the voices in order, from lowest to highest (B-T-A-S). This is probably another form of *anabasis* symbolizing the upward direction of the word "rufen".

Harmonic devices are also used to heighten emotionally laden texts. In *Einsamkeit* the chromatic line of the alto solo in measures 17 to 19 is provoked by the word "Qual" (torment), and a modulatory sequence in measures 13-24 of the first choral movement is probably suggested by the words "mit Ernst" (earnestly): F-Bb-Eb-Cm-Gm-F.[53]

In the bass aria of *Es naheten*, the dissonances (*parrhesia*) between the vocal bass and basso continuo are justified by the words "Kein starker braucht den Arzt" (he who is robust needs no physician). This sentiment apparently made Heinichen think of strong-willed independence.

Fig. 25 *Es naheten aber zu Jesu*, II, mm. 6-9

Very similar cross relations between vocal bass and continuo occur in *Es lebet Jesus unser Hort*, where, in the third movement, the bass sings the words "Jesus hat den Tod bezwungen" (Jesus has conquered death).

Expression of a General Affect

In our earlier discussion of overall structure we noted that varying degrees of sectionalization in Heinichen's works produce structures ranging from those consisting of a succession of well-defined, self-contained movements to ones comprising a series of connected sections. To the extent that Heinichen's movements employ the more modern compositional elements of recurring ritornelli, da capo structure, motivically independent instrumental lines, etc., they tend to achieve motivic unity and, hence, to express a single affect. These types of movements are in the minority, however. Most of them, although they clearly attempt to express the affects implied by isolated words and phrases with a variety of rhetorical figures, do not achieve a high degree of formal unity, the examples in Heinichen's treatise notwithstanding.[54] In *Lobe den Herrn*, for example, the first choral movement consists of four sections in alternating allegro and adagio sections.

That Heinichen was just beginning to learn the new style with its emphasis on unity of affect becomes evident when we compare individual movements of these works with the examples appearing in his treatise. Despite their brevity, most of the examples in Heinichen's treatise carry designations such as vivace, un poco allegro, furioso, cantabile, amoroso, etc. According to Quantz, such designations informed the performer of the intended affect.[55] In his German church works, Heinichen more often than not omits such indications, although he does use terms such as allegro, adagio, or vivace in one-third of the movements or sections.[56]

Furthermore, all of the examples in Heinichen's practical demonstration are scored for solo voice, obbligato, and continuo, and many essential aspects of the affective representation appear primarily in the accompaniments. To the extent that individual movements of Heinichen's German church works have obbligato parts, they, too, may achieve a unified affect. Many of his movements (especially the choral ones), however, use the older compositional styles in which the instruments double the voice parts or echo the text-determined vocal motives in a concertante exchange. In such movements the nature of the texts confirm and reinforce the older style. Being scriptural or, when newly composed, moralistic or dogmatic,[57] they do not yet contain the subjectivism of the later cantata, a subjectivism that was particularly well suited to the structural technique of unifying each movement with a single affective representation.

It is precisely in the newer-style cantatas that Heinichen achieves unified affects in the individual movements. Of these, many contain sentiments of joy, most frequently expressed with constantly running sixteenth notes, leaping intervals, or triple meter, all of which are typical devices of the time. Concerning the appropriateness of using large intervals to express joy, Mattheson wrote,

> Since...joy is an expansion of our soul, thus it follows reasonably and naturally that I could best express this affect by large and expanded intervals.[58]

Heinichen also uses triplet rhythms to express joy. In *Gelobet*, V, *Der Segen*, II, and *Ach, was soll ich Sünder machen*, VIII, he achieves unity with obbligato parts characterized by continuous triplets.

One anomaly occurs in *Gegrüsset*, where four out of the five movements use triple meter (although two of the four also include sections in common meter). Although the greater part of the libretto (a paraphrase of Mary's annunciation) is joyful and therefore suits triple meter, the second movement clearly does not. It is difficult to understand Heinichen's choice of triple meter for these words:

How can I, as virgin, be with child?
This cannot be, o frightful torment!

Other movements with unified affects express emotions of anger or strength, and they, too, typically employ rapid notes and large intervals. In some cases Heinichen uses a technique that Mattheson associates with stubborness, namely, "when one writes...passages which one is resolved not to change cost what it may."[59] In the bass aria of *Es lebet*, the vocal bass clashes frequently with the continuo bass as a result of this technique. Only the opening measures are reproduced here.

Fig. 26. *Es lebet Jesus unser Hort*, III, mm. 1-4

A similar example occurs in *Es naheten*, II.[60]

The affinity of these more lively affects with the theatrical style was noted by both Heinichen and Mattheson. Heinichen wrote,

> I would never suggest to anyone to fill up the theatrical style with too many serious inventions like these. For pathetic, melancholic, and phlegmatic music...is not well suited to the theatrical style, and one uses serious pieces simply for judicious changes. And if their lordships, the poets, overload us with pathetic and sorrowful arias, we must try to sweeten these either with mixed inventions or effective accompaniments; or in those arias containing a double affect, one bases the invention more generally on the lively element rather than the serious one.[61]

Mattheson thought similarly:

> One does not need...profundity with theatrical pieces; indeed, this goes to some extent against the character and purpose of plays, whose marks of distinction is always something of the playful and fictitious...[62]

Some other devices normally associated with lively affects do not appear in Heinichen's church works, however. Reverse-dotted rhythms and ornaments, both being devices Quantz associated with expressions of gaiety, are not to be found.[63]

In several movements Heinichen apparently choose 6/8 meter to express aristocratic graciousness as suggested by the word "grace" ("Gnade"). One example is the choral codetta to the duet in *Gelobet sei der Herr*. Here the dotted eighth notes enhance the feeling of a courtly dance.

Fig. 27. *Gelobet sei der Herr*, VII, mm. 20-22

In *Lobe den Herrn* the entire alto aria ("gracious, good, and full of mercy") is set in 6/8 meter, but in the final chorus, where "Gnade" would be better translated "mercy," Heinichen chooses common meter. In *Meine Seele erhebet den Herrn* the alto duet is in 6/8 meter and marked "affettuoso." Although "grace" is not mentioned until measure 41, the theme of the entire aria text is the graciousness of God.

Although Heinichen used harmonic devices to heighten emotion-laden texts,[64] he forcefully dismissed the affective significance of keys:

> ...one can compose the same words and affects in various, and according to the old theory, opposing keys. For that reason, what previous theorists have written about the properties of the modes are nothing but trifles, as if one mode could be merry, another sad, a third pious, heroic, warlike, etc. Indeed, if these imaginary properties had any inherent correctness, the slightest change of temperament used for them (in which instrumental parts are never completely accurate) as well as changes of *Chorton*, *Kammerton*, French, and the extravagant Venetian tunings would cause continual shipwrecks...[65]

Heinichen does, however, prefer minor keys for the more somber texts such as those in *Ach, was soll ich Sünder machen*.[66] In festive cantatas Heinichen sometimes prefers keys with flats rather than the more customary sharp keys. *Gelobet*, for instance, is primarily in F major, while *Lobe den Herrn* and *Gegrüsset seist du* are both in Bb major. *Meine Seele erhebet den Herrn* and *Es lebet Jesus unser Hort*, however, are both in the more traditional key of C major.

To sum up Heinichen's text treatment in his German church works, we may conclude that, although he was sensitive to the declamation of his texts and interested in highlighting affect-laden words and phrases, he was only just beginning to create unified movements expressing single emotional states. While this lack of expressive unity in Heinichen's cantata movements reflects the composer's youthfulness and inexperience, it also indicates the transitional state of the German cantata at this time, for the cantata was just beginning to incorporate the Italian theatrical style with its emphasis on self-contained, expressively unified movements.

Chapter 8. Notes

1. See Ziegler's definition of madrigalian verse in chapter 2.

2. These may both be stanzas from an unidentified chorale.

3. See chapter 2.

4. *Herr, nun lässest Du*, movements III, IV, VI, VII; *Gelobet*, III. These designations appear in tacet parts.

5. Seiffert, pp. LXXVI, LXXVII.

6. Vossler, p. 45.

7. Some of the recitatives end with a cavata. For further discussion of this matter see chapter 10.

8. Christian Hunold [Menantes], *Die allerneuste Art zur reinen und galanten Poesie zu gelangen* (Hamburg, 1707), p. 74. This book is a plagerization of Neumeister's Leipzig lectures. See below and chapter 2.

9. Westrup, *Bach's Cantatas*, pp. 17, 18. For a discussion of the relationship between sacred and secular spheres in Lutheran theology, see chapter 5. See also Dürr, *Die Kantaten*, 2:666.

10. Westrup, *Bach's Cantatas*, p. 18.

11. Westrup, *Bach's Cantatas*, p. 43. The aria text is translated by Westrup, *Bach's Cantatas*: "Great Lord, powerful King, beloved Savior, how little regard hast thou for earthly pomp." The problem with setting this text is that two affects are suggested: pomp and humility. In deciding between such double affects when composing in the theatrical style, Heinichen suggests a composer choose the more lively one. Bach's setting follows this rule. See Heinichen, *General-Bass*, p. 47, trans. Buelow, "Heinichen's General-Bass," p. 592.

12. Robert Freeman, "La Verita Nella Ripetizione," *Musical Quarterly* 54 (1968): 208-227.

13. Freeman, p. 225.

14. Westrup, *Bach's Cantatas*, p. 56.

15. Heinichen, *General-Bass*, trans. Buelow, "Heinichen's General-Bass," p. 581. It is for this reason that a one-on-one association of figures with affects was never standardized in the Baroque era. Instead, these figures were used only "to decorate and elaborate on a basic affective representation and to add dramatic musical stress to words and poetic concepts." See Buelow, "Rhetoric and Music," *New Grove*, 15:800-801.

16. Heinichen equates these three sources for invention with the rhetorical *loci topici*, but Mattheson points out that they comprise only part of the *locus circumstanttiarum* which itself is but one of the fifteen sources that together make up the *loci topici*. See Mattheson, *Capellmeister*, p. 297. Mattheson's listing (see page 285) is virtually identical with that used by Christian Hunold in his treatise, *Die allerneuste Art zur reinen und galanten Poesie zu gelangen*, (Leipzig, 1715). See pp. 541, 542. This book was an unauthorized publication of Erdmann Neumeister's lectures delivered in 1695 at the University of Leipzig and was published under the pseudonym "Menantes." It is quite likely that Hunold's (Neumeister's) book served as the most immediate source for both Mattheson's and Heinichen's ideas, even though the rhetorical procedure for generating ideas in this way can be found as far back as such classical authors as Quintillian. See Quintillian, *Institutiones Oratoriae*, trans. H.E. Butler, 4 vols. (Cambridge: Harvard University Press, 1922), vol. 2, p. 193.

17. In total, Heinichen gives examples of sixteen affects: fury, quarrelsomeness, pomp, persistence ("eternal pursuit of fortune"), fickleness, instability ("ever-changing or calamity-bearing fortune"), amorousness, passion ("burning fire of love"), flirtatiousness, tenderness, the "sighs of love," anxiety, mutual love, bantering, and dark shadows. See also George J. Buelow, "The Loci Topici and Affect in late baroque Music; Heinichen's practical demonstration," *The Music Review*, August 1966, pp. 161-176.

18. Heinichen, *General-Bass*, p. 88, trans. Buelow, "Heinichen's General-Bass," p. 613.

19. Heinichen, *General-Bass*, pp. 23-24, trans. by Buelow, "Heinichen's General-Bass," pp. 572-574.

20. Heinichen, *General-Bass*, p. 24, trans. in Buelow, "Heinichen's General-Bass," p. 573, edited by this writer.

21. Heinichen, *General-Bass*, p. 31, trans. in Buelow, "Heinichen's General-Bass," p. 580.

22. Quantz, *Flute*, p. 336. See also Hill, p. 201 ff.; Mattheson, *Capellmeister*, p. 202.

23. Part II, chapter 8.

24. Mattheson, *Capellmeister*, p. 371.

25. Mattheson, *Capellmeister*, p. 376.

26. Mattheson, *Capellmeister*, pp. 370-371.

27. Mattheson, *Capellmeister*, pp. 377-378.

28. Schmitz, p. 43.

29. Compare the last movement of *Historia der Auferstehung Jesu Christi* by Schütz.

30. Since this cantata does not have distinct movements, we speak here of sections.

31. Mattheson, *Capellmeister*, Part II, chapter 8.

32. Mattheson, *Capellmeister*, p. 396.

33. The actual punctuation is frequently missing in the manuscripts.

34. Mattheson, *Capellmeister*, p. 390.

35. Mattheson distinguishes among three types of exclamation. This one is of the first type. See Mattheson, *Capellmeister*, p. 400.

36. Mattheson, *Capellmeister*, p. 398.

37. Mattheson, *Capellmeister*, p. 402.

38. Mattheson, *Capellmeister*, p. 396.

39. The study of rhetoric comprises four aspects: Inventio (the invention or discovery of ideas related to the subject), Dispositio or Elaboratio (the arrangement of the content into a systematic order of six parts: Exordium, Narratio, Propositio, Confirmatio, Confutatio, and Conclusio), Decoratio (the creation of affects through effective use of language), and Pronuntiatio or Elocutio (methods of delivery including the use of gesture). Rhetorical figures belong to the category of "Decoratio." See Hans Heinrich Unger, *Die Beziehung zwischen Musik und Rhetorik im 16.-18. Jahrhundert* (Würzburg: Konrad Triltsch, 1941), pp. 3-11. Regarding the relationship between music and oratory, Quantz wrote,

> Musical execution may be compared with the delivery of an orator. The orator and the musician have, at bottom, the same aim in regard to both the preparation and the final execution of their productions, namely, to make themselves masters of the hearts of their listeners, to arouse or still their passions, and to transport them now to this sentiment, now to that.

See Quantz, *Flute*, p. 119.

40. See George Buelow, "Rhetoric and Music," p. 793.

41. Mattheson, *Capellmeister*, p. 483.

42. Buelow, "Rhetoric and Music," p. 793.

43. Buelow calls this category "Hypotyposis figures," a term derived from Burmeister. See Buelow, "Rhetoric and Music," p. 798.

44. Mattheson, *Capellmeister*, pp. 413-417.

45. Another madrigalism depicting quantity occurs in *Lobe den Herrn* on the text "heilet alle deine Gebrechen." Whereas the tutti reinforcement at the cadences in measures 73 and 75 is not unusual, the interjection in measure 70 on the word "alle, alle" is striking.

46. Mm. 12, 13, 18, 19, 22.

47. *Es naheten*, III, *Es lebet*, soprano duet, *Meine Seele*, soprano duet.

48. *Herr, nun lässest Du*, tenor aria. The convention of giving melismas to such terms of haste was specifically criticized by Mattheson, who pointed out that "whoever has speed tends otherwise not to hesitate long." See Mattheson, *Capellmeister*, p. 416.

49. *Lobe den Herrn*, V.

50. *Es lebet*, final chorus.

51. Also mm. 23-24.

52. The first exposition is for voices and continuo, the second includes instrumental doublings.

53. For a further discussion of these measures, see chapter 12.

54. Heinichen's treatise was, of course, written much later than the compositions under examination.

55. Quantz, *Flute*, p. 126.

56. In *Gott ist unsere Zuversicht*, a cantata that consists of eleven connected sections, not one carries any kind of tempo designation.

57. See chapter 5.

58. Mattheson, *Capellmeister*, p. 104.

59. Mattheson, *Capellmeister*, p. 108.

60. See above.

61. Heinichen, *General-Bass*, p. 47, trans. Buelow, "Heinichen's General-Bass," p. 592.

62. Mattheson, *Capellmeister*, pp. 213, 214.

63. Quantz, *Flute*, pp. 98, 125. A few trills such as those in *Herr*, III are exceptions to this generalization.

64. See earlier discussion.

65. Heinichen, *General-Bass*, pp. 83-84, trans. in Buelow, "Heinichen's General-Bass," pp. 608, 609.

66. Since only two movements actually use the chorale tune, the remaining movements are not musically bound to the chorale.

9.
The Structure of the Choral Movements

We have already seen a difference between Heinichen's choral and solo movements in the type of texts used for each, as well as in the placement of each within the overall structure of the work. Even it if could be conclusively demonstrated that some of the choral movements were intended for soloistic performance,[1] their role within the overall architectural framework, as well as their structure and style, relate them more closely to the ensemble movements than to the solo movements, and for that reason they will be discussed here.

To a large extent, the structures of Heinichen's choral movements are determined by their texts. In cases where a short text is given extended treatment, the movement tends to possess greater formal unity. Longer texts, on the other hand, tend to produce modular structures in which the sections exhibit contrasting styles. In all of his choral movements, Heinichen draws on the traditional choral styles of his time: fugal, concertante, and imitative motet style. In movements that combine styles, one style tends to be emphasized over the others, and the contrasting sections can then be viewed as introductions, interludes, or codas. For this reason we will categorize movements according to their prevailing compositional style.

Fugal Movements

Heinichen's attitude toward counterpoint changed over the course of his life. During his student days he was totally absorbed with it. This interest waned in later years, however, for reasons Heinichen himself clearly explains.[2] Since Heinichen's comments reveal not only his own attitude toward counterpoint but also the extent to which he subscribed to the aesthetic values of the new *galant* style, we quote him here at length.

Once and for all it should be reported that when the word counterpoint is mentioned in this treatise it is not meant *In sensu lato*, nor *Pro compositione in genere*, nor *Quasi punctum contra punctum*, nor *Nota contra notam*, but strictly for those compositions in which themes are used [in a contrapuntal manner]. Therefore, only those musicians can be called contrapuntists and arch-contrapuntists who seek the *Summum bonum* or the entire art of music in the study of counterpoint only. I am very fond of counterpoint, and in my youth I was an ardent champion of it; as in the past, in the future too I shall continue to demonstrate my willingness to haggle with fugues, double fugues, and other artifices of themes on paper in the pious church style. I cannot deny, however, that after many years of experience I have lost my previous enthusiasm for it and absolutely cannot bear our excessive misuse of forced counterpoints, in which for the most part (and I do not say completely) nothing has validity unless it is a pedantic counterpoint, and in which generally the artificial play with notes on paper is given out as the most noble and most artful form of music. This pretext is equally absurd for all sensible practicing musicians, and whatever the counterpoint-potentates may babble, one can satisfactorily destroy their weak arguments. Counterpoint serves a two-fold good purpose in music if it is cleansed of all useless classifications, sterile devices, and forced pedantries, and if only the true *Inventa* (which tyrannize our Ear the least) are chosen. First, [counterpoint] serves students and beginners in composition. With counterpoint they learn to climb or to spell, and with these given and restricted themes and toilsome exercises they are forcibly taught skilful progressions or *Passus compositionis*, just as the dancing or fencing master forces students first to make well-formed steps of the dance or a good body posture for fencing before showing them the true art. For such instructions the arch-contrapuntists are the very best suited, but one must not allow students to remain too long in apprenticeship, or else they will become as pedantic as their teachers.

Secondly, counterpoint serves church music if it is mixed, according to the style of good church composers, with other techniques of good taste. Here is really its place, and here the contrapuntist can best show his learned schooling. In addition, because our usual pious church music (more in Germany than in other countries) tolerates neither too much fire, inspiration, nor gay ideas, thus sometimes even a contrapuntist with little taste and invention can slip through at the very first. For after he has a bit of a theme or something of a musical idea and has captured it at the twelfth, then he whips it through all the usual transpositions and common inversions; this then is called erudition, and the man has accomplished Herculean feats. What, however, should I say about the overwhelming amount of stereotyped counterpoint? I will always unpack my Seven Articles of Faith, notwithstanding *praevia protestatione solenni* that I do not speak of discarding all counterpoint but only of *de nimis abuso* of the same. Together with all experienced musicians who believe in the true *Finis musices*, I can say that: (1) Most of the [contrapuntal] *inventa* (with few exceptions) are based on the visual and lifeless manipulations of notes but not on the actual sound. (2) That the more one sinks into the excesses of such stereotyped artifies, the more one necessarily must depart from the Ear and the true *Finis musices*. (3) That, therefore, those lines of a composition (not the entire piece, for there one can alternate) must be considered *inter casus raros & accidentales* or rare masterpieces, in which considerable sterile art is combined with equal amounts of good taste. (4) That the excessive abuse of too much counterpoint is the shortest path to musical pedantry, ruining many fine talents that otherwise could have been developed into something outstanding. (5) That, for the most part, counterpoint in itself is something laborious (like the farmers' work when they must load manure into wheelbarrows) but not artistic once one has learned the routine. (6) That one can make a dull contrapuntist *par force* out of any dumb boy but not a composer with good taste. (7) Finally, that there are many more beautiful and artistic things in music to promote the *Finis musices* than the forced rules of counterpoint. "Indeed!" say the embittered contrapuntists, "but one can unite art (paper art) with good taste." Answer: these gentlemen never observe their own watchword, for if one listens to their very best music it sounds as if someone were beating the dust out of an old woman's fur coat, or (as others say) as if an abecedarian were spelling out something, understandable as syllables and words, but not the full sense or connection [of these words in sentences]. In short, when the performance is finished one does not know what the fellow meant to say with it. True, now and then a good composer will show that one can unite counterpoint and good musical taste, *sed non omnes capiunt hoc verbum*. And even if we argue *a po[s]tiori* what can or ought to happen in nature, it still remains an eternal truth, that the excessive cultivation of counterpoint ruins good music and will ruin many fine natural talents born to music. So much for now concerning the abuses of counterpoint.[3]

Almost all of Heinichen's works have at least one movement that is predominantly fugal, most typically this is the first vocal movement (following the introductory sonata). In keeping with Heinichen's view that church compositions should mix counterpoint with other techniques, these fugues are often introduced by homophonic, at times concertante, sections.[4] The fugue itself is usually associated with a key phrase of text justifying the more extended treatment. Most of the fugal sections are not long, however, ranging in length from seven- or eight-measure fugatos[5] to thirty-five- or forty-measure fugues.[6]

The Fugue Themes

One of the most striking characteristics of Heinichen's fugue themes is that they are so harmonically conceived. Most of them are written in major keys, precluding the chromatic alterations inherent in minor scales. Many of them outline the tonality through triadic or scalar figures. In the following example (which is the opening statement of the fugato from which it is taken), the theme is really only an elaborated ascending scale. Yet even this tonally conceived line gives way to harmonic considerations by omitting the fifth scale degree.

Nun so fahr ich Him – – – – mel auf,

Fig. 28. *Herr, nun lässest Du*, VII, mm. 79-80

Sometimes the tonality is outlined twice, first with leaps, then with a scale:

Fig. 29. *Herr, nun lässest Du*, V, mm. 20-21.

The triadic leaps of the following subject were probably suggested by the text.

Fig. 30. *Gelobet sei der Herr*, II, mm. 23-25

In the following example, the octave leaps actually obscure the minor tonality because of the scale degrees on which they fall. The intent was, no doubt, to produce a picture of "battering."

Fig. 31. *Der Herr ist nahe*, II, mm. 17-19

Most often the fugue themes do not modulate. When such a theme begins on the fifth scale-degree and drops to the third (as Heinichen's frequently do),[7] the resulting intervallic adjustment in the answer usually presents the critical leading tone in a very conspicuous position and greatly strengthens the sense that the fugue is tonally bound. In *Mag auch ein Blinder*, Heinichen presents two such fugue themes. In both expositions, the answers are intervallically adjusted so that the second pitch is the seventh scale degree; in the latter case, however, Heinichen chooses the lowered seventh instead of the leading tone and in this way begins a modulation to the dominant minor.

Fig. 32. *Mag auch ein Blinder*, I, mm. 15-19

Fig. 33. *Mag auch ein Blinder*, IV, mm. 20-23

The contours of Heinichen's fugue themes are generally quite standard. Most of them span the traditional compass of a sixth,[8] although a few restrict themselves to a fifth,[9] and some cover an octave. Those that span the eight notes are generally scalar in shape, ascending from the tonic to its octave. The rather unusual subject from *Der Herr ist nahe* (see above), although stretching a minor ninth, is really constructed on the usual sixth (tonic to submediant), with the dominant and submediant degrees doubled at the lower octave. The other subjects move fairly predictably from the tonic to dominant or vice versa. A few return to the tonic. Although Schmitz found that the fugue themes of Heinichen's Masses often repeated motives (and texts), producing a tendency toward classical periodicity, this trend is not yet to be seen in the German church compositions.[10]

Overall Structure of the Fugal Sections

The fugal expositions of these works differ from those in the Masses on a number of counts. In general, they are much more rigid. While Schmitz found that the fugues in the Masses have periodic entries in only one-third of the cases, the proportion in the German church compositions is much higher. These entries are usually close, spaced at two-, two-and-one-half-, three-, or three-and-one-half-measure intervals. The pitch sequences are also rigid, holding strictly to the tonic-dominant pattern.[11]

The fugues in these works are further differentiated from those in the Masses by their order of entries. While Schmitz found almost only high to low voice or low to high voice entry sequences (with twice as many of the former), here we find many mixed-order types.

Some of the fugue subjects are first introduced as free-standing solos, before being treated contrapuntally. In *Lass dichs nicht irren*, the seven-and-one-half-measure fugue theme of the opening choral movement is introduced by the alto, then repeated at the fifth by the tenor, at which point a regular exposition commences. In *Mag auch ein Blinder*, both of the imitative movements introduce their themes this way. In the first movement, the conversational character of the text (which consists of two rhetorical questions) is emphasized by separating the subject and countersubject in the tenor introductory statement.

T: Question #1 (= subject)   Question #2 (= c.s.)
              A: Question #1 & #2 (= s. + c.s.)

Fig. 34. Separation of subject and countersubject in *Mag auch*, I

Two instrumental statements of the theme follow. They act like an episode in separating the introductory statement from the regular exposition that follows. In the fourth movement, a four-measure theme is introduced by the tenor then repeated at the fifth by the violin before it is treated in the usual fugal manner. Here, too, the instrumental statement serves to separate the introduction from the exposition.

The fugal structure in the fifth movement of *Lobe den Herrn* is unusual in a number of ways. The first exposition immediately presents a stretto between the first two voices. This pairing of voices is repeated three times in the third exposition[12] and may have been occasioned by the text taken in its entirety.[13] The middle exposition introduces the voices at more normal spacings of one-and-one-half- and two-measure intervals. The episodes that separate these three expositions are also unusual and will be discussed below.

Quite frequently Heinichen's countersubjects are written in such a way that when they are put with the subject they sound like an accompaniment rather than independent counterpoint. In the fifth movement of *Herr, nun lässest Du*, the countersubject is a sequential repetition of the second part of the subject, allowing melismas of parallel sixths.

Fig. 35. *Herr, nun lässest Du*, V, mm. 43-44

In the final movement of *Einsamkeit*, the countersubject is again harmonically derived from the subject, consisting of arpeggios.

Fig. 36. *Einsamkeit, o stilles Wesen,* VIII, mm. 11-14

Although the countersubject is often harmonically dependent on the subject, the rhythm is frequently a differentiating factor, as in this example from the last movement of *Es lebet Jesus.*

Fig. 37. *Es lebet Jesus unser Hort,* VII, mm. 4-6

In *Der Herr ist nahe,* an interesting rhythmic interplay results when subject and countersubject of the second movement are combined.

Fig. 38. *Der Herr ist nahe,* II, mm. 20-21

Some of Heinichen's two-part fugue themes are constructed in such a way that they can be overlapped with the countersubject in a three-part counterpoint. This happens in the short fugue that begins the opening choral section of *Der Segen des Herrn*. The entries occur at one-measure intervals, and the permutation produces the following pattern:

```
S        A    B    C
A             A    B    C
T                  A    B    C
B                       A    B    C
Vln                          A    B
```

Fig. 39. *Der Segen des Herrn*, choral fugue

In *Ach, was soll ich Sünder machen*, two statements of the countersubject are sometimes combined with one of the parts of the fugue theme. Normally this countersubject is a syncopated descending line. When two simultaneous statements of the countersubject occur, one is pushed onto the beat, so that their movements are staggered. This happens with the first appearance of the bass, which starts with the countersubject before presenting the fugue theme.

Fig. 40. *Ach, was soll ich Sünder machen*, II, mm. 35-37

We noted earlier that instrumental entries of the fugue theme sometimes serve as episodes. In other cases, they expand the texture of the exposition by adding an additional statement of the subject. Examples of this can be found in the fugal expositions in *Der Segen des Herrn* (m. 24), *Ach, was soll ich Sünder machen* (I, m. 42), and *Es lebet*, where the Tenor I is not given a regular fugal entry, but the bass enters twice, and the final clarini entry brings the total to seven:

| B | | T2 | | A |(T1)| S2 | | S1 | | B | |Cl.1|

Fig. 41. Fugal entries in *Es lebet*, VII, mm. 1-13

The episodes in Heinichen's fugues are almost always thematically related to the expositions. On occasion, the material is taken from the countersubject.[14] In *Ach, was soll ich Sünder machen*, the two episodes are only one measure in length (mm. 46, 60). Both are tutti parlando statements of the opening motive of the fugue theme. In the first episode, the original text is used; in the second one, the text from the end of the fugue theme is combined with the opening motive in the same chordal style.

meinen   Jesum lass ich nicht.

Fig. 42. *Ach, was soll ich Sünder machen*, II, m. 60

Most often, however, episodic contrast is achieved by shifting the focus to the instruments. We saw earlier how those expositions that introduced the themes as free-standing solos used instrumental entries to separate these introductions from the regular expositions. This technique is also used to separate expositions in *Herr, nun lässest Du*,[15] *Lobe den Herrn*,[16] and *Es lebet Jesus unser Hort*.[17] In this last example, the episode consists of three one-measure statements in a concertante exchange by the winds, strings, and voices respectively.

The fugal section in the final chorus of *Einsamkeit* really has no episodes. Instead, an exposition by the solo voices is immediately followed by a tutti exposition that retains the same order sequence but adds instrumental doublings. A similar structure is found in the second movement of *Gelobet sei der Herr*. In both examples, a full cadence marks the end of the first exposition.

Since most of Heinichen's fugues are complexes within the structure of larger choral movements, they are usually fairly short, concluding after two expositions. In cantatas like *Mag auch ein Blinder* and *Lass dichs nicht irren*, the solo introductions of the theme (which could perhaps be regarded as expositions) are followed by only one imitative exposition in each case. The fugatos, of course, have only one series of theme statements.[18]

In later expositions, entries of the subject, whether vocal or instrumental, are frequently paired with another voice written in parallel thirds or sixths.[19] This love for parallel thirds is especially obvious in *Der Segen des Herrn.*

Fig. 43. Parallel thirds in *Der Segen des Herrn,* mm. 30-33

As the fugues draw to their conclusion, the vertical emphasis implied by the pairing of voices invariably becomes stronger, and they usually end with a strong homophonic close. In *Herr, nun lässest Du*, the seven-measure closing of the first chorus is given special weight with a *grave* tempo and a concertante exchange in which a chordal statement by the solo voices is echoed by the instruments then followed by a final tutti.

The Introductory Sections

Most of the fugal sections are prefaced with homophonic sections. Almost always this mottolike opening presents the first part of the *dictum*, although occasionally a short text serves both opening and fugue.[20] Sometimes the textures employ tutti block chords in which the instruments basically double the voice parts.[21] In such cases the instruments are often used to bridge the choral phrases. More frequently, Heinichen employs a concertante interplay between voices and instruments and even between voice pairs. In *Herr, nun lässest Du* (mvt. II and V), *Der Herr ist nahe* (mvt. II), and *Gelobet sei der Herr* (mvt. II), this interplay is further enhanced by soli/tutti contrasts. The thematic material in such concertante sections is usually determined by text rhythms then treated in a responsorial fashion between voices and instruments. On occasion, contrasting material is given to the instruments. In *Lass dichs nicht irren* (mvt. I), an instrumental introduction provides a sequential figure that is later alternated with parlando choral statements.[22]

Fig. 44. *Lass dichs nicht irren*, I, mm. 7-9

In *Einsamkeit*, the last movement begins with block chords then proceeds with a 1+3 texture for the words "before they call."[23] In relation to the fugue that follows, this homophonic introduction is slow, consisting of quarter and half notes, compared with the eighths and sixteenths of the fugue. For this reason the "allegro" marking at the fugue probably refers to a relative rather than absolute increase in tempo.

A few of the introductory sections are characterized by imitative textures. In the fourth movement of *Mag auch ein Blinder*, overlapping entries are used to stress the accusatory mood of the text.

Fig. 45. *Mag auch ein Blinder*, IV, mm. 1-2

The six-measure introduction reaches a climax with a tutti statement of this motive. Since only the continuo has been accompanying the voices thus far, the abrupt entry here of the instruments is startling and focuses the listener's attention on the fugue theme that immediately follows.

The fugue in *Ach, was soll ich Sünder machen* is prefaced with two musical sections, each with its own portion of the text. In the first fifteen measures, the violins play the opening of the chorale tune in two-measure fragments, while the vocal parts present independent material in a contrapuntal texture that gradually becomes chordal. The entire section is built on an E pedal tone. The second section takes its cue from the emotion of fear implied by its text. For this reason, Heinichen chooses *stile concitato* in a concertante dialogue between voices and instruments.

Fig. 46. *Stile concitato* in
Ach, was soll ich Sünder machen, II, mm. 18-20

The Concertante Movements

Only a few movements are in concertante style throughout. These include two movements in *Lobe den Herrn*[24] and the first vocal movements of *Meine Seele erhebet den Herrn* and *Es lebet Jesus unser Hort*. The celebratory texts in all of these cantatas make the concertante style a natural choice. In addition to these entire movements, we could add the introductory sections of the type mentioned earlier, most notably the choral openings of *Gelobet* and *Einsamkeit*[25] and the fifth movement of *Herr, nun lässest Du*.

The relatively low proportion of concertante movements shows that they are not nearly as important in the cantatas as in the Masses,[26] and generally the style is more old-fashioned. Whereas the concertante movements in the Masses use ·concerto structures and procedures that Heinichen probably learned while he was in Italy,[27] these works employ a style closer to that of the Venetian concertante motet. The component phrases of Heinichen's texts become the bases for a series of sections, each with its own character.[28] The thematic material in the instrumental parts is usually derived from the vocal parts, and there are no recurring ritornelli.[29] Within this general stylistic framework, Heinichen explores the various ways in which musical dialogue can be established.

Most commonly, a chordal vocal statement in syllabic declamation (parlando) is echoed by the instrumental ensemble and finally climaxed in a tutti. In some instances, the instrumental version may be somewhat ornamented, as in the fifth movement of *Herr, nun lässest Du.*

Fig. 47. *Herr, nun lässest Du*, V, mm. 4-5

Imitative sections may also be echoed by the instruments as in this example from *Gelobet*, II.

Fig. 48. *Gelobet sei der Herr*, II, mm. 8-10

In *Meine Seele erhebet den Herrn*, Heinichen has four sound groups at his disposal, with which he explores various combinations: brasses, strings, and two SATB choirs. In the instrumental introduction, the winds alternate with the strings. In tutti sections, the winds are often paired with choir I, the strings with choir II. When he wishes to reduce the texture as much as possible, Heinichen begins with one unaccompanied voice, then adds the other voices of that choir with continuo. This choral statement is then echoed by the other choir. In the second section of the text ("und mein Geist freuet sich"), Heinichen begins with this procedure then repeats it in an intensified manner by beginning with the unaccompanied basses of *both* choirs (m. 38), adding layers of sound until he achieves a grand tutti.

```
mm.           |30        35        40        45

clarini       |              XX  XX      XXXXXXXXX
clarini       |              XX  XX      XXXXXXXXX
trombe        |              XX  XX      XXXXXXXXX
tamburo       |              XX  XX      XXXXXXXXX

vl.           |          XXXXX         XXXXXXXXXXXXXXX
vl.           |          XXXXX         XXXXXXXXXXXXXXX
vl.           |          XXXXX         XXXXXXXXXXXXXXX

S             |     XXXXX X XX    XXXX X XXXXXXXXXX
A             |      XXXX X XX         X XXXXXXXXXX
T             |      XXXX X XX         X XXXXXXXXXX
B             |      XXXX X XX    XXXXX X XXXXXXXXXX

S             |XXXXX    X XXX    XXXXX X XXXXXXXXX
A             |XXXX     X XXX        X X XXXXXXXXX
T             |XXXX     X XXX        X X XXXXXXXXX
B             |XXXX     X XXX    XXXXXX X XXXXXXXXX

B.c.          | XXXXXXXXXXXXXXXX XXXXXXXXXXXXXXXXX
```

Fig. 49. *Meine Seele erhebet den Herrn*, I, 30-46

A similar sixteen-part texture characterizes the triumphant ending of the first chorus in *Es lebet Jesus unser Hort.*

In cases where Heinichen sets a solo voice off against a larger ensemble, he most often chooses the soprano. Sometimes these solo sections are quite lengthy. In *Lobe den Herrn*, an accompanied soprano solo lasts fourteen measures before cadencing with a choral tutti. In the ninth movement of the same cantata, an introductory motto statement is followed by a solo sequence for soprano, alto, and tenor/bass duet respectively. Of these passages, the soprano solo is the only one that has the entire text, and in the following section (mm. 19-26) the soprano again leads the choir in a 1+3 texture. In the final (and only choral) movement of *Gegrüsset seist du*, on the other hand, Heinichen consistently introduces each tutti section with an alto solo, the middle voice of the five-part vocal texture.

Heinichen also likes to contrast tutti sections with duets. These are usually melismas in parallel thirds or sixths. In the last movement mentioned above, the final five-measure tutti is prefaced by two measures of just such melismas played by the violins. Vocal duets of the same type separate tutti sections in the second movement of that cantata.[30] In the only choral movement of *Meine Seele* (see above), the duets occur between like voice parts of the two choirs and are quasi-canonic, producing the same effect.[31] The soprano duet that begins the choral opening of *Es lebet* is also imitative but is written in such a way as to produce contrary motion after the entry of the second voice.

Imitative Motet Style

Although many of the movements we have just discussed incorporated aspects of old motet style (such as a sectionalized form based on the phrase structure of the text), the concertante elements in these movements (such as rhythmically independent instrumental parts and the resulting interplay between instruments and voices) were clearly the stronger of the two influences.

Concerning the old motet *alla breve* style Heinichen wrote,

> This antique, affective style is certainly the most beautiful and convenient in which a composer can best show his fundamental understanding and exactness in composing. For the chords in this style must at all times be pure, their progression and resolution strict and removed from all liberties, the *cantabile* preserved without numerous leaps in all parts. The latter (should be) laden with syncopations and beautiful suspensions of consonances and dissonances, and all the parts (should be) filled throughout with affective thoughts, themes, and imitations (but) without anything fanciful in character. Here one seeks the strict composer.[32]

Only one of Heinichen's movements is marked ₵. It appears at the end of *Der Segen des Herrn* and is a setting of I Timothy 4:8, a text with a reference to timelessness ("...having promise of the life that now is, and of that which is to come."). The first phrase of the text is presented in two successive points of imitation (twelve, and twelve and one-half measures long, respectively). The first of these is in strict imitation and accompanied only by continuo. The second point is treated more freely, and string doublings are added. Noteworthy is the violin I part, whose independent line, in effect, expands the texture to five voices for the rest of the movement. The second (and last) phrase of text is treated more freely throughout. It begins with a soprano/bass duet in which the soprano line deviates slightly from the norm in order to produce a suspension against the bass. The dissonance is emphasized with a trill in the continuo bass.

Fig. 50. *Der Segen des Herrn*, mm. 152-154

The *cantabile* character that Heinichen mentioned is preserved throughout the movement. The lines flow in gentle rhythms of mostly half- and quarter-note values, and the melodic movement is largely by step.

Sections or movements in a more loosely-imitative style are found elsewhere in Heinichen's cantatas. The opening narrative of *Es naheten aber zu Jesu* possesses the dramatic qualities characteristic of Passion settings, and Heinichen uses imitative style to represent the disorder of the *turba* after an introductory solo by the tenor "evangelist".

Fig. 51. *Es naheten aber zu Jesu*, I, mm. 21-24

In the generally concertante opening choral movement of *Lobe den Herrn*, one of the Allegro sections (mm. 29-49) is written in a loosely imitative style in which only the opening motive stays the same after the initial set of entries.

Fig. 52. *Lobe den Herrn*, II, mm. 33-35

The instruments double the voices but occasionally also add additional thematic entrances at vocal cadences.

The Chorales

Over half of Heinichen's German church compositions end with a chorale. The trend during the eighteenth century was for chorale settings to become increasingly simple[33] or to be omitted entirely.[34] Heinichen's simplest settings have no elaboration at all, and the instruments play *colla parte*.[35] In some works, Heinichen alternates unadorned chorale phrases with instrumental interludes. In *Herr, nun lässest Du*, the interludes are all derived from the twenty-four-measure instrumental introduction, which is finally repeated in its entirety as a da capo. While the ritornelli help unify the movement, they also provide contrast with the choral phrases; a contrast that is emphasized by silencing even the continuo during the choral passages. *Der Herr ist nahe* also has its chorale phrases interspersed with instrumental interludes. Further interest is added by an elaborated figured bass line, which, however, stops for the nine-measure instrumental coda.

Instrumental obbligato parts are used in a number of settings to provide musical interest. The chorale in *Der Segen des Herrn* (it appears as the second-last movement) has independent violin parts of constant triplets that frequently move in contrary motion and contrast with the duple eighths of the voice parts. The violas double vocal lines.

Fig. 53. *Der Segen des Herrn*, mm. 115-117

In *Lass dichs nicht irren*, the sixteenth-note figures of the unison violins bring back the material from the first movement (see above).

Fig. 54. *Lass dichs nicht irren*, VIII, mm. 2-3

We have seen that *Mag auch ein Blinder* is similar to the above cantata in several ways. Its chorale setting, too, is similar, with the appearance of sixteenth-note runs in the violins. This time they are not in unison, however, nor do they relate to any previous thematic material.

Finally, we examine the chorale in *Es naheten aber zu Jesu*. It appears twice: one stanza is sung in the middle of the cantata, the other at the end. Each phrase of the text is introduced with a vocal solo that preserves the words but departs musically from the chorale model. Instrumental doublings appear in the choral passages and are given pulsing eighth notes for greater rhythmic thrust.

Fig. 55. *Es naheten aber zu Jesu*, V/X, mm. 1-3

Fig. 56. *Es naheten aber zu Jesu*, V/X, mm. 7-8

In summary we may conclude that, despite the reservations Heinichen expressed regarding the use of counterpoint, he still preferred the fugue over other compositional styles in his German church compositions. This preference likely reflects the early dates of these works, for the later Masses reportedly have a lower proportion of fugal movements and a correspondingly higher proportion of concertante movements. Even in the movements that are predominantly fugal, however, Heinichen's interest in harmonic considerations is clear. Homophonic introductions and conclusions are common, and even the counterpoint itself is always harmonically conceived. Aside from such fugal movements, ones in the strict *stile antico* of the motet are rare. Concertante movements are generally of a traditional sort, the text being introduced phrase by phrase in choral statements that are then echoed by the instruments. Finally, Heinichen's chorale settings employ some elaborations, chiefly in the form of instrumental obbligatos, but are still generally simple and, thus, conform to the eighteenth-century trend away from complex chorale settings.

Chapter 9. Notes

1. In *Einsamkeit*, for instance, the absence of ripieno parts for the fifth movement might argue for a soloistic interpretation. On the other hand, since none of the ensemble movements have "soli/tutti" markings, one might argue that the ripieno parts simply augmented a chamber choir. Since the text here is being literally depicted ("Where two or three gather..."), and since the orchestration consists only of continuo accompaniment, a performance by four soloists would appear preferable.

2. According to Schmitz, Heinichen's earlier Masses have more fugues than his later ones. See Schmitz, p. 55. During the last years of his life, Heinichen's interest in contrapuntal technique apparently revived, however, for according to Hiller, he was planning a contrapuntal Mass when he died. This Mass was to be in the style of Praenestino (Palestrina), Gasparini, Lotti, and especially Fux, and would include all types of counterpoints and canons. His intention was to publish the Mass in a book that would also include a systematic explanation of all "contrapuntal and canonic devices." See Hiller, pp. 224, 225.

3. Heinichen, *General-Bass*, pp. 6-9, trans. in Buelow, "Heinichen's General-Bass," pp. 556-560.

4. This was a standard pattern for *dicta* in the eighteenth century. See Feder, col. 601.

5. "Nun so fahr ich Himmelauf" in *Herr, nun lässest Du*, and "Wo zwei oder drei" in *Einsamkeit*.

6. Opening fugue in *Herr, nun lässest Du*.

7. *Herr, nun lässest Du*, I, *Lass dichs*, IV, *Mag auch*, I and IV, *Lobe*, V.

8. This is also true of his Masses. See Schmitz, p. 59.

9. *Der Segen des Herrn*, I, *Lass dich's nicht irren*, I.

10. See Schmitz, p. 59.

11. In movement V of *Herr*, the second exposition begins just after a modulation to the dominant, and the fugue returns to the tonic by means of a V-I-V-I series of entries. The fugue in *Gelobet* is an exception to the rule, with entries on F, F, G and G.

12. A/S in m. 25, Vln I/T in mm. 27-28, Vln II/B in m. 30.

13. "For as the heaven is high above the earth, so His mercy holds sway over those who fear him."

14. *Der Herr ist nahe*, II, mm. 29-31.

15. II, mm. 28-31.

16. V, mm. 13-16. The second episode (m. 24) in *Lobe den Herrn* consists of a one-measure modulation to the subdominant.

17. VII, mm. 14-16.

18. *Herr*, VII, mm. 79-85, *Lass*, IV, mm. 15-32, *Einsamkeit*, V, mm. 1-7.

19. Thirds are supplied by the instruments in *Gelobet*, II, mm. 26-27.

20. *Herr, nun lässest Du*, II.

21. *Lass dichs nicht irren*, IV.

22. This figure returns in the last movement of the cantata. See below.

23. See chapter 8.

24. II and IX.

25. The first choral movement is mvt. III.

26. Schmitz found forty-seven concertante movements and even one purely instrumental movement in the Masses compared with fifty-one fugal movements. See Schmitz, pp. 56, 108.

27. This includes, most significantly, thematically unified movements with recurring ritornelli. Schmitz points out similarities between various of Heinichen's Mass movements and Vivaldi's *Gloria*. Since Vivaldi composed this work in Venice while Heinichen was visiting that city (ca. 1715), Schmitz believes Heinichen learned many of his later techniques from Vivaldi. For comparisons between Heinichen and Vivaldi, see Schmitz, pp. 108-109, 119-121, 124-125, 127-132.

28. In mvt. II of *Lobe den Herrn* the sections are marked with contrasting tempi.

29. One exception can be found in *Meine Seele* where a truncated version of the instrumental introduction follows the opening vocal statement, a two-measure soprano duet.

30. Mm. 10-12, 13-14.

31. Mm. 8-9 (S1 and S2), mm. 13-14 (T1 and T2), mm. 18-21 (B1 and B2), mm. 23-25 (S1 and S2). Notice that there are two soprano duets but no alto duet.

32. Heinichen, *Der General-Bass*, p. 333, trans. in Buelow, *Thorough-Bass*, p. 135.

33. Feder, "Die Kantate", col. 601.

34. Feder, "Die Kantate," col. 601; Fritz Treiber, "Die thüringisch-sächsische Kirchenkantate zur Zeit des jungen J.S. Bach (etwa 1700-1723)," *Archiv für Musikforschung*, II(1937):137.

35. *Gelobet* and *Lobe den Herrn*.

10.
The Structure of the Solo Movements

The solo movements in Heinichen's German church compositions never carry designations such as aria, recitative, or arioso. This holds true of all the manuscripts, whether they be sets of performing parts or scores. In two sets of performing parts (*Herr, nun lässest Du* and *Gelobet sei der Herr*),[1] the term aria is used in the tacet parts. It is never used in the part that actually contains the solo, however. Two other sets of parts (*Der Herr ist nahe* and *Einsamkeit*) use the term solo in the tacet parts. These works, nevertheless, contain solo movements of all three types, with the recitative and arioso movements being far outnumbered by the arias.

Recitative and Arioso Movements

Many of the works have no recitative or arioso movements at all. In those that do, the recitatives fulfill a variety of structural functions. In *Lobe den Herrn*, a cantata that combines rhymed paraphrases of verses from Psalm 103 with literal ones, Heinichen gets through verse 12 the quickest way possible, by setting the literal scripture in a five-measure recitative. His reason for doing this appears to be a desire to maintain the symmetrical structure of the cantata. In its present form, the two arias in the first half of the cantata are counterbalanced with two in the second. The recitative is too short to upset this balance.[2]

In the chorale cantata, *Ach, was soll ich Sünder machen*, Heinichen similarly chose to set the second stanza as a modest ten-measure recitative for bass voice. Coming, as it does, after the involved opening chorus, this recitative, with its sustained string accompaniment, provides a moment of reflective pause before the bass aria that follows.

The architectural role of the recitatives in *Meine Seele erhebet den Herrn* has already been briefly mentioned in chapter six. After an opening *dicta*, selected verses of the Magnificat text are set as three tenor recitatives. They are separated by duets setting reflective texts for like voice parts. The recitatives are all short, measuring five, seven, and six measures, respectively.

A much longer recitative follows the opening *dicta* of *Lass dichs nicht irren*. For the most part, its twenty-four measures are fragmented into one-measure units, usually following the pattern (4/4 ♪♫ ♫|♩). Frequently, these fragments include repeated notes and outline a particular chord. The bass moves mostly in whole notes, and the overall effect is too static to be effective.[3] This static quality is also characteristic of the recitatives in *Es naheten* and *Mag auch ein Blinder*. The similarity of the two recitatives in *Mag auch ein Blinder* is remarkable:

So gehts der tief in blindem Irrtum steckt,dünkt

Fig. 57. *Mag auch ein Blinder*, II, mm. 1-2

Man weiss die kleinen Sünden da man doch grösser tat

Fig. 58. *Mag auch ein Blinder*, V, mm. 1-3

Altogether, Heinichen's recitatives tend to be tonally bound. In the seventh movement of *Lass dichs nicht irren*, for instance, a six-measure recitative (twenty-four beats) contains thirteen beats of D major. There is no interior modulation at all. Those recitatives that do modulate seldom do so as adventurously as Bach's, and they usually travel no farther afield than the dominant or parallel major/minor. Tonally unstable chords, such as diminished seventh chords, are only seldom used, particularly in the cantatas mentioned above. Examples of more interesting recitatives include the one in *Ach, was soll ich Sünder machen*, which moves from C major to B major, and movement V in *Meine Seele*, which makes effective use of diminished chords. The melodic movement at cadences is seldom the expected descending fourth of tonic to dominant scale degrees. In several cases, although the I-V melodic pattern is followed in the vocal part, the fifth scale-degree is first prepared with the sixth, as in this example from *Mag auch ein Blinder*.[4]

Fig. 59 *Mag auch ein Blinder*, V, mm. 11-12

This recitative from *Meine Seele* cadences, as do some others, with a melodically descending third.

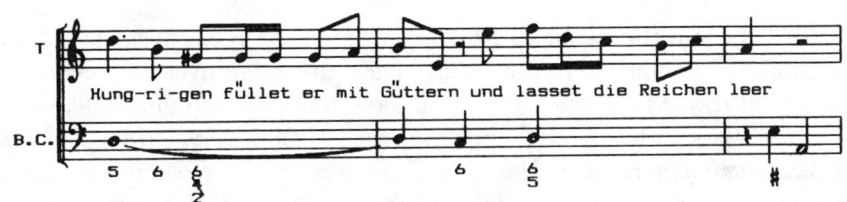

Fig. 60. *Meine Seele erhebet den Herrn*, V, mm. 5-7

The arioso ending of the final recitative in *Meine Seele* hints at a cadence in C with an implied G⁷ chord, then moves unexpectedly to G.

Fig. 61. *Meine Seele erhebet den Herrn*, VII, mm. 5-6

In the recitative from *Ach, was soll ich Sünder machen*, the voice part cadences with a V-I movement, but the tonic harmony is avoided in the accompanying parts. This deceptive cadence is then immediately followed by an authentic cadence:

- ficht, meinen Jesum lass ich nicht

Fig. 62. *Ach, was soll ich Sünder machen*, II, mm. 8-10

All of Heinichen's recitatives (even the secco recitatives) tend to have a *cantabile* character. It is not unusual for the recitatives to become even more lyrical toward the end, and some move directly into an arialike *cavata*.[5] The three works where this happens are *Lass dichs nicht irren*, *Es naheten*, and *Mag auch ein Blinder*: the three cantatas that are similar in so many other ways. *Lass dichs* and *Mag auch ein Blinder* each have two such recitative/*cavata* combinations. In each case, the *cavata* is strophic. Usually the two strophes are assigned to contrasting voice parts. An exception is the second example in *Lass dichs*, where an arioso[6] for alto is directly followed by a two-strophe aria, both strophes being assigned to the alto.

In two instances, the strophic aria is prepared by an instrumental figure at the end of the recitative.[7] In both cases, the figure is based on material from the following aria, and this relationship helps bind the two sections together.

Two ariosos can be found in *Es naheten aber zu Jesu*. In movement III, a two-measure narration by the tenor is followed, without pause, by a forty-two measure arioso for bass, accompanied by continuo alone. It is declamatory and includes a great deal of syllabic text-setting with frequent repeated notes. Important words are set as melismas, however, and the melody has a distinct *cantabile* quality. This is especially evident in the triple section that ends the movement with the text "freuet euch mit mir..." The other arioso is movement VIII, a counterpart to the above arioso, on the other side of the structural arch.[8] This movement is accompanied by the strings, which share some of the voice part's motivic material.

The sixth movement of *Herr, nun lässest Du* is designated as an aria in the tacet parts but exhibits characteristics of an arioso, especially in the adagio section, where syllabic declamation is accompanied by descending violin arpeggios and a pulsing bass. The harmonic modulations of this section make it particularly effective.[9] The fourth movement of *Ach, was soll ich Sünder machen* is, in many ways, similar. Also for bass voice, this movement has pulsing eighth notes that move chromatically in all three accompanying violin parts, as well as the continuo. The text-setting is largely syllabic, with numerous repeated notes corresponding with the pulsing duples of the accompaniment.

The Arias

A study of the arias reveals a variety of types that can, nevertheless, be divided generally into four groups:

1. Arias characterized by simple melodies with step-wise motion, and syllabic declamation
2. Arias differentiated from the above type by more complex structures
3. Operatic arias without da capo
4. Operatic da capo arias

The arias belonging to the first two categories exhibit the simplicity of the archaic strophic aria. Only *Lass dichs*, *Mag auch*, and *Es naheten* contain solo movements that are actually strophic, however, and in the first two of these cantatas, the strophic movements are really *cavate*.[10] A closer look at these *cavate* reveals some interesting architectural similarities. Movement III of *Lass dichs* has an A B A form and incorporates a ritornello (played by strings) that is expanded for the introduction and conclusion. The first strophe is given to the tenor, the second to the soprano. The strings continue to play during the vocal sections, and since their accompaniment material is related to the ritornello, the structure is partially obscured.[11]

	Rit.	‖: T/S+Str.	Rit.	T/S+Vl.	Rit.	T/S+Str.	Rit. :‖
	(4)	(2)	(2)	(3)	(2)	(2)	(4)

| | | A | | B | | A | |

Fig. 63. Three part structure in *Lass dichs nicht irren*, III

The repetition of the A section (both words and music) in a ternary form is also found in movement III of *Mag auch* (also a *cavata*), but in this case the instrumental interludes are not real ritornelli. In this example, too, the second A section is written out.

A comparison of the second *cavata* in each of the above two cantatas also reveals a parallel construction; in this case, both movements have a two-part structure in which the first section presents only voice and continuo, the second, only the instruments. Although the two *cavate* differ greatly in length, the basic structure is the same.[12]

```
Lass dichs                          Mag auch

‖  Voice + B.c.  |  Instr.  ‖    ‖  Voice + B.c.  |  Instr.  ‖

|     7 mm.      |  6 mm.  |    |     28 mm.     |  23 mm.  |
```

Fig. 64. A comparison of *Lass dichs*, VI, and *Mag auch*, VI

A strophic aria in *Es naheten* (movement IX) follows the same pattern but differs in its alteration of 3/4 and 4/4 meters. The other strophic aria in this cantata is accompanied by strings throughout; most of the time the strings simply play quarter note chords on the first and third beats.

The texts of the *cavate* in *Lass dichs* and *Mag auch* are striking for their blatant moralizing. The following example appears in *Lass dichs*, III:

Was Gepränge und Gesänge
Sind bei grossen Leichen doch.
Wird der Arme hingetragen,
Wird man wenig nach ihn fragen,
Sterb er oder leb er noch.

(What pomp and singing
There is at important funerals.
But if the poor man is carried away,
Few ask
Whether he is dying or still lives.)

In *Mag auch*, a chattering declamation results from assigning separate syllables to leaping sixteenth notes.

und ver-lass den Affen Wahn, ver-lass den Affen Wahn

Fig. 65. *Mag auch ein Blinder*, III, m. 21

Arias that are not strophic but that have the melodic simplicity of the strophic aria can be found in other church compositions by Heinichen. The alto aria of *Lobe den Herrn flows* in a gentle 6/8 meter, with vocal cadences being punctuated by woodwind interludes one to four measures in length.[13] The tenor aria of the same work is another example of the simple cantabile style. Here, not only the voice but also the two viola parts that accompany the voice throughout the aria move in relatively slow note values (quarter notes and eighths) and mostly by step.

A few arias, although similar to the above arias in their melodic movement, also employ the more complex motto technique in which a melodic phrase is sung by the voice, echoed by the instruments, then taken up again and extended by the voice. Often this opening phrase becomes a unifying element for the whole movement. In the ninety-one-measure soprano aria of *Ach, was soll ich Sünder machen*, the opening phrase is expanded periodically into what eventually becomes a four-phrase ritornello.[14] The reappearance of this ritornello at the end of the movement corresponds to a return to the original key. Soprano and instruments alternate throughout.[15] This aria, like some of those cited below, has no instrumental introduction.

```
|S |I |  S  |I |   S   |    I    | S  |I |  S   |    I    |

|4 |4 | 4+4 |3 | 4+3+3 | 4+4+3+3 | 10 |9 |  14  | 4+4+3+4 |
|a |a | a b |c | b c c | a b c c |    |  |      | a b c c |
 GM                                Em              GM
```

Fig. 66. Structure of *Ach, was soll ich Sünder machen*, VII

This additive procedure is even clearer in the tenor solo of *Der Segen des Herrn*. Here, too, the instruments echo the voice in their interludes.

T	I	T	I	T	I
2	2	3+2	3+2	3+3+3+(4+6+5)	3+3+5
a	a	a b	a b	a b b c	a b c

Fig. 67. Additive procedure in *Der Segen des Herrn*, mm. 66-114

The short alto solo in the same work also begins with a motto that is repeated after an instrumental response then given its completion. The interlude in this case does not repeat the vocal motive but answers it.

Vns.

A

Die blos-se Arbeit   Die blos- se Arbeit machts nicht aus

Fig. 68. *Der Segen des Herrn*, mm. 39-40

In the tenor aria of *Der Herr ist nahe* we find a songlike aria in which solo vocal phrases alternate with a thematically independent ritornello. Although the aria is still through-composed, the ritornelli provide a unity not present in those arias where the instruments simply echo the vocal phrases. The additive procedure is also evident here, but since the instruments do not imitate the voice, we cannot speak of an actual motto aria.

Many of Heinichen's solo arias and duets incorporate at least some of the compositional techniques of the contemporary opera aria without, however, adopting the da capo form: recurring ritornelli, ostinati, word and phrase repetition, and, invariably, more demanding vocal lines.

The formal unity of these movements spans a wide spectrum. Least unified, usually, are the through-composed movements in which vocal phrases alternate with instrumental interludes. Most frequently, such interludes echo the preceding vocal phrases.[16] This responsorial principle is expanded to polychoral dimensions in the tenor duet of *Es lebet Jesus*. Two long sections for voices and continuo are separated by interludes that are thematically related to the foregoing vocal duet and in which responsorial statements between the strings and winds are climaxed with tutti statements.

In the short duet for alto and tenor in *Gelobet sei der Herr*, Heinichen achieves a quasi-ternary form (and hence greater unity than in the examples cited above) by making the first and last pairs of such statements similar.[17] The instrumental echoes in these two sections are, in fact, identical. A brief modulation to the relative major in the middle section helps delineate the form.

A/T	I	A/T	I	A/T	I
2.5	3.5	4	1.5	4	3.5
A		B		A	

Fig. 69. *Gelobet sei der Herr*, VII

In the third movement of *Lobe den Herrn*, the instrumental interludes are simply thematically unrelated cadential figures. A certain sense of unity is provided by the bass in these interludes, however, which always consists of running sixteenth notes and, in that respect, imitates the vocal line. In the bass aria of the same work, a florid bass line that is separate from the continuo bass (played by bassone and chalcedono) operates in a similar way. At the start, the chalcedono accompanies the voice throughout, while the bassone joins during the florid interludes. As the movement progresses, however, both of the obbligato bass parts accompany the singer, at times continuing their sixteenth notes during the vocal phrases.

In several of his solo movements, Heinichen uses a bass ostinato as a unifying device. One of the more tightly organized movements is the bass aria in *Gelobet sei der Herr*. The four-and-one-half-measure ostinato has two parts and is sometimes extended by repeating the B section. Toward the end of the aria, two statements of the B section are transposed up a fifth.[18] Only three measures contain filler material (F).

```
A   B   B   A   B   F   B   A   B  (B   B)*  F   A   B   B
2  2.5 2.5  2   2   2   2   2   2   2    2   1   2   2   3
                                              * transposed
```

Fig. 70. Ostinato structure in *Gelobet sei der Herr*, IV

In the duet of *Herr, nun lässest Du*, the treatment of the ostinato is less literal, appearing in its original form mostly in the interludes.[19] In the bass aria of *Es lebet*, the ostinato is identical with the often-repeated opening vocal phrase, and the two lines grapple in a graphic depiction of the text. As the movement modulates from A minor to the relative major, the phrase is transposed.

Fig. 71. *Es lebet Jesus unser Hort,* III, mm. 9-10

In movement IV of *Der Herr ist nahe,* a descending scalar bass figure played by the bassoon alternates with an arpeggiated one played by the violins, while the continuo gives minimal support, often playing only on the first and third beats of the measure. Heinichen's intent was, no doubt, to depict the struggle described in the text.[20] He introduces the two combatting figures in the eight-measure introduction, then uses them throughout the movement as a unifying device. Sometimes the two figures exchange places, as in measure 10.

Fig. 72. *Der Herr ist nahe,* IV, mm. 10-11

Many of Heinichen's more unified movements incorporate ritornelli and some degree of recapitulation. Although ritornelli are usually associated with da capo form, they can also be found in movements without da capo. We have already mentioned a few examples of such movements in our discussion of motto arias. Other examples include the bass aria of *Es naheten,* in which a ritornello marks the end of the first and third parts. Although the ritornello confirms a three-part form, the sense of recapitulation is initially suggested by a four-measure bass solo with continuo reminiscent of the movement's opening.

B.c.	B+B.c.	Rit.	B+B.c.+Vls.	B+B.c.	Rit.
4	4	3.5	14.5	4	5

Fig. 73. Ternary form in *Es naheten aber zu Jesu*, II

In the opening section of the alto aria of *Es lebet Jesus*, the ritornello consists of an ascending chromatic line, played by the flute.

Fig. 74. *Es lebet Jesus unser Hort*, V, mm. 4-5

During the vocal phrases, the flute is either silent, or it imitates the voice.[21] In the second (Allegro) section of the aria, the flute abandons its ostinato figure and accompanies the voice in thirds and sixths that are imitatively derived.

Some of Heinichen's arias show the beginnings of da capo form in their repetition of the instrumental introduction at the end of the movement. Sometimes this repetition is literal and is, therefore, simply indicated with a dal segno or da capo rubric. Such is the case in the alto aria of *Der Herr ist nahe*. In this aria, however, the instrumental introduction is prefaced by a short vocal motto. When the instrumental section is repeated at the end of the aria, a repetition of the motto is avoided by means of a dal segno rubric. The introductory ritornello also provides the thematic material for the short interludes that appear in the first vocal section of the aria.[22] Before the opening ritornello reappears, a section for alto (designated "A" in the diagram) and continuo alone, modulating briefly to the parallel minor, provides contrast.

A		Rit.		A+Rit.		A		Rit.	
3		16		31		15		16	

Fig. 75. Structure of *Der Herr ist nahe*, V

The structure of the tenor aria in *Einsamkeit* is very similar. In this case, however, the vocal motto appears after the instrumental section, and so a da capo rubric can be used.[23] With the exception of a two-measure instrumental response to the vocal motto, the inner ritornelli are usually four measures long and alternate with vocal phrases of the same length.

Rit.		T/Rit.		Rit.	
24		82		24	

Fig. 76. Structure of *Einsamkeit, o stilles Wesen*, VII

The structure of the tenor duet in *Meine Seele* also has a motto *after* the instrumental introduction, and so a da capo rubric can be used here as well. In this aria, however, not only the inner ritornelli are derived from the instrumental introduction but also the vocal lines themselves. Another observable difference between this aria and the one in *Einsamkeit* is the less symmetrical phrase structure here.

In the alto duet of *Meine Seele*, Heinichen chose to end the movement with a slightly altered version of the instrumental introduction. Other than an exchange between the two violin parts, the changes are minor, but they nevertheless required rewriting the section at the end. The inner ritornelli are based on this material as usual.

In movement VII of *Es naheten*, Heinichen uses the dal segno for exactly the opposite purpose to that in the aria from *Der Herr ist nahe*. The structure of this aria is like that of the da capo examples cited above: an instrumental introduction is followed by a vocal motto, which is repeated and extended after an instrumental interlude.[24] At the end of the aria, Heinichen uses the dal segno to avoid repeating the instrumental introduction, choosing to repeat the opening vocal phrase (with motto) instead.

We come finally to Heinichen's full-fledged da capo arias. As we would expect, this category includes the longest solo movements.[25] It also includes some relatively short movements. The da capo duet in *Es lebet Jesus* is especially short (48 measures). In two instances (*Gelobet*, III; *Es lebet*, VI) the da capo sections contain some changes and are written out. In the former case the changes are minor; in the latter, the modifications include a slight change of text as well as an extended final cadence.

The overall shape of Heinichen's da capo arias usually follows the accepted proportional plan, in which the first of the two sections is given greater length. The relative difference in length between the two sections varies from a ratio of 3:2[26] to one of 4:1.[27] The two arias in *Einsamkeit* reverse the emphasis by making the second part significantly longer than the first. This is especially striking in movement IV, an alto aria with a B section that is almost twice the length of the A section. A similar ratio occurs in the soprano aria of *Gelobet*. Here, the da capo is written out and contains minor changes.

Usually the two sections of the aria are differentiated with a modulation to the relative major/minor tonality. In this matter, too, the arias of *Einsamkeit* are unconventional. In the C major alto aria, although the second section begins in A minor, it shifts abruptly to F major after eight measures and remains in that key until the da capo, producing a plagal relationship at that point. In the sixth movement of the same cantata, the B section continues in the D minor tonality of the A section, only reaching the relative major in measure 23. The B section then modulates back to D minor and finally cadences on A minor.

In the third movement of *Herr, nun lässest Du*, the B section begins and ends in the A major tonality of the first section but modulates to B minor in the interim. The contrast produced within the B section by this modulation to B minor is heightened by a tempo change and the reintroduction of the oboe obbligato. The only factors differentiating the A and B section, on the other hand, are the change of meter (3/2 to C), and the reduction of texture (the oboes are dropped).

A change of tempo also divides the B section of the tenor aria of *Herr, nun lässest Du* into two parts. Since no modulation is involved, however, and since more factors differentiate the A and B sections of the aria than in the previous example,[28] a three-part da capo form is left intact.

Although omission of the obbligato instruments is often used as a means of differentiating the B section, contrast can also be achieved by changing the style of the obbligato. In *Einsamkeit*, VI, the obbligato violins (I and II playing in unison) have an idiomatic figure consisting of Alberti-like arpeggios to depict the text "Ich will künftig disputieren."[29] In the B section, the violins switch to cantabile lines that, now alternate with the vocal phrases, now move in tenths with the voice. Especially striking is the duet in measures 31-35 on the text "führt er mich schon bei der Hand."[30]

sage führt er mich schon bei der Hand

Fig. 77. *Einsamkeit, o stilles Wesen*, VI, mm. 31-33

Da capo arias that incorporate ritornello procedures are also common. Most frequently, these occur within the A section. In movement III of *Der Herr ist nahe*, an eleven-measure ritornello whose first phrase corresponds with the opening vocal phrase,[31] begins and ends the A section of the aria. By means of motto procedure, this phrase is echoed by the violins after the initial vocal statement. The later interludes (except, of course, the one that ends the A section) are not closely related to the ritornello, however.

Rit.	Alto + interludes	Rit.	Alto	da capo
11	30	11	25	
Dm			FM	

Fig. 78. *Der Herr ist nahe*, III

A similar structure characterizes the soprano duet of *Meine Seele*. In the A section, the violins play a unison obbligato that is thematically derived from the ritornello. This obbligato disappears in the expected manner at the beginning of the B section but reappears once as a brief interlude.[32]

Rit.	S+S+Vls.	Rit.	S+S	da capo
5	17	5	9	
FM			Dm	

Fig. 79. *Meine Seele erhebet den Herrn*, II

The bass duet of this cantata follows the same plan, with a ritornello beginning and ending the A section. As is often the case in arias using motto procedure, this ritornello is derived from the opening vocal figure. In this instance, the correspondence is not literal; while the duet begins with ascending C major arpeggios (sung canonically), the trumpet obbligato reverses this direction.

We may summarize our structural examination of the solo movements with several generalizations. Recitatives do not appear often and, when they do, they are usually insignificant, both in terms of length and expressiveness. The arias, on the other hand, span a wide style spectrum, ranging from simple, strophic ones with syllabic, step-wise moving melodies to operatic, da capo arias unified with recurring ritornelli. In between these two extremes are a variety of specimens including some that have the simplicity of the first type but also independent, recurring instrumental parts, and operatic arias with motivic unity but without da capo.

Chapter 10. Notes

1. The later version of this cantata uses both "aria" and "solo" in the tacet parts.

2. See chapter 7.

3. Mattheson warns against such pauses and repetitions. See Mattheson, *Capellmeister*, p. 205.

4. Also mvt. II of the same cantata and mvt. II of *Lass dichs nicht irren*.

5. Neumeister points out that whatever such a movement may be called, it is set as an arioso. Hunold, p. 228.

6. The step-wise movement of the vocal line, and the melisma on "Prangen" suggest the designation "arioso".

7. *Lass dichs*, V, m. 11; *Mag auch* II, m. 12.

8. For further discussion of this cantata's symmetrical structure, see chapter 7.

9. For a further discussion, see chapter 12.

10. See above. Librettists who designated certain of their texts *cavata* include J.G. Neukirch and Neumeister. See Brausch, p. 62.

11. In the diagram the numbers indicate the numbers of measures. The repeat signs indicate successive stanzas.

12. The vocal line of the example cited from *Mag auch* is written out twice, once in the alto clef, once in the bass clef. These two lines appear one above the other in scorelike arrangement, and are marked "v.1," "v.2," respectively. Although this practice was not uncommon (see Feder, col. 592.), this is the only time it occurs in these works. Since the manuscript is a score (and so would not be used by the singers), and since the previous two-strophe movement for tenor and soprano presents its line in the tenor clef only, it is unclear why the copyist went to the extra work of writing out this part a second time.

13. Perhaps this aria is related to the barcarole strophic aria type mentioned by Treiber. See Treiber, p. 147.

14. The alto aria in the same cantata has a similar, although less complex, structure in the second of its two parts.

15. In the diagram, instrumental sections are designated "I."

16. All four of the arias in *Gegrüsset seist du*.

17. Vocal phrase plus instrumental echo.

18. Mm. 20-23.

19. This duet is one of Heinichen's few "continuo arias." Another example is the alto aria in *Einsamkeit*. In many sectional arias, especially in the da capo arias, it is common for one section to have only continuo accompaniment.

20. "Jesus hat den Stich erlitten."

21. Sometimes this imitation is canonic.

22. There are three of these ritornelli. One of them overlaps the vocal phrase by two measures (mm. 23, 24), another overlaps the vocal phrase completely (mm. 32-35).

23. Instead of a "dal segno."

24. In this case, the interlude echoes the vocal motto, so we may speak of *divisien* .technique.

25. *Herr, nun lässest Du*, III (136 mm.), IV (159 mm.) and *Der Herr ist nahe*, III (129 mm.).

26. *Herr, nun lässest Du*, IV.

27. *Meine Seele*, VI.

28. Reduction of texture, modulation to the relative major.

29. "I will henceforth argue my case."

30. "He leads me by the hand."

31. In the ritornello, this phrase appears canonically in the two violin parts.

32. Mm. 32-33.

11.
The Orchestral Parts

Orchestration

Günter Hausswald observes that the backbone of the orchestra in Heinichen's instrumental works is the string ensemble, usually in four parts, with instruments often merely implied by the choice of clefs.[1] This generalization also holds true for the German church compositions. In fact, seven of the fifteen cantatas have only string and continuo accompaniment, although oboes may well have doubled the violin parts in performance:[2]

Lass dichs: 2 (vl.), 2 (vla.), (S.A.T.B.), (B.c.)
Es naheten: 3 vl., S.A.T.B., B.c.
Mag auch: 2 (vl.), 2 (vla.), (S.A.T.B.), (B.c.)
Der Segen: 2 vl., 2 vla., S.A.T.B., B.c.
Ach, was soll ich: 2 (vl.), 3 (vla.), (cello), (S.A.T.B.), (B.c.)
Gegrüsset seist du: 2 (vl.), 1 (vla.), (cello), (S.S.A.T.B.), (B.c.)
Gott ist unsere Zuversicht: 2 (vl.), 1 (vla.), (S.A.T.B.), (B.c.)

Two other works have basically string accompaniment, but add a bassoon part that is, to a certain degree, independent of the continuo.

Der Herr: 2 vl., 1 vla., S.A.T.B. + rip., *fagotto*,[3] B.c.
Einsamkeit: 2 vl., 1 vla., S.A.T.B. + rip., *fagotto*, B.c.

The works that specify woodwinds in addition to the basic strings include:

Herr, nun lässest Du: 2 ob.,[4] *bassone*, 1 vl., S.A.T.B. + rip., B.c. (includes *fagotto*).
Gelobet: 2 ob., *bassone*, 2 vl., 2 vla., S.A.T.B. + rip., B.c.
Lobe den Herrn: 2 ob., *bassone*, 2 vl., 2 vla., S.A.T.B., B.c. (includes *chalcedono*).
Heilig ist der Herr: 2 ob., 2 vl., (S.A.T.B.), B.c.(includes *fagotto*).

Two works include brass:

> Meine Seele: 2 clarini, 1 tromba, tamburo,[5] 2 vl., 1 vla., S.A.T.B./S.A.T.B., B.c.
>
> Es lebet: 2 clarini, 2 trombe, 2 ob., 1 fl.,[6] 2 vl., 3 (vla.), (S.S.A.T.T.B.), (B.c.).

Noteworthy is the incomplete complement of strings in Herr, nun lässest Du, a cantata that is, otherwise, fully orchestrated. Also of interest is the changing ratio between violin and viola parts, which varies from 3:0 to 2:3. It should also be mentioned that the entire ensemble is never heard in Es lebet; the woodwinds only appear in later movements as replacements for some of the brass.[7] The appearance of a chalcedono in Lobe den Herrn was probably influenced by Telemann, who used this instrument frequently in his church cantatas,[8] while the simultaneous use of two bassoon types likely reflected the popularity this instrument enjoyed during the eighteenth century.

The Sonatas

Most of Heinichen's works begin with a separate instrumental sonata.[9] These sonatas are generally short movements that, in some cases, are further sectionalized. Thus, for instance, the sonata of Herr, nun lässest Du consists of two parts: the first introduces thematic material used in the following choral movement, the second presents a chorale that reappears in the opening chorus and in later movements as well. The sonata of Einsamkeit is also in two parts; the second similarly introduces a cantus firmus that may well be a chorale.[10] Unlike the sonata from Herr, nun lässest Du, however, the one from Einsamkeit has an opening section that is thematically independent from the following vocal movement.[11]

Although Heinichen's younger contemporary Johann Scheibe recommended no more than two sections in a sonata beginning a vocal work,[12] Heinichen begins Der Herr ist nahe with a three-part, slow-fast-slow sonata, and Ach, was soll ich with a four-part sonata alternating common and triple meters.

The thematic relationship of the sonata to the following vocal movement varies with the cantata. Some sonatas introduce, or at least foreshadow, the motivic material to come.[13] Others are thematically independent.[14] In the works where the instrumental introduction is part of the choral movement, the instrumental material almost invariably introduces the vocal themes; an exception to this is the introduction of *Es naheten*. There, an introduction using the dotted rhythms of the French Overture creates a sense of dramatic expectation before moving directly into a tenor narration.

Instrumental Style

Heinichen's instrumental style varies with the type of movement. In choral movements that are predominantly contrapuntal, the instruments adopt the vocal style, either doubling the voices or participating independently in the imitation.[15] Although the system of voice doubling changes, a frequent pattern is for the violin II to double the soprano, the violin I to double the alto at the higher octave, and a viola to double the tenor. In the score manuscripts, the doublings are often only partially written out. Usually a few notes signal which part is being doubled. Thereafter the staff is left blank until the instrument switches to another part, at which time an additional few notes appear in the manuscript to indicate the switch. Even in movements where the instruments primarily reinforce the vocal parts, occasionally one of them is given the prominent harmonic function of alone carrying the third of the chord. This happens in the closing measures of *Gott is unsere Zuversicht*, where the third is conspicuously absent in the choral parts in measures 193, 196, and 198. Each time it appears only in the highest instrumental part as a Picardy third. In *Meine Seele*, I, m. 44, the third likewise appears in the highest instrumental part but also an octave lower in the alto part of one of the two choirs.

More idiomatic instrumental styles appear in the nonimitative movements. Arpeggiated figures and rapid, scalar figures are featured prominently in the violin parts. Thus, for example, the adagio of the bass aria "Mein Augenblick" in *Herr, nun lässest Du* is accompanied throughout by descending violin arpeggios. The sonata of the same work includes a chorale accompaniment in which an arpeggiated figure is alternated between the violins and the basses.

Fig. 80. *Herr, nun lässest Du*, I, mm. 15-17

Such arpeggiated accompaniments are harmonic rather than thematic and, insofar as they subordinate the instruments to the voice, approach a more classical style of instrumental writing.[16] Drum basses also belong to the more modern style of accompaniment[17] but are utilized in only a few of Heinichen's movements.[18] Repeated sixteenth notes for strings in the style of Vivaldi are another type of nonthematic accompaniment figure and can be found in some of the festive, concertante movements.[19]

When accompaniment figures are given a more definitive shape, they begin to take on the character of an obbligato. The cyclical theme, appearing in the violin part of the first and last movements of *Lass dichs*, falls into this category,[20] as does the violin ritornello of the soprano duet in *Meine Seele*.[21] The violin obbligato in the bass aria of *Einsamkeit* is given individual character by means of occasional thirty-second notes.

Fig. 81. *Einsamkeit, o stilles Wesen*, VI, mm. 1-2

Chorales are frequently accompanied by violin figurations that are idiomatic in style.[22] In movement VI of *Ach, was soll ich Sünder machen*, the tenors sing the chorale cantus firmus, while the violins play an obbligato that includes two-octave leaps.

vol — len   Freud

Fig. 82. *Ach, was soll ich Sünder machen*, VI, mm. 19-21

Fanfare figures consisting of arpeggios and repeated notes characterize some of the brass parts,[23] and a scalar ostinato with dotted rhythm in the duet of *Herr, nun lässest Du* is particularly suited to the bassoon, as are some of the fast passages in *Heilig ist der Herr*.

One of Heinichen's greatest compositional skills was his handling of orchestral timbres.[24] This skill can already be seen in the cantatas that, as we have demonstrated, were composed relatively early in his career. Although the mixing and contrast of timbres is, to a certain degree, precluded in the compositions with only string accompaniment,[25] an examination of the others reveals effective use of timbral contrast. In *Meine Seele* and *Es lebet*, the winds and strings are contrasted in alternating polychoral blocks of sound. In *Lobe den Herrn*, concertante exchanges between winds and strings include both homophonic blocks and florid duets.[26] In the last movement of that cantata, Heinichen shows his understanding of the affinity between string and voice timbres by doubling the voices with strings and assigning concertante echoes to the contrasting woodwinds.[27]

Heinichen also achieves effective contrast between movements. The orchestration of *Es lebet* illustrates this:

I.	clarini, trumpets, strings, continuo
II.	clarini, trumpets, strings, continuo, chorus
IIIa.	continuo, bass
IIIb.	clarini, trumpets, continuo, bass
IIIc.	clarini, trumpets, strings, continuo, chorus
IV.	oboes, trumpets, strings, continuo, tenor duet (duet alternates with ensemble)
V.	flute, continuo, alto

VI.   oboes, trumpets, continuo, soprano duet (duet alternates with ensemble)

VII.   clarini, trumpets, strings, continuo, chorus

Within tutti movements, Heinichen frequently builds climaxes by adding instruments and voices layer by layer. In fugal sections, the first exposition may be accompanied by continuo alone, while subsequent expositions are strengthened by instrumental doublings.[28]

Heinichen's orchestrations are, at times, significant for the instruments that have been omitted. The omission of the flutes and oboes in the tutti movements of *Es lebet* may have been done for reasons of contrast. Perhaps they were intended to play *colla parte*. The reduction of the string group to violins in the otherwise elaborately orchestrated cantata *Herr, nun lässest Du* must have been a deliberate choice, however.

Another striking effect is the omission of the continuo at various points in these works. A very effective example of this technique occurs at the end of the duet in *Herr, nun lässest Du*.[29] Here the tutti sopranos begin to sing the chorale stanza "Lass dein Engel mit mir fahren"[30] completely unaccompanied. The effect produced is one of ethereal innocence, especially if this line is sung softly by boy sopranos.

Other writers have noted the effective orchestrations in Heinichen's Masses and instrumental works.[31] In the German church compositions, too, although they are early works, we see evidence of Heinichen's skill as an orchestrator. Because Heinichen composed in a generally simple and uncluttered style, his use of timbral contrast, idiomatic instrumental writing, and the calculated inclusion or omission of particular instruments at specific points all produce effective, if not strikingly dramatic, results.

Chapter 11. Notes

1. Hausswald, *Instrumentalwerke*, p. 124.

2. In the chart, instrumental or vocal designations only implied by clef are put in parentheses.

3. For a discussion regarding the difference between *fagotto* and *bassone*, see chapter 6.

4. Oboes in Heinichen's cantatas are always labelled *hautbois*.

5. Tympani

6. "*Traverso*"

7. Unless, of course, they doubled other parts in performance.

8. See chapter 6.

9. *Gegrüsset* begins immediately with a tenor solo.

10. This tune reappears in the following soprano solo.

11. This section is characterized by imitative interplay between the two violins.

12. Johann Scheibe, *Critischer Musikus*, No. 65, p. 601 quoted in Hauswald, *Instrumentalwerke*, p. 61.

13. The sonatas of *Herr, nun lässest Du, Gelobet, Einsamkeit, Lobe den Herrn, Es lebet*.

14. In *Der Herr ist nahe*, and *Ach, was soll ich*.

15. For a discussion of the structural significance of their participation, see chapter 9.

16. Schmitz observes that Heinichen's later Masses have less of the thematic-style accompaniments than the earlier works. see Schmitz, p. 167.

17. Burney considered drum basses an important aspect of modern style. See Burney, II:796, 802, 806, 822.

18. *Ach, was soll ich*, VI; *Es naheten*, IV.

19. For example, *Meine Seele*, I.

20. See chapter 9.

21. See chapter 10.

22. See chapter 9.

23. *Es lebet*, III; *Meine Seele*, I, VI.

24. See Schmitz, p. 123 and Hausswald, *Instrumentalwerke*, p. 143. How thoroughly Heinichen had grasped the principles of orchestration by the end of his career, can be seen in a discussion of unisons that appears in his treatise. See Heinichen, *General-Bass*, pp. 60-61.

25. The violin pizzicato in movement III of *Lass dichs* is an exception to the usual homogenous string sound.

26. Movement I.

27. The *bassone* plays in consort with the oboes, while the *chalcedono* plays with the continuo bass.

28. For a further discussion of these techniques, see chapter 9.

29. Also *Ach, was soll ich*, VII, mm. 51-52; *Einsamkeit*, VII, mm. 25-27; *Heilig*, mm. 13-17.

30. "Let thine angel travel with me."

31. See Schmitz, *Messen*, p. 123 and Hausswald, *Instrumentalwerke*, p. 143.

12.
Heinichen's Musical Language

Melody

In our earlier discussion of Heinichen's fugal movements, we found his fugue themes to be largely diatonic and often built on triadic or scalar figures. This characterization also holds true for his melodies generally.[1] Only occasionally do they strike one as being imaginative or inventive.[2] Modulations, if they occur, are usually to the dominant or relative major/minor. Chromaticism is scarce. The fact that so many of his movements are in major keys further discourages chromatic alterations. One interesting melody, combining modulation, chromaticism, and leaps of a sixth, appears in the alto aria of *Ach, was soll ich Sünder machen*.[3]

Fig. 83. *Ach, was soll ich Sünder machen*, V, mm. 7-9

Another chromatic melody occurs in the alto aria of *Einsamkeit*, the chromaticism occasioned by the word "Qual."

Fig. 84. *Einsamkeit, o stilles Wesen,* IV, mm. 16-18

Usually, however, the melodies are less distinguished. The opening melody of the tenor aria in *Es naheten* is fairly typical.

Fig. 85. *Es naheten aber zu Jesu,* VII, mm. 4-8

The structures of Heinichen's solo melodies generally fall into two categories. The florid, operatic melodies usually display the assymetrical phrases and sequential development of Baroque *Fortspinnung*. In the first bass aria of *Herr, nun lässest Du,* this technique produces a particularly long melody.

Fig. 86. *Herr, nun lässest Du*, III, mm. 54-65

The violin obbligato in *Herr, nun lässest Du*, IV, is spun out for twenty-nine measures.[4] Because time groups are alternated with rhythm groups, the phrasing is confused in some measures.

Fig. 87. *Herr, nun lässest Du*, IV, mm. 31-40

Heinichen's simpler melodies, on the other hand, often show post-Baroque clarity and symmetry. Although it can be argued that some of these arias (especially the strophic arias) are actually archaic rather than progressive, the presence of more modern techniques, such as regular ritornello structures, already indicates the introduction of *galant* style. Movements in triple meter are almost invariably of this type, their symmetrical phrase structure influenced, no doubt, by the dance associations of triple meter.[5] Since examples of this type of melody have been given in our previous discussion of ritornelli,[6] we will not repeat them here.

The degree of virtuosity is, of course, much greater in melodies of the first type. Even the most florid melodies, however, are generally characterized by the *cantabile* that Heinichen prized so highly.[7] Vocal ranges and tessituras are moderate,[8] although the tessituras of the higher voices is more demanding in the choral movements with six or eight vocal parts.[9] Heinichen's greatest demands on the singer occur in the melismas that contain successive leaps. In each case, these passages are occasioned by their texts. The alto aria of *Es lebet* illustrates the connection.[10]

Fig. 88. *Es lebet Jesus unser Hort*, V, mm. 22-24

Occasional melismas are too long to be sung in one breath. This example occurs in the tenor aria of *Herr, nun lässest Du*.

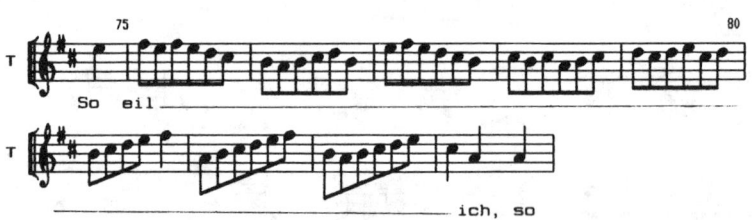

Fig. 89. *Herr, nun lässest Du*, IV, mm. 75-83

Ornaments are scarcely ever indicated, although Heinichen would have expected embellishments in the arias.[11]

Rhythm and Meter

Heinichen's surface rhythms are characterized by a relative simplicity and homogenity that are, at least in part, identifiable with the "ease and naturalness" for which he strove.[12] Because Heinichen often sets texts syllabically, the rhythms of a high proportion of the vocal parts and their imitating instrumental counterparts are text-determined. In the vocal melismas, sixteenth-note movement is the rule, although occasional thirty-second notes can be found.[13] Regularly dotted rhythms are rare in both vocal or instrumental parts (including the sonatas), although some can be found in certain arias.[14] Reverse dotting does not occur.

The one rhythmic novelty is Heinichen's use of triplets. These usually occur on affect-laden words such as "murret,"[15] "lachen,"[16] "loben,"[17] "rasen,"[18] or "erfreuet"[19] and produce a striking effect each time because they appear suddenly within a phrase of predominantly duple rhythms. In only one case do triplets occur simultaneously with duplets.[20]

Triplets also occur in the accompaniments of two homophonic movements. In the chorale that ends *Ach, was soll ich Sünder machen*, the violin obbligato is built on a one-measure motive that begins with an eighth-note triplet.

Fig. 90. *Ach, was soll ich Sünder machen*, VIII, mm. 1-2

In movement V of *Gelobet*, the continuo plays scalar triplets throughout, while the violins and oboes alternate triplets with dotted rhythms. Since the dotted rhythms would probably have been accommodated to the triplets, the entire movement could more correctly have been notated in 12/8 meter.[21]

Heinichen's choice of meters demonstrates a slightly greater dependence on common meter than is evident in Bach's cantatas.[22] Next to common meter, Heinichen favors 3/4, a meter he usually reserves for arias that are then marked "adagio." Unlike Bach, he seldom uses 3/8. Only once does he use ₵, in a movement written in the archaic motet style.[23]

Harmony

That Heinichen considered music's vertical dimension the proper point of departure for the study of composition is clear from the title of the second edition of his treatise: "The Thorough-bass in Composition, or: a new and thorough instruction for advancement...also in composition itself." The introductory remarks elaborate this perspective:

> No music connoisseur will deny that the *Basso Continuo* or so-called thorough-bass, is next to [the art of] composition, one of the most important and most fundamental of the musical sciences. For from what source other than composition itself does it spring forth? And what actually is the playing of a thorough-bass other than to improvise upon a given bass the remaining parts of a full harmony, or to compose to [the bass]?...The thorough-bass, like composition itself, leads to the complete investigation of the entire musical edifice.[24]

Heinichen's preoccupation with harmony can also be seen in the musical textures of his compositions; even his counterpoint invariably seems harmonically conceived and is sometimes little more than animated homophony. Despite this interest in harmony, Heinichen's works usually show remarkably little harmonic originality. Modulations within movements, when they occur, are usually predictable and unadventurous. Most often such modulations move to the dominant or the relative major/minor. In view of his claim to have independently discovered the circle of fifths while still a student,[25] one would have expected more adventurous modulations. Heinichen's fugues, for instance, often have successive expositions in the original key,[26] resulting in a stasis that contrasts sharply with the harmonic growth found in Bach's fugues. Even the harmonic contrast between movements is often minimal, especially in the following works:

Herr, nun lässest Du	6 of 8 movements in A major
Es naheten	7 of 10 movements in G major
Der Segen	all sections in G minor
Einsamkeit	6 of 8 movements in F major

There are some passages, however, that are striking enough to deserve special mention. Perhaps the most imaginative is the tonally unstable adagio of the second bass aria in *Herr, nun lässest Du*. Basically in A minor, this passage becomes tonally ambiguous when the modulations implied by the melody (to F major and D minor) are undermined by the harmonic progressions of the accompaniment.

Fig. 91. *Herr, nun lässest Du*, VI, mm. 13-18

In the tenor duet of *Es lebet*, the harmony contradicts the movement of the bass itself when the traditional V - I cadence is replaced by iii^6 - I. Heinichen repeats the pattern four times,[27] so there can be no question of a mistake. Since our ear expects the dominant chord, the D sounds like an appoggiatura that, however, never resolves to the C.

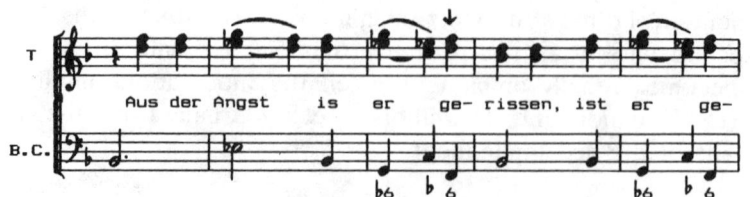

Fig. 92. *Es lebet Jesus unser Hort*, IV, mm. 14-18

Another harmonically interesting passage occurs in *Einsamkeit* and involves the imaginative use of secondary dominant chords. A modulatory sequence on the words "mit Ernst" first moves by falling fifths then, after switching to the relative minor, reverses its direction in the circle of fifths, eventually arriving back in the original tonality.

FM - BbM - EbM - Cm - Gm - Dm - FM.

The resolutions of the secondary dominants in the first part of the sequence are embellished with subdominant chords of the new tonality.

FM	F^7	Eb^6	F$^{6/5}$	BbM	Bb^7	Ab^6	Bb$^{6/5}$	EbM
I	V^7/IV	IV^6/IV	V$^{6/5}$/IV	IV				
				(I)	V^7/IV	IV^6/IV	V$^{6/5}$/IV	IV
								(I)

Fig. 93. Harmonic sequence in *Einsamkeit, o stilles Wesen*, III, mm. 13-15

An extended pedal tone is used in only one work. In *Ach, was soll ich Sünder machen*, the entire first section of the opening choral movement, totalling fifteen measures in length, is built on a pedal tone. This opening is then followed by a section in *stile concitato*, whose energetic rhythms produce an effective foil to the static introduction.

Heinichen's harmonies often have an immediate, if perhaps superficial, appeal.[28] That Heinichen consciously strove for this "agreeableness" is clear from numerous statements in his treatise and shows the extent to which he subscribed to the aesthetic values of the *galant* style.

> I will give a single little word containing... the true boundaries and the heart of music, and it is in four letters, *Goût*.[29]

According to Heinichen, music posesses *goût* if it

> ...for the most part, and ordinarily pleases 1) both educated and uneducated, 2) individuals of completely different temperaments and humors, 3) in various parts of the world where tastes are completely different and has the public approval.[30]

If immediate appeal was the mark of a good composition, then general dislike was the sign of a poor one.

> Those contrapuntists, however, who are not endowed with good taste and who know only how to handle notes accurately, are pursued by the natural punishment, indeed, the original sin: their music is not liked by a single living soul.[31]

For models of simplicity and grace, Heinichen looked to France.

> One nation (Germany) believes art is only that which is difficult to compose; another nation (France), however, seeks a lighter style and correctly states that it is difficult to compose light music or to possess a light style...[32]

We have already noted Heinichen's limited harmonic vocabulary, a quality characteristic of the *galant* style. Other *galant* aspects in Heinichen's harmonies include his clear preference for major tonalities[33] (the ratio is about 2:1 in favor of major keys) and his love for parallel thirds and sixths.[34] In *Heilig ist der Herr* Heinichen introduces bass figures in the continuo and bassoon parts that, when taken together, outline each triad. Together, the two parts resemble an Alberti bass. Each instrument only contributes part of the triad, however.

Fig. 94. *Heilig ist der Herr*, II, mm. 7-9

While Heinichen's harmonies are generally consonant, and the harmonic progressions simple, occasional pungent dissonances are also characteristic, and Heinichen considered these "the most beautiful materials in music."[35] Many of these dissonances are text-determined.[36] One type of cadential dissonance should still be mentioned however, the so-called "Corelli clash."[37] In this formula, the tonic scale-degree is combined first with the supertonic, then the leading tone, before resolving to a unison, as in this example from the alto aria of *Es lebet*.

Fig. 95. *Es lebet Jesus unser Hort*, V, mm. 17-18

This formula only appears in a few works: *Es naheten aber zu Jesu, Lobe den Herrn, Es lebet Jesus unser Hort*, and *Gegrüsset seist du holdselige Maria*.

As an advocate of the fashionable *galant* style, Heinichen composed in an agreeable yet superficial manner. Diatonic, often scalar, melodies in major keys, passages in parallel thirds or sixths, harmonically conceived counterpoint, and simple, homogenous rhythms all contribute to the "ease and naturalness" for which he strove. This agreeableness does not always make up for an evident lack of inventiveness, however, a shortcoming that can at least partially be explained by the fact that Heinichen composed these works relatively early in his career.

Chapter 12. Notes

1. We are interested here primarily in solo melodies (both vocal and instrumental). Melodies in accompaniments or concertante textures are, to a large degree, harmonically determined.

2. To be sure, this was an age of transition, in which artifice and inventiveness were prized less highly than naturalness, ease, and simplicity. See Heinichen, *General-Bass*, p. 24 (footnote); George J. Buelow, "In defence of J.A. Scheibe against J.S. Bach," Royal Music Association - London: *Proceedings* 1974-75, p. 96.

3. Biplanar melodies such as this one appear infrequently. Additional examples may be found in *Der Herr ist nahe*, II (fugue theme), V.

4. Mm. 23-51.

5. See *Der Herr*, III, V, VI; *Einsamkeit*, VII; *Ach, was soll ich*, Vb, VII; *Meine Seele*, IV (in 6/8); *Es lebet*, IV. Contrasting sections without ritornello may be less symmetrical. See *Der Herr*, III.

6. See chapter 10.

7. Heinichen, *General-Bass*, p. 23.

8. Ranges generally stay within the staff, although the bass frequently goes as high as C or D.

9. *Es lebet* and *Meine Seele*. In these cantatas, the instrumental parts are more likely to cross each other.

10. For a further discussion and examples, see chapter 8.

11. Heinichen, *General-Bass*, p. 83.

12. See above.

13. See *Es naheten*, V; *Lobe*, VII.

14. *Herr*, III, VIIa; *Lobe*, VII.

15. *Es naheten*, II.

16. *Es naheten*, VII.

17. *Einsamkeit*, IV.

18. *Meine Seele*, VI.

19. *Meine Seele*, II.

20. *Meine Seele*, II, m. 18.

21. The *bassone* part of source #504 does, in fact, notate it in 12/8 meter. The other bass parts are notated, for some inexplicable reason, in 12/16.

22. Heinichen has about three times as many movements or sections in common meter as any other kind.

23. *Der Segen*, VII. See also chapter 9. In his treatise, Heinichen called ₵ the overture meter. See Heinichen, *General-Bass*, p. 348. Quantz associates ₵ with the *galant* style. See Quantz, *Flute*, p. 65.

24. Heinichen, *General-Bass*, p. 1, trans. Buelow, "Heinichen's General-Bass," p. 551.

25. See chapter 3.

26. This is a typical weakness found in many fugues of the time. See Treiber, p. 147. One exception to this generalization is *Lobe*, V. After the second exposition, a one-measure episode modulates to the subdominant. The third exposition then modulates via a V/ii back to the tonic.

27. Mm. 3-4, 6-7, 16-17, 18-19.

28. The foregoing examples are exceptions to this generalization.

29. Heinichen, *General-Bass*, p. 22, trans. Buelow, "Heinichen's General-Bass," p. 571.

30. Heinichen, *General-Bass*, p. 13, trans. Buelow, "Heinichen's General-Bass," p. 563.

31. Heinichen, *General-Bass*, p. 25, trans. Buelow, "Heinichen's General-Bass," p. 574.

32. Heinichen, *General-Bass*, p. 10, trans. Buelow, "Heinichen's General-Bass," p. 560.

33. Heinichen's choice of specific keys is unrelated to affect (see chapter 7). For this reason, we need not be surprised that the festive cantata *Lobe den Herrn* is written in Bb major.

34. See *Lobe*, I, mm. 10-13 (oboes). See also many of his vocal duets.

35. Heinichen, *General-Bass*, pp. 225-226. Concerning the mix of consonance and dissonance in the *galant* style, Quantz wrote, "[If a melody] is to have a galante air, it must contain more consonances than dissonances... [although] dissonances must be used from time to time to rouse the ear." See Quantz, *Flute*, p. 91.

36. See chapter 8.

37. Robert Donington suggests the "Corelli clash" may have been resolved with a conventional trill. See Robert Donington, *The Interpretation of Early Music*, New Version (London: Faber and Faber, 1977), p. 250.

13.
Conclusions

Heinichen's fifteen German choral church compositions, with the possible exception of *Heilig ist der Herr* (because of its more modern bass and phrase structure), all appear to be early works. Since Heinichen's duties as chapel master of the Dresden court concerned primarily the Catholic chapel, while the Protestant chapel remained the responsibility of his predecessor, Johann Christoph Schmidt, Heinichen had little reason to compose Protestant music in Dresden. During his Italian visit, too, Heinichen had no cause for writing Protestant works. Most probably, therefore, these compositions were written in Leipzig before Heinichen left for Italy. Perhaps they were performed at the New Church whose musical activities attracted many of the university students. It is possible, however, that some of Heinichen's works were performed in Dresden under Schmidt's direction for, by the time Heinichen arrived there, Schmidt had ceased composing, and the court prided itself in performing only works by its resident composers.

Despite the fact that the term cantata was not often used in Heinichen's day for church compositions, Heinichen's works have many of the elements we now consider definitive characteristics of that genre. Most are between fifteen and twenty minutes long, and are divided into relatively independent sections. *De tempore* designations are specified for many of them; for others, their place in the church calendar can be determined from their texts. Most of the texts are compilations of scripture, rhymed poetry, and/or chorale stanzas. Often there is a close relationship between the cantata libretto and the applicable Gospel lesson.

For all of these reasons, we may call most of these compositions cantatas. A clear exception is *Heilig ist der Herr* whose length, structure, and text identify it as a communion motet. *Der Segen des Herrn* and *Gott ist unsere Zuversicht*, because of their brevity and the absence of distinct movements, may be regarded as transitional forms between the motet and cantata genres.

When we compare Heinichen's works with Bach's cantatas (which have become normative for the genre), we find significant differences. Most of Heinichen's works are shorter, and individual movements have less motivic unity. The melodies are simpler, often consisting of scalar or triadic figures, and the declamation is frequently syllabic. Thus, Heinichen's melodies are inherently more vocal than Bach's but also less distinctive. Heinichen's harmonic vocabulary is far more limited, and chromaticism is less common. His harmonic rhythm is slower, and major keys are more prevalent. Since Heinichen's textures are always harmonically conceived, he never achieves truly contrapuntal textures as Bach does. Heinichen's works also contain none of the elaborate chorale settings found in Bach's cantatas.

In general, then, Heinichen's cantatas are more superficial that Bach's but, on the other hand, are more accordant with the prevailing aesthetic values of the *galant* style. Despite such progressive elements, however, Heinichen's works are not yet fully developed examples of the madrigalian cantata. They contain only a few recitatives or da capo arias. Few movements are thematically unified with instrumental ritornelli. The orchestration is effective but usually modest and is often thematically dependent on the vocal parts. Concertante movements often still use the old Venetian style, and the texts do not yet have the strong mystic elements characteristic of the later cantata.

In view of Heinichen's detailed demonstration (in his treatise) of ways that texts may generate musical ideas, the music-text relationship becomes an important point of departure for any examination of Heinichen's own compositions. Our study reveals that while Heinichen does express the affective significance of isolated words and phrases with a wide variety of rhetorical figures, he does not often unify his movements well enough to express one prevailing affect effectively. This lack of motivic and expressive unity within movements, along with some of the other characteristics noted above, not only indicates that these works are youthful compositions but also exemplifies the transitional state of the German cantata at the beginning of the eighteenth century. In short, Heinichen's works are facile examples of German church music during a time of stylistic transition, written by a young composer just beginning to enjoy popular acclaim.

Bibliography

Manuscript Sources

Berlin, D.D.R. Deutsche Staatsbibliothek, MSS *Heinichen autogr. IN, 30210* (Heinichen excerpts), *30221* (Heinichen excerpts).

Dresden. Sächsische Landesbibliothek, MSS *Mus. 2398-E-500* to *Mus. 2398-E-509* inclusive.

Published Sources

Heinichen, Johann David. *Heilig ist Gott der Herr (Ein deutsches Sanctus)*. Full score. Edited by Melvin P. Unger. Stuttgart: Carus-Verlag, 1988.

Heinichen, Johann David. *Herr, nun lässest du deinen Diener in Friede fahren*. Full score. Edited by Melvin P. Unger assisted by Wolfgang Horn. Stuttgart: Carus-Verlag, in preparation.

Unger, Melvin P. "The German Choral Church Compositions of Johann David Heinichen (1683-1729)." 2 vols. D.M.A dissertation, University of Illinois at Urbana-Champaign, 1986. The appendix includes full scores of all Heinichen's German choral church compositions.

Reference Literature

Adrio, Adam, and Forchert, Arno. "Das Vokalkonzert." *Die Musik in Geschichte und Gegenwart*. 16 vols. Edited by Friedrich Blume. Kassel: Bärenreiter, 1949-1979, vol. 7 (1958), cols. 1560-1569.

Becker-Glauch, Irmgard. "August der Starke." *Die Musik in Geschichte und Gegenwart*. 16 vols. Edited by Friedrich Blume. Kassel: Bärenreiter, 1949-1979, vol. 1 (1949-1951), cols. 841-842.

Becker-Glauch, Irmgard. *Die Bedeutung der Musik für die Dresdener Hoffeste bis in die Zeit Augusts des Starken*. Kassel: Bärenreiter, 1951.

Becker-Glauch, Irmgard. "Dresden, Von den Anfängen bis zum Tode Augusts der Starken. *Die Musik in Geschichte und Gegenwart*. 16 vols. Edited by Friedrich Blume. Kassel: Bärenreiter, 1949-1979, vol. 3 (1954), cols. 757-771.

Berner, Alfred. "Hebenstreit." *Die Musik in Geschichte und Gegenwart.* 16 vols. Edited by Friedrich Blume. Kassel: Bärenreiter, 1949-1979, vol. 6 (1957), cols. 3-6.

Blankenburg, Walter. *Wege der Forschung.* Vol. 170: *Johann Sebastian Bach.* Darmstadt, 1970. Cited in Günther Stiller, *Johann Sebastian Bach and Liturgical Life in Leipzig,* p. 143. St. Louis: Concordia, 1984.

Blume, Friedrich. *Protestant Church Music; a History.* New York: W.W. Norton & Co., 1974.

Bose, Fritz. "Quantz, Johann Joachim." *Die Musik in Geschichte und Gegenwart.* 16 vols. Edited by Friedrich Blume. Kassel: Bärenreiter, 1949-1979, vol. 10 (1962), cols. 1797-1806.

Brausch, Paul Friedrich. "Die Kantate: Ein Beitrag zur Geschichte der deutschen Dichtungsgattungen, I: Geschichte der Kantate Gottsched." Ph.D. dissertation, University of Heidelberg, 1921.

Brown, Dale. *Understanding Pietism.* Grand Rapids: William B. Eerdmans Publishing Co., 1978.

Brown, Howard Mayer and McKinnon, James W. "Performing Practice." *The New Grove Dictionary of Music and Musicians.* 20 vols. Edited by Stanley Sadie. London: Macmillan & Co., 1980, 14:370-393.

Buelow, George J. "Johann David Heinichen." *The New Grove Dictionary of Music and Musicians.* 20 vols. Edited by Stanley Sadie. London: Macmillan & Co., 1980, 8:438-439.

Buelow, George J. "In defence of J.A. Scheibe against J.S. Bach." *Proceedings.* London: Royal Music Association, 1974/75.

Buelow, George J. "Johann David Heinichen's Der General-Bass in der Composition." Ph.D. dissertation, New York University, 1961.

Buelow, George J. "Music, Rhetoric and the Concept of the Affections: a Selective Bibliography." *Notes: The Quarterly Journal of the Music Library Association* 30 (1973-4):250-259.

Buelow, George J. "Rhetoric and Music." *The New Grove Dictionary of Music and Musicians.* 20 vols. Edited by Stanley Sadie. London: Macmillan & Co., 1980, 15:793-803.

Buelow, George J. "The Loci Topici and Affect in late baroque Music; Heinichen's practical demonstration." *The Music Review* August 1966: 161-176.

Buelow, George J. *Thorough-Bass Accompaniment according to Johann David Heinichen* Berkeley and Los Angeles: University of California Press, 1966. Out of print 1983.

Burney, Charles. *A General History of Music.* London: 1776-1789; new ed., London: Frank Mercer, 1935; reprint ed., New York: Dover, 1957.

Buszin, Walter E. "Criteria of Church Music in the Seventeenth and Eighteenth Centuries." *Festschrift Theodore Hoelty-Nickel: a Collection of Essays on Church Music.* Valparaiso, Indiana, 1967, pp. 14-21.

Buszin, Walter E. "Music of the Lutheran Church." *The Encyclopaedia of the Lutheran Church.* Edited by Julius Bodensieck. Minneapolis: Augsburg, 1965, 2:1676-1685.

David, Hans T. and Mendel, Arthur, eds. *The Bach Reader.* Revised ed., New York: W.W. Norton & Co., 1966.

Donington, Robert. *The Interpretation of Early Music.* New Version., London: Faber and Faber, 1977.

Dürr, Alfred. *Die Kantaten von Johann Sebastian Bach.* 2 vols. Kassel: Bärenreiter, 1971.

Eitner, Robert. *Biographisch-Bibliographisches Quellen-Lexicon.* 10 vols. S.v. "Heinichen." Leipzig: 1905.

Eller, Rudolf. "Leipzig: II. Vom Westfälischen Frieden bis zum Ausgang des 18. Jh." *Die Musik in Geschichte und Gegenwart.* 16 vols. Edited by Friedrich Blume. Kassel: Bärenreiter, 1949-79, vol. 8 (1960), cols. 545-560.

Feder, Georg. "Die protestantische Kirchenkantate." *Die Musik in Geschichte und Gegenwart.* 16 vols. Edited by Friedrich Blume. Kassel: Bärenreiter, 1949-79, vol. 7 (1958), cols. 581-608.

Freeman, Robert. "La Verita Nella Ripetizione." *Musical Quarterly* 54 (1968): 208-227.

Fürstenau, Moritz. *Beiträge zur Geschichte der Königlich Sächsischen musikalischen Kapelle.* Dresden: 1849.

Fürstenau, Moritz. *Zur Geschichte der Musik und des Theaters am Hofe zu Dresden.* 2 vols. Dresden: 1862; reprint ed., Hildesheim: Georg Olms, 1971.

236

Galling, Kurt. "Bibelübersetzungen. IV. Deutsche Übersetzungen." *Die Religion in Geschichte und Gegenwart*. 3d ed. Edited by Kurt Galling. Tübingen: J.C.B. Mohr (Paul Siebeck), 1957-1965, 1:1201-1210.

Georgiades, Thrasybulos. *Music and Language*. Translated by Marie Louise Göllner. Cambridge: Cambridge University Press, 1982.

Gerber, Christian. *Historie der Kirchen-Cermonien in Sachsen*. Dresden and Leipzig, 1732. Cited in Günther Stiller, *Johann Sebastian Bach and Liturgical Life in Leipzig*. St. Louis: Concordia, 1984.

Gerber, Ernst Ludwig. "Heinichen." *Neues Historisch-Biographisches Lexicon der Tonkünstler*. 2 vols. Leipzig: 1812-14; reprint ed., Graz: Akademische Druck und Verlaganstalt, 1969.

Gill, Donald. "Colascione." *The New Grove Dictionary of Musical Instruments*. 3 vols. Edited by Stanley Sadie. London: Macmillan & Co., 1984, 1:434-436.

Härtwig, Dieter. "Schmidt, Johann Christoph." *Die Musik in Geschichte und Gegenwart*. 16 vols. Edited by Friedrich Blume. Kassel: Bärenreiter, 1949-79, vol. 11 (1963), cols. 1858-1861.

Harwood, Ian. "Colascione." *The New Grove Dictionary of Music and Musicians*. 20 vols. Edited by Stanley Sadie. London: Macmillan & Co., 1980, 4:523-524.

Hastings, Arthur; Walker, Thomas; Warren, Charles; Sadie, Stanley. "Concerto: 1. Terminology to c. 1670." *The New Grove Dictionary of Music and Musicians*. 20 vols. Edited by Stanley Sadie. London: Macmillan & Co., 1980, 4:627-628.

Hausswald, Günter. "Johann David Heinichen." *Die Musik in Geschichte und Gegenwart*. 16 vols. Edited by Friedrich Blume. Kassel: Bärenreiter, 1949-1979, vol. 6 (1957), cols. 46-51.

Hasswald, Günter. *J.D. Heinichens Instrumentalwerke*. Leipzig, 1937.

Heinichen, Johann David. *Der General-Bass in der Composition*. Dresden, 1711, photographic reprint edition, Darmstadt: fotokop wilhelm weihert, 1969.

Held, K. *Das Kreuzkantorat zu Dresden*. Leipzig, 1894.

Hertzsch, E. "Farben." *Die Religion in Geschichte und Gegenwart*. 3d ed. Edited by Kurt Galling. Tübingen: J.C.B. Mohr (Paul Siebeck), 1957-1965, vol. 2, cols. 874-876.

Hill, John Walter. "The Life and Works of Francesco Maria Veracini." Ph.D. dissertation, Harvard University, 1972. U.M.I. Research Press, 1979.

Hiller, Johann Adam. "Lebenslauf des Herrn Johann David Heinichen." *Wöchentliche Nachrichten und Anmerkungen die Musik betreffend.* Leipzig, 1766 and following years; reprint ed., Hildesheim: Georg Olms, 1970, 1:213-217, 221-225.

Hofmann, E.H. *Capella sanctae crucis. Der Dresdner Kreuzchor in Geschichte und Gegenwart.* 2d ed. Berlin, 1957.

Horn, Wolfgang. *Die Dresdner Hofkirchenmusik 1720-1745. Studien zu ihren Voraussetzungen und ihrem Repertoire.* Joint publication. Kassel: Bärenreiter-Verlag; Stuttgart: Carus-Verlag, 1987.

Hunold, Christian [Menantes]. *Die allerneuste Art zur reinen und galanten Poesie zu gelangen.* Hamburg, 1707.

Irwin, Joyce. "German Pietists and Church Music in the Baroque Age." *Church History* 54 (1985):29-40.

Kliefoth, Theodore Friedrich Dethlof. *Liturgische Abhandlungen.* Vol. 4: *Die ursprüngliche Gottesdienst - Ordnung in den deutschen Kirchen lutherischen Bekenntnisses, ihre Destruction und Reformation.* 2d ed. enl. Schwerin, 1858.

Kolneder, Walter. "Fagott." *Die Musik in Geschichte und Gegenwart.* 16 vols. Edited by Friedrich Blume. Kassel: Bärenreiter, 1949-1979, vol. 3 (1954), cols. 1717-1731.

Kraft, Günther. "Zeitz." *Die Musik in Geschichte und Gegenwart.* 16 vols. Edited by Friedrich Blume. Kassel: Bärenreiter, 1949-1979, vol. 14 (1968), cols. 1188-1192.

Kretzschmar, H. *Bachkolleg: Vorlesungen über J.S. Bach. Leipzig,* 1922. Quoted in Günther Stiller, *Johann Sebastian Bach and Liturgical Life in Leipzig.* St. Louis: Concordia, 1984.

Krummacher, Friedhelm. *Die Choralbearbeitung in der protestantischen Figuralmusik zwischen Praetorius und Bach.* Kassel: Bärenreiter, 1978.

Krummacher, Friedhelm. "The German Cantata to 1800." *The New Grove Dictionary of Music and Musicians.* 20 vols. Edited by Stanley Sadie. London: Macmillan & Co., 1980, 3:702-713.

Leaver, Robin A. and Bond, Ann. "Martin Luther." *The New Grove Dictionary of Music and Musicians.* 20 vols. Edited by Stanley Sadie. London: Macmillan & Co., 1980, 11:365-371.

Leibniz, J.F., ed. *Leipziger Kirchen-Andachten: Darinnen der Erste Theil, Das Gebetbuch oder die Ordnung des gantzen öffentlichen Gottes-Dienstes durchs gantze Jahr...Der Ander Theil, Das Gesangbuch...*Leipzig, 1694. Quoted in Günther Stiller, *Johann Sebastian Bach and Liturgical Life in Leipzig.* St. Louis: Concordia, 1984.

Leipziger Kirchen-Staat: Das ist, Deutlicher Unterricht vom Gottes-Dienst in Leipzig. Leipzig, 1710. Quoted in Günther Stiller, *Johann Sebastian Bach and Liturgical Life in Leipzig.* St. Louis: Concordia, 1984.

Liliencron, Rochus von. *Liturgisch-Musikalische Geschichte der Evangelischen Gottesdienste von 1523 bis 1700.* Schleswig, 1893; reprint ed., Hildesheim: Georg Olms, 1970.

Luther, Martin. *Formulae Missae et Communionis.* Wittenburg, 1723. Translated by Bard Thompson. *Liturgies of the Western Church.* Philadelphia: Fortress Press, 1982, pp. 106-122.

Luther, Martin. *The German Mass and Order of Service.* 1526. Translated by Bard Thompson. *Liturgies of the Western Church.* Philadelphia: Fortress Press, 1982, pp. 123-137.

Marpurg, Friedrich Wilhelm. "Herrn Johann Joachim Quantzens Lebenslauf von ihm selbst entworfen." *Historisch-kritische Beyträge zur Aufnahme der Musik* I, 3. Stück. Berlin, 1755.

Mattheson, Johann. *Das beschützte Orchestre.* Hamburg, 1717.

Mattheson, Johann. *Der vollkommene Kapellmeister.* Translated by Ernest C. Harriss. Ann Arbor: U.M.I. Press, 1981.

Mattheson, Johann. *Grundlage einer Ehren-Pforte.* Hamburg, 1740; reprint ed., Berlin: Leo Liepmannssohn, 1910.

Melchert, Hermann. "Das Rezitativ der Kirchenkantaten J.S. Bachs." *Bach-Jahrbuch* XIV (1958):5-83.

Mendel, Arthur. "On the Keyboard Accompaniments to Bach's Leipzig Church Music." Music Quarterly 36 (1950):339-362.

Mendel, Arthur. "On the Pitches in Use in Bach's Time." *Music Quarterly* 41 (1955): 332-354, 466-480.

Mendel, Arthur. "Pitch in Western Music since 1500, a Reexamination." *Acta Musicologica* 50 (1978):1-93.

Mendel, Hermann. "Heinichen." *Musikalisches Conversations-Lexicon.* Berlin, 1875.

Menke, Werner. *Thematisches Verzeichnis der Vokalwerke von Georg Philipp Telemann.* Vol. 1: *Cantaten zum Gottesdienstlichen Gebrauch.* Frankfurt: V. Klostermann, 1982-.

Neumann, Werner and Schulze, Hans-Joachim, eds. *Bachdokumente.* 3 vols. Leipzig: Bach-Archiv, 1963-1972.

Neumeister, Erdmann. *Geistliche Cantaten statt einer Kirchen-Music. Die zweite Auflage Nebst einer neuen Vorrede auf Unkosten Eines guten Freundes.* Weissenfels, 1704.

Neumeister, Erdmann. *Fünfffache Kirchen-Andachten bestehend in theils eintzeln theils niehmals gedr. Arien, Cant. u. Oden auf alle Sonn- u. Fest-Tage des gantzen Jahres.* Leipzig, 1716/1717.

Neumeister, Erdmann. *Fortgesetzte Fünfffache Kirchen-Andachten in Drey neuen Jgn. auf alle Sonn- und Fest- auch Apostel-Tage; denen noch beygefügt andere Geistl. Kirchenstüche u. Gedichte.* Hamburg, 1726.

Neumeister, Erdmann. *Dritten Theil der fünfffachen Kirchen-Andachten.* Hamburg, 1752.

Noack, Friedrich. "Christoph Graupner als Kirchenkomponist." Supplement to *Denkmäler Deutscher Tonkunst* LI-LII. Leipzig: Breitkopf & Härtel, 1926.

Noack, Friedrich. *Christoph Graupner: Ausgewählte Kantaten.* Wiesbaden: Breitkopf & Härtel, 1960.

Noack, Friedrich. *Christoph Graupners Kirchenmusiken: ein Beitrag zur Geschichte der Musik am landgräflichen Hofe zu Darmstadt.* Leipzig: Breitkopf & Härtel, 1916.

Phillips, Walter Alison. "Vestments." *Encylopaedia Brittanica,* 1959 ed. London: Benton, 2:108-112.

Quantz, Johann Joachim. *On Playing the Flute.* Translated by Edward R. Reilly. London: Faber & Faber, 1966.

Quintillian. *Institutiones Oratoriae.* 4 vols. Translated by H.E. Butler. Cambridge: Harvard University Press, 1922.

Ranke, Ernst. *Der Fortbestand des herkömmlichen Perikopenkreises von geschichtlichem und praktisch-theologischem Standpunct aus.* Gotha, 1859.

Raynor, Henry. *A Social History of Music.* New York: Taplinger Publishing Co., 1978.

Reed, Luther D. *The Lutheran Liturgy*. Revised ed., Philadelphia: Muhlenberg Press, 1947.

Rhodes, J.J.K. and Thomas, W.R. "Pitch. 2. Baroque Chamber Pitch, Ellis and Praetorius." *The New Grove Dictionary of Music and Musicians*. 20 vols. Edited by Stanley Sadie. London: Macmillan & Co., 1980, 14:781-785.

Riedel, Friedrich Wilhelm. "Johann Kuhnau." *Die Musik in Geschichte und Gegenwart*. 16 vols. Edited by Friedrich Blume. Kassel: Bärenreiter, 1949-1979, vol. 7 (1958), cols. 1878-1887.

Riemer, Otto. "Florilegium Portense." *Die Musik in Geschichte und Gegenwart*. 16 vols. Edited by Friedrich Blume. Kassel: Bärenreiter, 1949-1979, vol. 4 (1955), cols. 429-432.

Rilling, Helmuth. "Bach's Significance." Translated by Gordon Paine, *The Choral Journal* vol. 25, no. 10 (June, 1985):7-14.

Ronan, Colin Alistair. "The Gregorian Calendar." *The New Encyclopaedia Britannica* (Macopaedia). 15th ed. Toronto: Benton, 1974, 3:602-603.

Ruhnke, Martin. "Georg Philipp Telemann." *The New Grove Dictionary of Music and Musicians*. 20 vols. Edited by Stanley Sadie. London: Macmillan & Co., 1980, 18:647-659.

Sachs, Curt. *Handbuch der Musikinstrumentenkunde*. Leipzig, 1930; reprint ed., Hildesheim: Georg Olms, 1967.

Samuel, Harold E. "Johann Philipp Krieger." *The New Grove Dictionary of Music and Musicians*. 20 vols. Edited by Stanley Sadie. London: Macmillan & Co., 1980, 10:268-270.

Scheibe, Johann Adolf. *Critischer Musikus*. 2d ed. Leipzig, 1745.

Schemelli, Georg Christian. *Musicalisches Gesang-Buch*. Leipzig, 1736; reprint ed., Hildesheim: Georg Olms, 1975.

Schering, Arnold. *J.S. Bach und das Musikleben im 18. Jahrhundert*. Leipzig, 1941. Cited in Günther Stiller, *Johann Sebastian Bach and Liturgical Life in Leipzig*. St. Louis: Concordia, 1984.

Schering, Arnold. *Johann Sebastian Bachs Leipziger Kirchenmusik*. 3d ed. Wiesbaden: Breitkopf & Härtel, 1968.

Schering, Arnold. *Musikgeschichte Leipzigs von 1650 bis 1723*. Leipzig, 1926.

Schmid, Heinrich. *Doctrinal Theology of the Evangelical Church*. Translated by Charles Hay and Henry E. Jacobs. 3d ed. Revised. Minneapolis: Augsburg Publishing House, 1961.

Schmidt, Eberhard. *Der Gottesdienst am Kurfürstlichen Hofe zu Dresden. Ein Beitrag zur liturgischen Traditionsgeschichte von Johann Walter bis zu Heinrich Schütz*. Göttingen: Vandenhoeck & Ruprecht, 1961.

Schmidt, Eberhard. "Die Messen J.D. Heinichens." Ph.D. dissertation, University of Hamburg, 1967.

Schmitz, Eugen. *Geschichte der Weltlichen Solo Cantata*. Leipzig, 1714; reprint ed., Hildesheim: Georg Olms.

Schnoor, Hans. *Dresden: Vierhundert Jahre Deutsche Musikkultur*. Dresden: Dresdner Verlagsgesellschaft, 1948.

Schrade, Leo. "Bach: The Conflict Between the Sacred and Secular." *De Scientia Musicae Studia atque Orationes*. Edited by Ernst Lichtenhahn, Bern, 1967. Quoted in Joyce Irwin, "German Pietists and Church Music in the Baroque Age," *Church History* 54 (1985):29.

Seibel, Gustav Adolph. *Das Leben des königl. Polnischen und kurfürstl. Sächs. Hofkapell meisters Johann David Heinichen...und thematischen Katalog seiner Werke*. Leipzig, 1913.

Seiffert, Max, ed. Forword to "Johann Philipp Krieger." Vol. 53/54 (1916) of *Denkmäler Deutscher Tonkunst*. Leipzig: Breitkopf & Härtel, 1892-1931, pp. V-LXXXVI.

Sicul, Christoph Ernst. *Neo annalium Lipsiensium Continuatio II: Oder des mit 1715ten Jahre Neuangegangenen Leipziger Jahrbuchs Dritte Probe*. Leipzig, 1717. Quoted in Günther Stiller, *Johann Sebastian Bach and Liturgical Life in Leipzig*. St. Louis: Concordia, 1984.

Siegele, Ulrich. "Bach's Ort in Orthodoxie und Aufklärung." *Musik und Kirche* 51 (1981). Quoted in Joyce Irwin, "German Pietists and Church Music in the Baroque Age," *Church History* 54 (1985):30.

Smend, Friedrich. *Bach in Köthen*. Berlin, 1951. Quoted in Günther Stiller, *Johann Sebastian Bach and Liturgical Life in Leipzig*. St. Louis: Concordia, 1984, p. 149.

Snyder, Kerala Johnson. "Erdmann Neumeister." *The New Grove Dictionary of Music and Musicians*. 20 vols. Edited by Stanley Sadie. London: Macmillan & Co., 1980, vol. 13:155.

Söhngen, Oskar. "Bach und die Liturgie." *Der Kirchenmusiker* I (1950). Quoted in Günther Stiller, *Johann Sebastian Bach and Liturgical Life in Leipzig*. St. Louis: Concordia, 1984.

Spener, Philip Jacob. *Pia Desideria*. Translated and edited with introduction by Theodore G. Tappert. Philadelphia: Fortress Press, 1964.

Spitta, Philipp. *Johann Sebastian Bach*. Translated by Clara Bell and J.A. Fuller-Maitland. 3 vols. New York: Dover Publications, 1951.

Spitta, Philipp. *Musikgeschichtliche Aufsätze*. Berlin, 1894.

Stiller, Günther. *Johann Sebastian Bach and Liturgical Life in Leipzig*. Translated by Herbert J.A. Bowman, Daniel F. Poellot, and Hilton C. Oswald. Edited by Robin A. Leaver. St. Louis: Concordia, 1984.

Stoeffler, F. Ernest. *German Pietism during the Eighteenth Century*. Leiden: E.J. Brill, 1973.

Stoeffler, F. Ernest. *The Rise of Evangelical Pietism*. Leiden: E.J. Brill, 1971.

Tagliavini, Luigi Ferdinando. "Erdmann Neumeister." *Die Musik in Geschichte und Gegenwart*. 16 vols. Edited by Friedrich Blume. Kassel: Bärenreiter, 1961, vol. 9 (1961), col. 1401.

Tanner, Richard. *J.D. Heinichen als dramatischer Komponist*. Leipzig, 1916.

Terry, Charles Sanford. *Joh. Seb. Bach, Cantata Texts Sacred and Secular With a Reconstruction of the Leipzig Liturgy of his Period*. London, 1926.

Thompson, Bard. *Liturgies of the Western Church*. Philadelphia: Fortress Press, 1982.

Treiber, Fritz. "Die thüringisch-sächsische Kirchenkantate zur Zeit des jungen J.S. Bach (etwa 1700-1723)." *Archiv für Musikforschung* II (1937):129-159.

Unger, Hans Heinrich. *Die Beziehung zwischen Musik und Rhetorik im 16.-18. Jahrhundert*. Würzburg: Konrad Triltsch, 1941.

Vockerodt, Gottfried. *Missbrauch der freyen Kunste, insonderheit Der Music*. Frankfurt, 1697. Quoted in Joyce Irwin, "German Pietists and Church Music in the Baroque Age," *Church History* 54 (1985):37.

Vossler, Karl. *Das deutsche Madrigal: Geschichte seiner Entwickelung bis in die Mitte des XVIII Jahrhunderts*. Weimar, 1898.

Wackernagel, Philipp. *Das Deutsche Kirchenlied*. 5 vols. Leipzig, 1864; reprint ed., Hildesheim: Georg Olms, 1964.

Werner, Arno. *Städtische und fürstliche Musikpflege in Weissenfels bis zum Ende des 18. Jahrh.* Leipzig: Breitkopf & Härtel, 1911.

Werner, Arno. *Städtische und fürstliche Musikplege in Zeitz*. Leipzig, 1922.

Westrup, Jack with Walker, Thomas; Heartz, Daniel; and Libby, Dennis. "Aria." *The New Grove Dictionary of Music and Musicians*. 20 vols. Edited by Stanley Sadie. London: Macmillan & Co., 1980, 1:573-579.

Westrup, Jack. "Cavata." *The New Grove Dictionary of Music and Musicians*. 20 vols. Edited by Stanley Sadie. London: Macmillan & Co., 1980, 4:35.

Westrup, Jack. "Cavatina." *The New Grove Dictionary of Music and Musicians*. 20 vols. Edited by Stanley Sadie. London: Macmillan & Co., 1980, 4:35.

Westrup, Jack. *Bach's Cantatas*. British Broadcasting Corporation, 1966. Seattle: University of Washington Press edition, 1969.

Whittaker, William Gillies. *The Cantatas of Johann Sebastian Bach*. 2d ed. 2 vols. London: Oxford University Press, 1964.

Wilhelm, Imanuel. "Johann Adolph Scheibe: German Musical Thought in Transition." Ph.D. dissertation, University of Illinois, 1963.

Wolff, Christoph. "Motet" III, 1., 3. *The New Grove Dictionary of Music and Musicians*. 20 vols. Edited by Stanley Sadie. London: Macmillan & Co., 1980, 12:637-638, 640-641.

Zahn, Johannes. *Die Melodien der deutschen Evangelischen Kirchenlieder*. 6 vols. 1889; reprint ed., Hildesheim: Georg Olms, 1963.

Zander, Ferdinand. *Die Dichter der Kantatentexte Johann Sebastian Bachs*. Ph.D. dissertation, University of Cologne, 1967.

Ziegler, Caspar. *Von den Madrigalen/ Einer schönen und zur Musik bequemsten Art Verse/ wie sie nach der Italianer Manier in unserer Deutschen Sprache auszuarbeiten/ Nebenst etlichen Exempeln.* Wittenberg, 1653; 2d ed, 1685. Cited in Karl Vossler, *Das deutsche Madrigal: Geschichte seiner Entwickelung bis in die Mitte des XVIII Jahrhunderts*. Weimar, 1898.

Index